Praise for *The M[...]*

"Inspiring without being preachy, V[...]
appeal to today's youth." —*Publishers Weekly*

"Uplifting . . . Wilson candidly shares the eye-opening details of his time in prison with a prose style that moves with directness and refreshingly unfettered honesty. . . . A smoothly written memoir steeped in positive reinforcement and hope for the future."

—*Kirkus Reviews*

"Wilson's voice comes through loud and clear in this memoir that should have wide appeal." —*Library Journal*

"*The Master Plan* is less of a roadmap and more of a philosophy that we should all take to heart: We are all better than our worst decision, our sense of justice should honor the redemptive possibilities inherent in every person, and our destinies are truly intertwined."

—Wes Moore, author of *The Other Wes Moore*

"This is a brave book, full of thought-provoking insight on criminal justice, the modern prison system, and the possibility of redemption. And yet what sticks with me most is the beautiful, heartbreaking mother-son relationship. . . . Thank you, Chris Wilson, for taking us into the cave, so that we can better understand the light."

—Beth Macy, bestselling author of *Dopesick* and *Factory Man*

"A brutally confessional indictment of mass incarceration in America."
—Taylor Branch, Pulitzer Prize winning author of *Parting the Waters*

"*The Master Plan* adds a personal narrative to Michelle Alexander's *The New Jim Crow*, making it equally important. Chris Wilson is our generation's go-to voice on mass incarnation and redemption. Not only does he brilliantly articulate his struggle, he offers a clear path to what needs to be done if we truly want reform. The difference between Wilson and other scholars is that he doesn't only talk about the ills of the system—he's survived that system and changed his life, and now spends his time helping other people do the same. This book will change the world."

—D. Watkins, bestselling author of *The Beast Side* and *The Cook Up*

"A bright light in a moment of moral darkness. Chris Wilson's story is both a triumph and a call to arms on behalf of the incarcerated."

—Nathalie Molina Niño, CEO of BRAVA Investments and author of *Leapfrog*

The
MASTER
PLAN

My Journey from
Life in Prison
to a Life of Purpose

CHRIS WILSON

with Bret Witter

G. P. Putnam's Sons
New York

PUTNAM
— EST. 1838 —

G. P. PUTNAM'S SONS
Publishers Since 1838
An imprint of Penguin Random House LLC
penguinrandomhouse.com

All uncredited photos are courtesy of the author.

The Library of Congress has catalogued the G. P. Putnam's Sons
hardcover edition as follows:

Names: Wilson, Chris, author. | Witter, Bret, author.
Title: The master plan : my journey from life in prison to a life of
purpose / Chris Wilson ; with Bret Witter.
Description: New York : G. P. Putnam's Sons, 2019.
Identifiers: LCCN 2018041588| ISBN 9780735215580 (hardcover) |
ISBN 9780735215603 (ebook)
Subjects: LCSH: Wilson, Chris. | Criminals—Rehabilitation—United
States—Biography. | Businessmen—United States—Biography. |
Self-realization. | Conduct of life.
Classification: LCC HV6248.W4987 A3 2019 | DDC 338/.04092 [B] —dc23
LC record available at https://lccn.loc.gov/2018041588

First G. P. Putnam's Sons hardcover edition / February 2019
First G. P. Putnam's Sons trade paperback edition / February 2020
G. P. Putnam's Sons trade paperback ISBN: 9780735215597

Printed in the United States of America
8th Printing

Book design by Katy Riegel

To my mom

Author's Note

AT THE REQUEST of my publisher and legal counsel, some names, places, and dates in this book have been changed to protect the people involved and those still hurting over events described here. I know, for them, this telling will be hard, and I am sincerely sorry for that pain, but I believe that as long as people are dying in our streets, stories like this need to be told. Please respect the privacy of those affected. Thank you.

At some point between my sentence reduction and my release, I lost the paper copies I had made over the years of my Master Plan. I now have only the last version, which I wrote for my judge and which is pictured in this book. I had stored the list on a floppy disk, which I kept in my cell, but every time I updated it I saved over the previous version, so those older versions are lost. I re-created the older versions of the Master Plan in this book by starting with this most recent version and making an educated guess at when items were added.

Contents

PART 2
The Middle Passage

PART 3
The Master Plan

PART 4
The Middle Passage, Part 2

PART 5
From Plan to Action

EPILOGUE
Moving Forward

Foreword

I FIRST MET Chris Wilson five years ago when a mutual friend and prominent local philanthropist convened a small group of local leaders to discuss Baltimore's future. The framing of the evening invited us "to envision Baltimore in 2033" in the hope that we might generate a handful of new solutions to some of Baltimore's deepest challenges. Over wine and good food, we considered the future of the city in the context of its declining population. We debated the obstacles to every child enjoying a quality education no matter where they attend school. We ruminated on the difficult fact that roughly 50 percent of Baltimore's adult population does not work, and together, we started to explore ways we might reverse that trend.

It was on this last point of conversation that Chris Wilson emerged. Soft-spoken and impeccably dressed in a crisp white dress shirt adorned with a royal purple tie, Chris described the plight of black men across the city. He highlighted the fact that half of Baltimore's black men are under some form of correctional control (i.e., in prison, paroled, or on probation). He conveyed, on a visceral level, the heavy stigma that burdens those caught up in the criminal justice system.

By virtue of their conviction, our brothers and sisters cannot vote; employers, time and again, refuse to hire them upon their return home after completing a simple background check. Chris spoke of the pain that too many feel when they return home from prison: despite having served their time and paid their debt, recently returned men and women cannot move forward from their crime or their previous lives behind bars because of discriminatory barriers and attitudes perpetuated across society. Chris painted a clear, compelling, and ultimately urgent portrait of a large swath of the black community: generations of black men and women lost not only behind bars but functionally "disappeared" upon their return to society.

Chris reminded us that these men and women don't disappear. They exist. They are real. Their hopes, dreams, and struggles are valid and they matter. Chris closed that night by sharing his dream: He wanted to build, with his own hands, companies that made people's lives better. He envisioned, for instance, a furniture company that would rehabilitate secondhand furniture as well as the prospects of the people whose hands created it. Chris believed that such a company would change the lives of the men and women who acquired critical skills behind bars but who returned home to find no avenues to employment. He also believed that a company led by the formerly incarcerated could alter our larger conversation about the people that we as a society are altogether too comfortable disregarding. Chris asked us a question: What if we didn't throw our people away? What would happen if we recognized their value? What would we discover about them? About us?

Something I learned in the course of writing *The Other Wes Moore* is that people are not only products of their environment but ultimately of their expectations. Who believes in us and to what end are among life's most important questions. In *The Master Plan*, Chris

Wilson challenges us to expect something more and different from the people we cast away. He challenges us to remember that they are our brothers and sisters, mothers and fathers, sons and daughters; through his words we come to regard the people we encounter throughout Chris's story with a level of dignity and respect rarely afforded to those housed or impacted by America's criminal justice system. Chris rightly highlights that for the *millions* of Americans who languish behind bars and the *millions more* who have returned home, the American Dream has been foreclosed. Chris inspires us to dream what could be if we supported those who return home from prison in rebuilding their communities, raising their families, and advancing their careers. He challenges us to think about the many ways the world might be different.

Chris's favorite story is the allegory of the cave by Plato. On several occasions, I've watched Chris relay the story in a speech and have always been moved by his telling of it. Chris's framing of modern inmates as prisoners in the metaphorical cave is heartbreaking because it forces us to fathom the dreary lives endured by men and women imprisoned behind bars. In our imaginations, we wrestle with the fact that for those in prison, life's simple gifts—fresh air, sunshine, blue skies—remain just beyond reach for years, decades, or quite possibly, life. Harder still to reconcile is the fact that despite those desperate and limited circumstances, these men and women never fail to dream or imagine a better life beyond the four walls that surround them. Chris presents us with those stories—the yearning hopes and dreams fueled by a desire for a better life—and in doing so, *The Master Plan* breaks open your heart. It renders our willful blindness to those imprisoned by our criminal justice system intolerable. *The Master Plan* is Chris Wilson's master work because it forces us to confront, and leave, our own "caves" by compelling us to empathize with the realities of those that we as a society have thrown away. We discover that we need these men and women in the fight to improve our communities and secure our future. And we are better for it. *The Master Plan* is less of a road map and more of a philosophy that we should all take to heart: we are all better than our worst decision, our sense of justice should honor the redemptive possibilities inherent in every person, and our destinies are truly intertwined.

—GOVERNOR WES MOORE
Baltimore, Maryland

Very soon after I went to live with Mr. and Mrs. Auld, she very kindly commenced to teach me the A, B, C. . . . Mr. Auld found out what was going on, and at once forbade Mrs. Auld to instruct me further, telling her, among other things, that it was unlawful, as well as unsafe, to teach a slave to read. To use his own words, further, he said, "If you give a nigger an inch, he will take an ell. A nigger should know nothing but to obey his master—to do as he is told to do. Learning would *spoil* the best nigger in the world. Now," said he, "if you teach that nigger (speaking of myself) how to read, there would be no keeping him. It would forever unfit him to be a slave . . ." These words sank deep into my heart, stirred up sentiments within that lay slumbering, and called into existence an entirely new train of thought. . . . From that moment, I understood [that reading and knowledge was] the pathway from slavery to freedom.

—FREDERICK DOUGLASS

Narrative of the Life of Frederick Douglass, an American Slave

PROLOGUE

One Shot

It's not the load that breaks you down,
it's the way you carry it.

—LENA HORNE

November 6, 2006

THEY CAME TO my cell at 4:00 a.m., but I was already awake, dressed and standing by my bunk. It wasn't that I couldn't sleep. Those days, I was sleeping better than ever. It was more like my body knew: *This is the moment, Chris. Ten years, four months in the making. Let's get it done.*

"You ready, Wilson?"

"I'm ready."

They walked me down the tier, everyone asleep at this hour, nothing but the sound of our shoes on the concrete floor, the doors buzzing as the guards pushed them open, then clanging shut as we left. They put the cuffs on to process me through the last gate, the guard whispering "Good luck, Wilson, we're rooting for you" as he locked the chain around my waist. When he stepped away, he was all business as usual.

The transfer bus took almost an hour: ten minutes through the rolling fields of Howard County; thirty on the interstate; another fifteen through the Washington, DC, suburbs of Prince George's County to the courthouse in Upper Marlboro, where my original trial had taken place. It was still dark, so there wasn't much to see past my own reflection looking back at me through the bars across the bus window.

In the basement of the courthouse: another set of doors and metal detectors, another set of procedures. They locked me in a holding cell with five members of the MS-13 street gang—skinny Salvadorans with tattoos on their faces, because MS-13 is no joke; the members are dedicated to the life. I wasn't chained, but I was in my prison uniform. I never wore it, because I wanted to look on the outside like the man I was inside, but it was required here. This was who the system said I was.

The Salvadorans watched me with suspicion as I slid onto the bench. I nodded, but nobody nodded back. Eventually, they started arguing in Spanish about whether I was a snitch, put in the cell to eavesdrop and gather information. They were in for a preliminary hearing, but the state had nothing, they said, so don't say nothing, especially around this *soplón*. I spoke fluent Spanish—I spoke three languages fluently, in fact, and I was working on Mandarin—but I didn't react. I didn't want to spook them. We were in the cell for almost two hours, and for the last hour nobody said a word.

"Inmate 265–975. Inmate Wilson. Let's go, Wilson."

"*No soy un soplón*," I said as I left. Just so they knew.

I rode up in the elevator with a black female bailiff. She was a grandmotherly type, her hair set, uniform pressed. She smelled nice. Nothing in prison smelled nice. "You have a good judge," she said. "She's a fair lady. What's your sentence?"

"Life."

"Oh," she said as her face dropped. For lifers, she knew, there was never good news. "Well, good luck."

Judge Serrette was on her high seat, studying me as I entered.

How many men like me has she seen today? I wondered. *How many this week? This month?* The jury box was empty, but the public benches were packed with bored people, mostly women and children, mostly black, waiting for their loved ones to be called. I searched the crowd, but nobody looked back. All these friends and family were here for other prisoners. I knew nobody was coming for me.

The only person there for me—my pro bono lawyer, Keith Showstack—was laughing and joking with the state's attorney. I had known Keith for more than seven years. I trusted him with my life. But when I saw him laughing with the state's attorney, it threw me, the old street mistrust coming back. *She's trying to keep me inside forever. Why you talking to her?*

Keith put his hand on my shoulder. He winked, like, *We got this, Chris.*

He looked confident, but Keith Showstack always looked confident. He looked confident the day I met him, in the lawyer's room at the Patuxent Institution, when I was a twenty-year-old lifer and he was a twenty-three-year-old family law intern with slicked-back hair and a South Boston accent so thick I could barely understand him. It took us six years and five rejections by the judge to get this sentence modification hearing—the only way a lifer like me could get out from under—but every three months Keith had slapped his ratty briefcase on the table at Patuxent, smiled like he knew every secret in the book, and said, "They turned down your request again, Chris. But don't worry."

Easy for you to say, when you get to drive home.

"Your Honor, we're prepared," he said, "if the court is ready."

The state's attorney hammered my crime, like I knew she would. A man was shot six times, Your Honor, she said. Shot in the middle of the chest. Shot in the lower right side of the chest. Shot in the right buttocks. In the right elbow. Shot in the hand, Your Honor, as he was running. Murdered, Your Honor, while running away.

"He will never be able to better himself," she said. "He will never be able to say I'm proud of myself, I got an associate's degree. He will never know his children. He will never know his grandchildren. He was shot down at thirty-one years of age. *That defendant*"—pointing at me—"without any thought to what his life was like, took it away."

The state's attorney sat down, and I could feel the spectators on their benches leaning forward, because this was more than a crime, it was a murder, and I was more than a prisoner. I had been sentenced to natural life in the penitentiary system of the state of Maryland at the age of seventeen, and I had only one shot, this shot, of ever walking out of my cell alive.

So everyone in that courtroom wanted to know what I had to say. Was I innocent? Was I falsely accused? Were there extenuating circumstances, like self-defense? The judge turned to me, like, *Well?* Not unkind, but curious. I hoped.

I took a deep breath. This was it. My life in a moment. My fate in a stranger's hands. My last chance, or I would die in a prison cell thirty, forty, fifty years in the future, an old man slurping watery farina from a plastic bowl. And yet I felt calm. I knew what I had to do.

"Your Honor," I said. "I want to tell you the truth."

PART 1

The Cave

How could they see anything but the shadows
if they were never allowed to move their heads?

—PLATO, "THE ALLEGORY OF THE CAVE"

Division Avenue

MY GRANDPARENTS, GRANDMA and Big Daddy, moved to Northeast Washington, DC, in 1948, when it was the black part of town. They bought a duplex and raised five children there, the youngest being my mom, who everybody called Mona after the *Mona Lisa*. That's what Big Daddy wanted to name her, Mona Lisa, but Grandma said you couldn't burden a child with a name like that. Grandma was always practical. So they named my mom Charlene, but ended up calling her Mona Lisa anyway, since Big Daddy refused to call her anything else. One way or the other, Big Daddy got his way.

I hear the neighborhood was nice back in the day. Big Daddy worked as a clerk in various government offices and drove a Capitol Cab. He made decent money, and I suspect most of the people in the neighborhood did, too, although it was segregation money, and there was only so much that ordinary black people could make. Working poor, but proud. Grandma stayed home with the children, and she worked hard, too. She had flowers along the street and a garden full of southern specialties like collard greens—Grandma was from a small town in North Carolina, Big Daddy from an even smaller town in Mississippi—and she kept the house spotless. Most of her children went on to successful lives, although Uncle Buddy still alternates between her basement and the street, and we lost Uncle Gerald to AIDS, which he caught from heroin needles.

Even when my sister and I were living with them in the 1980s, Grandma kept things square. Three home-cooked meals, chores after school. Wash your hands when you walk in the door and don't talk back. Church on Wednesday evening, no excuses. Big Daddy had his recliner and his television shows, and you didn't want to disturb his routine by forcing him to punish you, because he was a large and serious man. It was better to sit with him and watch.

Outside, though, the neighborhood was rough. The working black community had been transformed by housing projects, especially the 440-unit Lincoln Heights Houses. Fifteen depressing three-story cinder-block and brick buildings surrounded by dirt yards, the Houses threw a shadow over the neighborhood from the hill right behind Grandma's house. Three blocks away, next to the elementary school, was Clay Terrace, another 1960s-era government housing project. The Lincoln Heights crews and the Clay Terrace crews hated one another and were always beefing. My grandparents' duplex, with its tidy flowers and neatly trimmed plot of grass, was right in the middle.

It was fine during the day. There were kids on the block, and we played in the street. Heroin addicts wandered up from the bottom of the hill a few blocks away—heroin was the drug back then, and the block known as "the bottom" was where to buy it—but mostly it was kids playing chase, old heads on porches, nosy women hanging out of windows, and Doug E. Fresh and Slick Rick blasting all day.

But when the streetlights came on, the crews came out. Mostly I remember arguments, yelling that turned into fights and sometimes brawls. Car alarms going off, windows smashed. Guys tore bricks out of the border around Grandma's garden and used them as weapons, and Grandma went out the next morning, on her knees, and put them back in place. Back then, if it was gunshots, it was only three or four.

"Just keep your head down and your eyes to yourself," Grandma said as she ferociously brushed my hair before sending my sister and me off to school. "Don't talk to nobody and you won't have problems. God don't like the ugly."

It was three blocks to Richardson Elementary, with three ways to get there. I planned my route every day. It wasn't the dealers I wanted to avoid; it was the middle-school girls. They chased us, taunted us, and forced us to kiss them. I loved girls, even at seven years old. Most days I spent my lunch money on candy from the corner store to share with cute classmates. Those teenage girls, though, were terrifying.

I was never a good student. Too much anxiety. Even as a first grader, I stayed awake most nights, worrying about the yelling, the gunshots, the car tires squealing away. More than any other sound from my youth, that's what I remember: car tires squealing away. But I was smart. I read books. I joined the chess club. I was chosen for school trips to Baltimore and New York, where I toured the United Nations and saw the Statue of Liberty. I was even our class representative to CEO for a Day. We spent a few hours at a Safeway, learning how they ran a grocery store. It wasn't a CEO position, and it smelled like cabbage, but I guess they figured that this was the best kids from Lincoln Heights could hope for.

I can't remember how I discovered the Capitol View Library. It was nine blocks away, probably the farthest I had ever walked from my grandparents' duplex. Grandma scolded me when she found out I was crossing East Capitol Street, because it was a four-lane. She thought it wasn't safe, which is funny, because she insisted the neighborhood was fine.

"It's good here," she said, even when a teenager got shot on our block. "Just keep your eyes to yourself and pray. God don't like the ugly."

The library was where I got away from the tension of the street. It had a kids' room where the librarians read books. I remember a librarian telling us about the great library in Alexandria, Egypt, and how scholars came from all over the world to study there, and how boat captains stopped to have the librarians draw them maps before they headed out on long voyages. I thought, *Wow. There been libraries for two thousand years.* I pictured it like a tower, a thousand stories tall. I didn't know, until much later, the library in Alexandria burned down. I guess everything, eventually, burns down.

It was around then I started noticing the bullet casings and baggies—crack didn't come in vials in my area. The next minute, it seemed, I started seeing young men in nice cars and guys on porches, in broad daylight, putting coolers on the barrels of their guns and loading extended clips.

They'd catch me watching and nod. "That's an Uzi, young," they'd say, showing off. "You like it?"

My sister, Leslie, who was a year older and protective, talked me onto the school track team. I was the smallest kid in third grade and I had asthma, but Coach Pergerson took no pity.

"Every kid thinks they have asthma, Chris," he said, walking around in his skintight tracksuit. "You don't have asthma. You're just out of shape."

Even when I was sick and huffing, barely able to breathe, Coach Pergerson challenged me. "You wanna quit, Chris?"

"No, sir."

"You can quit running right now, Chris, but if you do, you better start walking, because you're off the team. I got no room for quitters. I'm looking for warriors!"

And just when my lungs were burning, and I felt like dying, my sister would run up beside me and whisper, "Don't quit, Chris. Keep going."

There was a fence separating the field from the Clay Terraces, and men would get up against it, drinking from bottles and laughing at us. We saw drug deals going down. One time, a stolen car being chased by the cops slammed through the fence and went skidding across the field in the middle of practice.

"Keep running! Push it!" Coach Pergerson yelled like he never even noticed.

I liked track—I liked being challenged. My passion, though, was books, especially after I discovered a section of child-friendly versions of classics like *Aesop's Fables* and the Greek myths. I checked them out, curled up in a sheet on the floor of my bedroom, and read until late at night. I had a bed, but I never slept in it. I was too worried about stray bullets coming in the window. Since the arrival of the Uzis and Mac-11s, it felt like stray bullets were always coming through windows on Division Avenue.

Who we at war with? I wondered, wrapping the sheet around me.

My favorite book was an illustrated version of Plato's "The Allegory of the Cave." In the story, a group of people live chained together in a cave. The only light comes from torches on the wall, and all that the captives can see is a screen where the shadows of people are always moving. Since they've never seen anything else, the people think the screen is the world and the shadows are real. They talk constantly about the shadows, arguing about who they belong to and what they are doing. They pride themselves on knowing more of those details than the people chained around them.

Eventually one person gets unchained, and he goes out of the cave. In my mind, the man closes his eyes, blinded by the bright sunlight, but when he finally opens them he sees color for the first time. He feels the wind on his skin, and he breathes fresh air. As his eyes adjust, he notices mountains in the distance, and green grass, and a waterfall. Birds fly past, riding the wind, and he realizes the screen was a lie. It wasn't the world. There was another world outside, bigger and more beautiful than those poor chained people could imagine. They just weren't allowed to go there.

Even at eight years old, I knew the story was about me, because I was living in that cave. The kids in Lincoln Heights talked all day about the neighborhood. They knew the crews. They analyzed the weapons, the stereos, the cars. That was all they cared about, because that was all they knew. Their world was eight or nine blocks, and most kids never left that cave. They didn't know there were places where people sat down in restaurants and ate meals; the only food they knew was carryout. They'd seen a swimming pool, maybe, but never a beach.

The Cosby Show? Please. A house? Nice clothes? A dad? Real life wasn't like that.

I remember having debates with my friends because they thought every white person was a racist. It was gospel truth to them that white people hated us and they kept us down so they could hoard the good things for themselves. Why wouldn't we think that? The only white people we ever saw in Lincoln Heights were cops, and those cops *did* hate us, and they *were* trying to keep us down. They never hung at the corner store or the block parties. All they did was eyeball us, harass us, make us feel like criminals, even though we were kids. Then suddenly, they barreled down the road twenty at a time in six-wheeled combat vehicles, battering down doors and throwing everyone to the floor. We couldn't point to one white cop in the neighborhood who wanted to do us any good.

So how did I know all white people weren't racists? Why did I believe in the world outside the cave?

Because I was the kid who got out of his chains.

My Mona Lisa Mom

I LIVED WITH my grandparents on Division Avenue during the week, but on the weekends my sister and I lived with my mom in Prince George's County. Her neighborhood, Temple Hills, was half an hour away, barely over the state line, but it was a different world. The houses were bigger. They had lawns. There were gas stations and a grocery store with vegetables. It was a mixed neighborhood, with white and black families living together. It even had a park, where my sister and I climbed trees.

Best of all, it had Mom.

Mom was a striver. Pregnant at sixteen, she finished high school and married the father of her child. She bought her first house at nineteen. She and Dad had four children in ten years—two boys a year apart, then a five-year gap before my sister and me. They divorced when I was eight months old. Mom was a nurse, but she went back to school and became a paramedic. That's when she sent my sister and me to live with her parents in Lincoln Heights, while my older brothers stayed with her. Being a paramedic meant twelve-hour shifts, including overnights. Leslie and I were too young to stay in the house alone.

But Mom was off every weekend, and seeing her each Friday was the highlight of my life. Whatever Mom wanted, I wanted. Whatever she said, that was truth. We went to the mall and she bought me Nike Air Max or Asics running sneakers. We played Monopoly and chess. Mom was a giver. When she came across wounded animals, she took them to the vet and found them good homes. If my friends went to the store with us, she bought them a little candy, too.

Mom was careful with her money. She knew the hard work it took to get ahead, and she was determined to teach me. She sat me down at the kitchen table and explained how much she made, and I couldn't believe it. We were rich! Then she explained insurance, the mortgage on the house, the electric bill, the groceries, and I was shocked because there wasn't anything left.

"That's life," she told me. "That's why you save your money. Don't buy cheap stuff. Wait until you can afford it, then buy something nice."

That's what Mom had done. She saved for her first house. Then she traded up to a nice four-bedroom split-level on a corner lot. It had a

Mom in her twenties

swimming pool, so Mom bought a karaoke machine and threw parties for her friends. They sang along to Whitney Houston, Sade, and especially James Brown. I remember watching from upstairs as Mom and her boyfriend, Ronald, clapped and danced to the Godfather of Soul. Sometimes, I was invited down to dance with her. I still love that music. *Say it loud, I'm black and I'm proud.*

Mom's best friend, Gwen, was

white, with long blond hair. I still remember the way it blew in the wind when she took me out for rides in her Corvette convertible. I loved those rides because I loved that car. It was so beautiful, I used to rub its curves. Sometimes we drove along the Anacostia River past the rich people's houses and boats, but mostly we just cruised with the top down. I was a different person in Gwen's Corvette. I was out of the cave. I felt like if this was happening—me, a pretty woman, the world's coolest car—then anything was possible.

I had a Matchbox car collection, and Mom always bought me the Corvettes because she knew how I felt about that car. If you work hard enough, she said, you'll have one of your own one day.

Grandma was steady as a rock. She was gonna stand in her duplex until time pushed her into the ground. I could count on her. But she was hard like a rock, too. She never asked how I was. She never talked about life. She never gave me a hug or said she loved me. Everything was by the book with Grandma, and apparently the book said, *No affection required.*

"I've cried all my tears," she told me once. I guess she'd shared all her love by the time I came along, too.

Mom loved me openly. She *enjoyed* me. Her smile made me believe that happiness was possible and that the world was more than hustling to put food on the table. Grandma taught me to work, but Mom taught me to dream. She was a nine-to-fiver, but she was always trying to get ahead. She and Ronald sat up at night, studying medical books so that they could get more paramedic certificates.

I had a sweet tooth. I loved candy. Mom suggested I sell it at school. "You can make good money," she said.

"What you mean?"

We were at the kitchen table, where Mom studied every night. I was young: my head barely cleared the edge.

"You know about supply and demand, right?" she asked.

"I guess . . ."

"If there's more buyers than sellers, you can sell for a higher price. If you're the only seller, you can name your price."

"I'm not the only seller," I pointed out. "What about the store?"

"Can kids go to the store during school?"

I shook my head no.

"That's called the Law of Scarcity. There are no other Blow Pops available at school."

My mind was rolling now. "So if they want them, they have to pay my price!"

"Not too high, though, Chris. Blow Pops cost, what, a dollar for five at the store? That's twenty cents. In school, kids might pay a quarter, or even fifty cents."

My jaw dropped. *Are you serious?*

"That's called entrepreneurship," Mom said.

Then give me some!

Before long, I was making a five-dollar profit a week. Then I convinced some friends to work for me, and I started making ten dollars. Now I could buy my girl chocolate milk at lunch, and soda after school. That's all I wanted, really, was to impress a few girls.

Life was running against me, though. This was the late 1980s, and crack was hitting hard. Murder rates were spiking in Lincoln Heights, and even in Temple Hills families were being torn apart by addiction. I was selling Blow Pops; other kids in my elementary school were carrying rocks. It was so violent on Division Avenue, the cops put twenty-foot-tall spotlights out on Grandma's block, making it impossible to sleep. Helicopters hovered overhead. The National Guard was in the streets. They had tanks, with battering rams for the doors. It was a war, and life feels cheap in times like that. When every month is worse than the last, people start grabbing hold of what they can.

My friends from Division Avenue said I didn't understand. They hated when I looked at them side-eyed, because they were nine years old and heading into the game. They were like, "What you know, Chris? Your mom got a house. Your mom got a pool." They thought I was living a life of luxury.

I suppose I was. I was out of the cave. And just being in the world? Understanding the possibilities? For a kid from the inner city, that changes everything.

But when you start from a place like Division Avenue, life's fragile. You don't get to make mistakes, because you don't have a safety net. Ronald developed a drinking problem. He had been a field medic in Vietnam, and he had nightmares. He screamed in his sleep. As a kid, I didn't understand. I didn't know why he drank until he passed out, or why he got up in the middle of *Platoon* or *Apocalypse Now*—he had a huge collection of war movies on VHS tapes—and walked away. When I found him later, sitting on his bed crying, I thought he was soft. Really, though, Ronald was sick.

So Mom kicked him out. And then she made her mistake, the one that shattered our family. She fell in love with the wrong man.

The Cop

HE WAS A police officer. They met on the job. As a paramedic, Mom met a lot of cops. She had a thing for cops. I think it was something about their power. Most men where we lived didn't have much power.

At first, things seemed good. I came home for the weekend and there was new stuff in the house: a six-hundred-gallon fish tank, a Bose stereo. The cop bought me video games and a Sonic 6 bike. I was nine when he moved in with Mom. With two incomes, they built a bar in the basement. Bought a sixty-inch television. Fixed the pool.

The next year, Mom got pregnant with my baby brother, Korey, and the family shuffled around. My oldest brother, Kenny, went to live with my dad, and my other brother, Derrick, came to live with my grandparents. Derrick and I never got along. He was six years older than me and always looking for a fight. By the time he got to Lincoln Heights, Derrick was running the streets and carrying guns. Mom thought Grandma's discipline might help. Unbelievable, thinking a move to Division Avenue would keep Derrick out of trouble. Division Avenue *was* trouble.

So I was super happy when, as part of the shuffle, Mom brought my sister and me to Temple Hills. That was the sixth grade, the happiest year of my life. It seemed like Mom and I were always together, talking, laughing, dancing. I wanted to start a lawn-mowing business, so Mom taught me how to work out the pricing. "Never sell yourself short, Chris," she told me. "But never cheat anybody, either." I went around the neighborhood and found customers. Mom spent her Saturdays driving me to my jobs.

She showed me how to court a lady. I always talked with Mom about my crushes—I was so open with her, she even helped me write love notes—so when I asked my first girl on a date, Mom made sure I knew how to treat her right. Always be respectful. Listen to her. Open doors. Keep promises, and never, ever lie. "Think about how you want your sister treated," she said. I was her youngest, except for baby Korey; I was always her "little man." She drove my dates and me to the ninety-nine-cent movies, then took us out afterward to eat.

For her birthday, Mom bought herself a necklace, then wrapped it so I could give it to her. Looking back, that's sad. No one gave my mother gifts. At the time, though, it made me feel close to her, like we had something special.

Then, one day, the cop punched her in the face. I was with my friends, and as soon as Mom left, they were like, "Dude, he just hit your mom."

"Nah," I said. "They just playin'."

My friends shook their heads. "They ain't playing, Chris."

I put it together then: All the times I came home to find holes in the walls or a broken chair. All the times Mom had bruises and excuses. I knew Mom and the cop argued. They had a baby together, but he was never home, and when he was home he was often drunk, blaring his terrible music at top volume while he ironed his uniform. I mean, I'd seen things. *I knew*, even before my friends called it out, but I'd been lying to myself. I was a kid, and I wanted the world to be perfect, and I always believed in Mom.

I tried to talk to her, but she shook her head. "Don't worry about it, Chris. It's complicated. It has nothing to do with you."

She wouldn't look me in the eye, and that made me sad, because that wasn't Mom.

I started crying. "Why are you with him, Mom?"

"You're too young, Chris," she said quietly. "You don't understand."

She started drinking. Mom usually drank when she was dancing and having a good time, but now she drank during the day. That was the cop's thing. He drank all day.

"I'm going to leave him," she said when I asked about her black eye.

She said that a lot. Sometimes she followed through and he was gone for a few days. But he always came back, and soon after, Mom went back to drinking.

I started going through his stuff when he was out. I found pictures of trashy women hidden in his drawers. "He's cheating on you, Mom," I said.

From the way she slumped, I knew it wasn't a surprise. He didn't even own a car. He was taking Mom's car out to meet other women. And she knew. *Mom knew.*

"Don't go through other people's stuff," she said.

"Why you defending him?"

I found guns in his dresser drawers and drugs in his duffel bag.

"He's a cop," Mom said. "They confiscate drugs all the time."

"And cops bring those drugs home? They hide the drugs in their bedroom?"

I guess she loved him, but he was killing her. She didn't smile like she used to, she didn't laugh. Gwen had stopped coming around with her Corvette, and most of her other old friends had stopped coming, too.

They fought: about the drugs, the women, the money. The cop hit my mother, choked her, punched her to the floor, then turned and blamed me. "You a snitch. This is on you."

She kicked him out, and I got my hopes up. But he was back a few days later, sitting with Mom on the sofa. He smiled when he saw me, put his arm around her. Then he came to my room and stood in the doorway. "You tried to get rid of me, huh? You little snitch. Well, I ain't going nowhere."

Sometimes Big Daddy showed up in his Oldsmobile, wearing his fraternity cap. He'd say he wanted to take me out, but I knew Mom had called him to take me away. We talked as he drove. "How you doing, Chris?" he'd ask, driving way below the speed limit.

"All right," I'd say, watching the other cars fly past us.

"I hear your grades are slipping. You got to study, son. Education is important."

"Okay," I'd reply, but what did *he* know? He wasn't there when Mom got punched in the face and fell to the floor. He didn't see it when the cop threatened me, pressing his gun to my head. He didn't go to bed hungry. He wasn't up all night, worried sick. I remember the school nurse taking me aside. She said I had a big bald spot on the back of my head. I was so nervous, I'd been pulling my hair out.

"How about those Redskins?" Big Daddy would say, one big hand on the wheel and his eyes on the road. "I think maybe they got it this year."

My cousin Eric saved me. He was four years older than me, a lifeguard at the Barry Farm Projects pool, and a ladies' man. I liked his style, his personality, everything about him. He lived in Southeast, across town, but when things got bad in Temple Hills, he and his sister, Angie, would come pick up my sister and me, no questions asked.

Eric gave me an escape. He gave me stylish clothes: Guess jeans, Used jeans, Fila sneakers. He took me to the go-gos on Friday and Saturday nights. These were small clubs, usually in strip malls or cribs, with live local bands like Rare Essence, Northeast Groovers, and Junkyard Band—eight or ten black men packed on a tiny stage laying down a heavy electric conga beat. Lights blinking, dance floor jammed with women. The nicest cars in the neighborhoods lined up for blocks. Eric was only sixteen, but he slipped me Miller Lite in red plastic cups and I followed him like a kid brother, feeling like I belonged.

It never lasted. After two or three days of my sleeping on his floor, Eric was always like, "Why you still here, cuz? Man up. Go home and face your problems."

But what was I going to do? Mom was shrunk into herself, not talking, or she had more bruises she didn't bother trying to explain. Things disappeared: the fish tank, the brass figurines Grandma had given her for her wedding.

When things got too rough, Mom called the cops. They confronted him. "You drunk? You break this table?"

He said, "Hold on now. I'm a police officer." Showing his badge.

"Okay, okay," they said, softening their stance, because cops took the aggressive approach with a black man unless he was one of their own. "Why don't you cool down? Do you have some place to go for the night?"

It always ended the same way: no report, no arrest, just a night away to sober up. Even if he threw a remote so hard that it shattered against the wall. Even if he left marks on a woman's face. Even if her twelve-year-old son was standing right there, watching, and the kid had a bruise on his face, too.

The next day, the cop was back in a brand-new outfit he'd bought with Mom's money, standing in my doorway. "I'm still here, Chris. This is my house now."

I was in the yard one day, minding my own business, when two scraggly dudes pulled up in a hooptie car. "This Mona's house?"

"Yeah. I'm her son. What you want?"

They pulled into the driveway and went inside. I knew those dusty dudes weren't right, so I paced. I probably climbed a tree, because that's what I did back then to escape my fear. Finally, I snuck into the garage and opened the door to the little bedroom Mom had built back there. The police officer, Mom, and the dusty dudes were sitting around a table covered in beer bottles and crack rocks.

Mom stared at me through the smoke, her mouth hollow, her eyes pleading. She looked down, and the cop stood up, blocking my view.

"Get the fuck out of here, boy," he said. "And close that door. You didn't see nothing."

He didn't have to tell me twice. I wanted that door closed. I went to my room and laid on my bed, waiting for Mom. I waited all night. It felt like she never came back.

Soon after, I stood up to the cop. He was beating my mother, and I grabbed the only weapon at hand: her hot curling iron. We were in their bedroom. Close quarters. I held out the iron, threatening to burn him. Mom was screaming, *Don't hurt him, Chris, don't hurt him.*

I looked at her, my heart breaking. Why'd she always side with him instead of me?

He lashed out and grabbed the curling iron from my hand. He smiled and stepped toward me, backing me into the corner. He was huge, a former marine. I was thirteen by then, but barely five feet tall. He looked down at me and laughed. I knew he was going to hurt me for real this time.

Instead, he handed me the curling iron. "Go ahead," he said. "Do what you came to do, little man."

Mom was screaming.

"Shut up, Mona," the cop said without looking away from me. "This little nigga ain't gonna do nothing."

He was right. I couldn't do it. I wanted to, but I wasn't like him. I couldn't hurt someone. And he would have killed me if I'd tried.

So I ran. I took three buses to Division Avenue, hating myself the whole way. My grandparents' house wasn't any better, because my brother Derrick was there. When I started hanging with Eric, Derrick took it as disrespect. He felt I should come to him, but he was a mean son of a bitch. He wore his jeans loose, his Timberlands untied, and his guns out. Derrick was small for his age, but I was six years younger and even smaller. Derrick beat me all the time. He'd do it to amuse his friends, but even after they stopped laughing and told him to be cool, he kept at it.

"Chris need this," he said, punching me as hard as he could. "Chris soft as shit."

So I'd call Eric and go out with his crew: Tyrone, Muhammad, Warren. Drinking. Dancing. Listening to rap in the parking lot after a go-go show. Eric with a Miller in his hand, leaning on his sister's Toyota Celica in the parking lot, Jay Jah in the backseat, rolling blunts.

"I see you looking at that girl, Chris. Go talk to her."

"No, I'm good."

"Don't be a pussy, Chris. Closed mouths don't get fed."

I did it for Eric. It was embarrassing, but I talked to those older girls, the kind that had intimidated me in elementary school, and just when I felt like their smirks would kill me, Eric always slid to my rescue. "Hey, that's my little cousin. He bothering you? I'm Eric, by the way."

Those nights at the go-gos with Eric, feeling like a grown man talking to real women even when I was only setting up my cousin, were the best of my young life.

And then I went home, and my video games were missing. The stereo disappeared. I got a job at a car wash—I was too young to work legally, so they paid cash under the table—but Mom stole my money. She turned mean when I tried to stop her. Now it wasn't just the cop and Derrick beating on me.

I went to Big Daddy. "They're on crack," I said.

Big Daddy confronted them, but they denied it. "He don't know what he's talking about, Big Daddy," Mom said. "Chris a troubled kid."

I stole the police officer's bulletproof vest. I thought he'd get in trouble for losing his equipment, maybe even get kicked off the force. It was dumb.

I tried to sell the vest at school. That was dumber. Someone ratted me out, and I got expelled.

My teachers took pity on me. My grades were bad, I was neglecting my work and falling behind, but they liked me. I think they saw something in me, or maybe they saw my hurt. They gave me the schoolwork for the rest of the year.

I stayed in the basement alone, doing schoolwork, reading books, looking after my three-year-old brother, Korey. My sister came home from school with the food and Pampers. She was strong. She was a freshman in high school and excelling even while taking care of us.

As soon as Leslie hit home, I was out. I had a Temple Hills crew, the kind of kids Grandma would call "bad influences." We were drinking and smoking blunts, but it was nothing, just being kids. They came from good homes with two parents, worked hard in school. Their families took me in when things at home got tight.

Or Eric came around and took me out with him. It was around

then he gave me my first gun. It was for protection, because young black men were dying in the streets, and guns were everywhere. After a while, you don't question it, because that's the cave. We'd be at a party, talking to girls. Someone would walk in the door and Eric would say, "We got to go, Chris, get the joints," meaning guns.

A couple times it was "We got to go," and the next second, "Run, run, run," and shots were being fired. I never fired my gun. I never saw Eric fire his gun, except for target practice in the alley with his dad, Uncle Gerald. Our guns were for deterrence, but they were necessary, because I saw four murders that year.

The first was at a go-go, a typical night. The crews were mixed up, bumping into one another, and by the time the club let out at 2:00 in the morning, emotions were high. There must have been three hundred people smoking, chatting in the parking lot, and suddenly: shots fired. Everyone screamed and scattered, but I had a panic reaction. I hit the ground.

"We got to go," Eric said, coming back to find me.

I looked up, and everybody was gone except a kid ten feet away in a puddle of blood. "We need to help him," I said.

"We need to go, cuz! Right now! Ain't no help for him!"

I turned fourteen on December 28, 1992, and celebrated with blunts and booze. A few days later, the cop came home drunk at 2:00 in the morning. Mom was with her friend Lisa, but the cop didn't care about acting right in front of guests anymore. I was in the basement, with my head down, listening to Mom scream, "Get off me! Get off me!" I jumped up when I heard something shatter.

It was the lamp. It was broken on the floor, and in the flickering light I could see the police officer with his hand on Mom's throat. He was yelling about who she'd been seeing that night.

Just some girlfriends, she said.

He slammed her into the hallway wall. He lifted her by the throat, turned, and slammed her into the other wall. It hurts, even now, to see it in my mind. Mom was kicking and screaming, but he pinned her to the wall with a forearm and jammed his fingers into her panties, yelling, "You're wet, Mona. I can feel it. You're wet. You been cheating on me."

I thought, *Get your gun, Chris. Get your damn gun.*

But I didn't. I took one step, then stopped. I couldn't do it. I hated him. He was killing us. But I didn't have the . . . courage, I guess, or maybe the heart.

Mom's friend Lisa jumped in. The cop turned and slammed her down so violently her head put a hole in the wall. She fell over, unconscious. Then he dropped Mom and came for me. He raised his gun, I stepped back, and he pistol-whipped me so hard I blacked out.

The next thing I heard was the pounding and grunting. I opened my eyes. I saw a broken lamp, Lisa lying on her side, a table, a chair, and the cop on the bed, in the next room, punching my mother. I could see his fist rising and falling, jackhammering her face until she finally stopped struggling and lay still.

All I remember after that was the quiet. The cop breathing heavily, staring down at what he'd done. It took him forever to catch his breath. Finally, he got up, grabbed a few items from the table, and walked out the door.

I pulled myself to Mom. She was trying to curl into a ball and hide, but I could tell her face was broken. I found out later he smashed the orbital bone of her right eye.

I was only fourteen, but I knew how to drive. So I dragged Mom to her car and laid her in the backseat. I meant to drive to the hospital, but I ended up at the police station. Mom was in bad shape. Her face was bloody and swollen. She was crying so hard her breath would catch, like she was choking.

The cops didn't care. They made her wait in a hard chair, without a towel or a drink of water. She fell and they didn't help her up. It was like they hated us for bothering them. I heard one mutter, "Stupid bitch. He's just going to get back in there."

They had been called to our house a dozen times. They knew the cop was an abuser. But Mom kept taking him back, so they didn't want to help her. They thought she got what she deserved.

Eventually, they took her statement, then sent her to the hospital. That's all I know. I remember arriving home to catch the morning school bus, no sleep at all, but the police report doesn't back that up. It says the attack happened after midnight on New Year's Day. January 2, 1993, was a Saturday. So either the police report is wrong, or I took my mother to the police station and nursed her back to health and caught the school bus on some other terrible morning I've been trying ever since to forget.

Broken

THE POLICE OFFICER was arrested, but the damage was done. Mom came home broken, with a bandage over her face and dark glasses because her cracked eye socket made her sensitive to light. She couldn't work. The paramedic service put her on disability, and she spent the next few weeks in bed, crying. She became addicted to her pain medication, especially after she began mixing it with alcohol. Mom never worked full-time again.

I was just as broken, in a different way. I was angry. I couldn't think about that night for years, especially after I found out the cop had been raping her, too. But I thought often about the way those cops at the station had spit on my mother.

I was angry: at *the* cop, at *those* cops, at *all* cops. When the cop pleaded out to sexual battery and assault and received less than three years, I lost my faith in the system. He destroyed my mother, on purpose, over a period of years, and he was going to get paroled in a year and a half.

And even after all that, Mom didn't cut him off. The cop called her collect from prison at least once a week, and she always accepted the charge. She was ashamed. She knew it was wrong. She knew it was hurting us. But the abuse had destroyed her self-worth. Even after he had almost killed her, Mom couldn't let that man go.

I didn't understand. I didn't know abuse could bind you to its cause, so I was angry at my mother. She had wanted to change him, I guess, but he had changed her instead, and what had she ever done but love him?

And what had I ever done, all those years, to stop him?

That hurt the most. Mom was in bed, in bandages, and I could have stopped it. With my gun. With the curling iron. But I was weak. It takes a powerful motivation to pull a gun on another human being—fear, delusion, cruelty, hate—and I didn't have it in me, not even for the cop. All my life, I'd taken the abuse. I wouldn't stand up, even for my mother's life.

You soft, Chris, I told myself. *You got to learn how to hurt.*

That's when I started carrying a gun every day. That's when I started seeing a gun not just as a deterrent but as a tool. It was the wrong response, I know that now, but I didn't know what else to do. It was only Leslie and me and our baby brother, Korey. Nobody came to help. Nobody asked, *So, was that terrible, Chris, when you saw your mother beaten and raped? Do you need to talk about that?* I had just turned fourteen. I needed my mother, and if she was gone, I needed someone to help me cope with the loss.

My anger exploded three months later, at a Little Caesars in Temple Hills. My friends and I had gone for a slice, and a crew we were beefing with cornered us. I said, "Come on, now, I thought that was squashed." But they were senior football players, and we were freshmen, and they thought they had us beat.

Until I pulled my gun.

They ran. I chased them half a block, firing over their heads. One of the bullets shattered the window of their car.

I ran home, half in shock, and switched guns. I knew I had to lie low, so I made plans to meet up with Eric on Division Avenue and stay with him in Southeast. But Mom was having a good day. She was at the kitchen table, smiling. So I stayed with her, talking and laughing, listening to James Brown. She was so gentle and soft-spoken, touching my arm, saying, "How you doing, Chris? You all right, son? I'm sorry about all this."

The phone rang. It was Eric. He was at my grandparents' duplex, chilling with Derrick. I thought, *Why you hanging with him?*

"I'll be right there," I said, but I never made it. The cops were waiting out front with a search warrant. They found two guns, but not the weapon I had fired. I remember the disappointment on Mom's face as they took me away.

"What have you done, Chris?" she whispered. She had been so happy that day, like her old self. And I ruined it.

She came to see me the next morning in lockup. She wasn't the smiling mom I'd sat with twelve hours earlier. She was the beaten woman I'd come to know.

"Eric's dead, Chris," she said.

I was like, *Nah, that ain't true.* But I could see it on her face. She looked hollow, like she was collapsing from the inside. And that's when I started coming undone, too.

ALL I GOT of the story was this: Eric and Derrick got tired of waiting for me and decided to grab a bite at the carryout. They left Grandma's yard by the back gate, like always. Two men were waiting in the alley. They opened fire with a submachine gun. Derrick made it back to the house. Eric died at the scene.

"Why'd they kill Eric, Derrick?" I asked my brother. This was months later, after I was out of detention and Derrick was out of the hospital. He had been shot seven times in that alley, but he got lucky, I guess.

"I don't know," he said.

"What did they want?"

"I don't know."

"Well, what did they say?"

"I don't know, Chris. I can't remember."

"*Who were they waiting for, Derrick?*" This was his neighborhood, after all.

"I don't know, Chris," Derrick snapped. "I don't know nothing. Leave me alone."

Derrick was strong in his secrecy, but eventually my aunt—Eric's mom—forced him to talk to the state's attorney. It was at my grandmother's house, after the cops had finally made an arrest. Derrick said fine, he'd talk, but someone had to go with him to the station. Mom was at the house, and other adults, too, but for some reason I was the one ended up going, just Derrick and me.

While Derrick was giving his statement, the state's attorney pulled me aside. *Come here, son. Let me show you something.* She had a big piece of paper spread out on a desk. It was a helicopter photo of the neighborhood, maybe ten blocks, with my grandparents' duplex near the middle. The photo had red X's all over it. I counted eighty, and I didn't get them all.

"Those are where someone was shot or killed in the last six years," she said. She pointed to an X in the alley. I knew the spot. *Don't tell me,* I thought. *Please don't say it.* "That's your cousin."

Then she showed me the crime scene photos. You know how people say the dead look peaceful, like they're sleeping? I guess it depends on how you die, because Eric's eyes were open. He was looking right at me, and he was scared. My cousin died in terrible pain.

"You're not going to make it," the state's attorney said. "Not the way you're going." She didn't know me, but she looked down at me anyway. "Do you guys even care if you live or die?"

If she was trying to scare me straight, she messed up. She hung me halfway between hatred for her and depression over my life, because I knew it was true, I wasn't going to make it, and there was nothing I could do to change that fact. Honestly, I don't remember another word. I don't remember leaving the police station. I remember seeing a stranger on the bus who was talking and laughing. I remember thinking, *How can you do that? How can you act like this is a normal day?*

That's how it always felt on the worst days. When I heard Eric had died. Sitting in school after Mom was beaten and raped. Intense anger, but also distance, like I wasn't there. I wasn't in the world. That's the weird part: I couldn't hear the woman on the bus, even though I could see her flapping her fool mouth.

Somehow, I ended up in Mom's basement in Temple Hills. I didn't know what to do. So I went to the bar, grabbed an unopened bottle of Rémy Martin, and put on my headphones. I drank and cried all night, listening to Eric's favorite music—Ice Cube, EPMD, NEG, "Fuck tha Police." There was half an inch in the bottom of the bottle when I realized it was morning. I decided to go to school. I don't know why.

My homey Butchie caught me on the sidewalk. He should have sent me home, but he gave me a ride. I walked through the front door of a high school I had already been expelled from with that empty bottle of Rémy in my hand . . . and I passed out cold.

They sent me to the hospital for alcohol poisoning. Then they sent me to counseling, but the counselor only asked me one question, over and over again: "Why are you trying to kill yourself, Chris?"

I said, "I'm not trying to kill myself, fool."

I'm just trying to survive.

Gladiator School

Three friends (all now deceased) and me (lower left) at the Hickey School

I STARTED CUTTING at Boys' Village. I stole a fork and jammed holes in my arm, then pulled it down to deepen the wounds. I unfolded metal paper clips to rip my flesh. I was having visions of Eric. Every time I closed my eyes, I saw my cousin on the ground, terrified, dying. The pain of cutting was nothing compared to that.

They put me in solitary. They gave me medicine. It caused hallucinations and made my depression worse. I started having fantasies about suicide. They transferred me to the Hickey School, Maryland's long-term prison school for juvenile offenders, and switched my medication. It didn't help. I pried industrial staples out of the walls and kept cutting.

At that time, Hickey was privately run, with a hands-on discipline policy. That meant the guards could physically restrain inmates if they deemed it necessary, which went about like this:

"Tuck in your shirt, inmate."

"It is tucked in."

"I said tuck in your shirt."

"I said . . ."

And before "inmate" could say any more, two guards knocked him to the ground, flipped him over, and handcuffed his arms behind his back. The guards were big, mostly ex-army or ex–law enforcement, and they were hired, I have no doubt, because of their enthusiasm for this kind of work.

The inmates responded to violence with violence. It felt like there was a fight every hour until lights-out. Once, an inmate locked himself in the guard cage of our thirty-person dorm and called in alerts to other parts of the campus. We watched through the window as the guards ran back and forth, looking for the problem. It was hilarious. Then kids started destroying anything they could get their hands on. I slipped back to my room and shut the door. When the guards figured out what was going on, they busted heads. Mostly, what kids learned at Hickey was how to fight—and fight the system.

I dreamt of Eric, in his Filas, chilling against his sister's car. Then I dreamt of him on the ground, wanting to talk, but with nothing left to say.

"You g-g-g-good, Chris?" Greg asked. He was a small kid from north DC with a serious stutter, and my closest friend inside.

"Nah," I said, meaning *Leave me alone*. I was so deep under, I felt like I was never coming up, and I wasn't sure I wanted to.

Then a family friend brought Mom to visit. She was wearing a tank top and I could see her ribs. Her hair was messed up. She kept repeating herself, like she couldn't remember where she was.

I turned to the family friend and snapped, "What's your problem? How could you let my mother out of the house like this?"

He just lifted his hands, like, *What can I do?*

On the way back to my dorm, I heard an inmate whisper, "Yo, Chris's mom on drugs."

He didn't say "crackhead." If he had, I'd have busted his mouth. I could feel the urge. It was the same one that had me ripping my arms with metal staples.

I called the family friend and told him, *Don't ever bring my mom to see me again.* That's how mad I was. How ashamed.

Hickey stressed physical fitness. We ran every morning, yelling cadences at the top of our lungs and making up rhymes: *I used to carry a Tec-nine—I used to carry a Tec-nine—now I'm running in a line!* We lifted weights. We never made it a day without someone being knocked down in the pit. That was part of the program. Hickey had the philosophy that violence built men. So I started hate-working on my body, getting my anger out, and I got strong. Eventually, they took me off the drugs. I became run leader of my group. I started thinking about the military. I was sentenced to Hickey until I was twenty-one. The army would take me then, I thought, because by then I'd be a killing machine.

Instead, they let me out after less than a year. I thought it was a court date, but when I arrived at the courtroom, Mom was there. My rejection stung her so bad she went to rehab and cleaned up. Somehow, she talked the state into letting me out.

"I have something to show you," she said proudly as she drove to Upper Marlboro, a middle-class neighborhood near Temple Hills. "I'm gonna buy that house," she said, pointing at a nice two-story with a FOR SALE sign in the yard. The house was freshly painted. Every yard on the block was trimmed. "You're going to a new high school. I've already enrolled you. We're gonna be good now, Chris."

God, I wanted that. I thought, *Maybe this is it. Maybe we're gonna be a real family now.* Mom was so convincing when she was clean.

But when we got home, my brother Derrick pulled me aside. "Come upstairs, little brother. I got a birthday present for you."

He pulled out two guns: a big one and a small one. "We gonna retaliate for Eric," he said.

I thought, *Yeah, I guess I knew it was going to be this way.*

I chose the bigger gun.

The House Becomes the Cave

THERE WAS NO new house, of course. No new school. Mom didn't make it a week before she was back in bed, drinking, crying, and popping her pain pills. She tried, I know. She was diagnosed as bipolar, but it was the drugs, and the alcohol she mixed with her medications, too. Some days she'd be smiling, doing her hair, singing. She'd say she was going to the grocery, gonna cook us a nice meal. But it never happened. Within days, if not hours, she was back in bed. Depressed. Addicted. Traumatized.

Leslie took care of the basics. She raised Korey, bought the groceries, and paid the bills, all while going to high school full-time.

I took care of the guns. There was no retaliation for Eric or anything like that. Instead, I knocked Derrick down. He was beating on Korey, just like he used to beat on me, and I squared him up.

"This gonna stop, Derrick," I said. "We ain't kids in here no more."

The cop was out of prison and stalking my mother. I don't know why. He didn't love her. He didn't want to spend time with his son. He just wanted to hurt us.

He harassed Mom with phone calls, leaving her in tears. He sat outside our house in a car, watching us, but always drove away before I could confront him. One night, I answered the phone instead of Mom. He didn't say anything, but I knew it was him. I could hear him breathing. So I pulled my pistol from my waistband. I put it to the phone so he could hear it when I slid back the bolt.

"We ain't kids in here no more," I said.

Mom's house was a hangout spot, like the front porch in *Boyz n the Hood*. People from the neighborhood were always around, drinking and smoking. It wasn't a crack house or anything. These weren't bad people. But we had a pool, a barbecue grill, and nobody in charge. Mom was too deep in her depression, or else she was the life of the party, dancing, drinking, people parked up and down the road.

I took it on myself to keep things straight. These people were twenty-five, thirty, and I was fifteen, but I broke up the fights. I kept things from getting smashed. I stopped the robberies, because in a house like that there's always someone jonesing, going through other people's shit. I even went as muscle when dudes bought drugs. I was a kid, but I felt like a man when they said, "Bring Chris. Nobody mess with Chris."

That's what my life was about: becoming so hard no one would mess with me. No one would come here, to my house, and hurt my mother.

One day, the cop fell through the living room ceiling. He had snuck through the attic door in the garage and was climbing along the rafters when he slipped. Mom was on the couch, with two friends, when he smashed through her coffee table. It would have been hilarious if I didn't know what he was capable of.

I wasn't there that day, but I told everyone I knew, "Bring guns when y'all come. We got enemies here."

I AMASSED A stockpile of weapons. Then I laid my hands on big metal, a hundred-shot Calico submachine gun, and I let it be known, *Chris Wilson is fully armed.* Those three months were the most peaceful of my teenage years. Nobody bothered me. Nobody bothered my mom. Even the ex-cop stayed down.

Then I was arrested for illegal gun possession. "What's wrong with you, Chris?" Mom said, like she just realized this wasn't normal. "Why aren't you in school?"

Because I'm here for you.

The court offered me a choice: Hickey or my father. He was a decent guy, I guess. Held down a good job as an electrician for Pepco. He took me in, but he never loved me. I had read in my mom's journal he didn't think I was his son. *That's why he left her,* I thought, hurting bad. *That's why she always called me her little man. That's why I was the one to give her jewelry on her birthday. Cuz it's my fault.*

But it didn't make sense. My father looked just like me! I was definitely his son, and I needed him to acknowledge that. I needed his love, especially with Mom slipping away. All he said was "I heard you were smart, Chris. I heard you were a good kid. Look at you now."

I said, "You don't know me. You don't care about me. You never even called me on my birthday."

He said, "Well, I didn't know when your birthday was."

I left. I went back to Mom, violating my court order. They were going to send me to Hickey, until Big Daddy convinced the judge to let me live with him on Division Avenue.

I never saw Grandma in Temple Hills. I never saw her out of her house, except walking four blocks to church three days a week. Big

Daddy was the problem solver. He loved his Mona Lisa, and he showed up in Temple Hills. He saw the house falling apart, the sketchy characters hanging around, the holes in the walls, and the empty refrigerator. When he demanded Mom clean herself up, she always said, "Yes, Big Daddy. I'll do better."

He'd start to leave, and she'd whisper, with her eyes on the floor, "I got bills stacking up, Big Daddy. Can you give me a little money to help out? I'll pay you back."

I was thinking, *No, no, no.* Mom spent the minimum on bills, rolling them to the next month as long as she could. She spent most of the money on alcohol. But Big Daddy couldn't help himself.

He tried to help me in the same way. He knew I had guns. He knew I was in the streets. He said, "Just finish high school, Chris. Then you can get a good job and move away from here."

I was fifteen. I hadn't attended school regularly in two years. Graduating was four years away, at least, and graduating didn't mean a job. There were no jobs for high school graduates from Lincoln Heights. And I was hungry *now*.

"You need money?" He peeled off a ten, his way of caring. "Get yourself something to eat."

Then Big Daddy started coughing. He was a big man, but that cough doubled him over. Big Daddy was a hero to me, but he was sick, and his time had passed. He didn't know the world I was living in.

Every child needs a safe space. They need love and, like, quiet to think. They need an adult they can talk to, and a hot meal on the table once in a while. I wasn't getting that. I was trying to provide that for my mother: get her fed, make her warm, keep her safe.

She'd beep me when I was out, because we had beepers then. I'd rush home, and she'd be crying, talking about killing herself. Or she'd be thankful, saying she loved me, I was her man, could I do her a little favor? Or she'd be so drunk, she didn't remember beeping me.

I wouldn't touch crack. I wouldn't sell drugs, not after what they'd done to my mom. But I needed that safe place, that break from the madness of the life, and I found it in PCP. "It makes you powerful," Eric's old friend Tyrone told me. "It makes you indestructible."

PCP messed with your mind. Smoking it straight made you feel hot. It made your skin itch. A few times, we got so high we took off all our clothes, in winter, and ran naked in the street. That's why they called the drug Buck Naked.

Mostly, though, I sprinkled it in weed. I still remember the smell of metal when it burned, and the crackle when I inhaled. It was an electric buzz, a bug zapper in my brain, and then I'd go numb. Nothing could hurt you on PCP because you couldn't feel a thing. Not the cold. Not a bullet. Not the pain.

I became paranoid on that stuff. I barely slept. I kept my hand near my gun. I always had the sniffles because I didn't own a winter jacket. Mom bought me one for my birthday, a nice Eddie Bauer parka with a fur-lined hood. Two dudes stole it off me at gunpoint when I stepped off the subway near Grandma's house. It was only the second time I'd worn it.

"God, Chris, you can't take care of nothing, can you? Why I give you anything?"

Those were bad times, violent times, and guys around me were dropping.

Tyrone got his face sliced from forehead to chin. He lost an eye.

Muhammad caught forty years. He killed his stepfather for abusing his mom.

They shot Little Anthony near the playground at the Lincoln Heights Houses. He wasn't the target; he wasn't even in the game.

Almost five hundred people a year were being gunned down in DC, and the Lincoln Heights Houses were in the middle of the war. Everybody knew if you saw a car you didn't recognize, you ran, but Little Anthony didn't run fast enough.

The cops stood around his body for hours. It wasn't an investigation; it was a message. *Just another dead black kid. That's what he gets for living here. That's what you animals deserve.* It was the same way they'd treated Mom at the station. The way the state's attorney said, "Do you people even care?"

Then Jay Jah got his. We were walking down the street and he slipped away, pulled a knife on a guy in a carryout. I'd seen him do it a dozen times, just show the knife and wait. He'd get a twenty-dollar bill, and we'd roll on. This time, without a word, the man pulled a gun and unloaded a clip. Ten shots, point-blank, into Jay Jah's face and chest. The man was an undercover cop, and he tore my friend apart. Jay Jah knew he was doomed. He always talked about going out gangster, like Scarface. When he fell, though, he had tears in his eyes.

I got PTSD off that, and a lot of other things, too. That's what my prison therapist told me years later. He said my early life was a tour of duty in a combat zone, and I had to face the damage it had done. But I never woke up screaming like my mother's old boyfriend Ronald. I just stopped believing in a future. *We all going out,* I thought, *but none of us making it out.*

So when I found out Big Daddy had terminal cancer, I wasn't shook. I felt like I was joining him soon. I had an idea the dead were on the other side, waiting for me. I had more people over there I loved than I had people still beside me.

"Don't trip, Chris," my sister said. "We gonna make it. We gonna travel the world."

The world? Nah, this was my world here: these blocks, this house, my mom. And Leslie, she loved me, I know that, but this wasn't the third-grade track team anymore. Leslie was going at her own pace, sprinting to get away. She was working two jobs. Saving her money. Acing high school. If I couldn't keep up, she was cutting me loose.

I don't blame her. She had to do for herself. One of the hardest parts of growing up the way we did was that family is a weight. You want to help, but they pull you down. Mom. Derrick. Me. Even my oldest brother, Kenny, was in the bottle for years. There was a point, for Leslie, where she had to cut the line or drown.

And it wasn't like I was jogging, trying to keep up. I was staggering. Leslie knew it. Everyone knew it. They could see it on my face. PCP will make you untouchable, but only because it kills you inside. The sunken place, right? That's where I was. The place where nobody can touch you or hear you scream.

Darico, my inspiration

Then my son, Darico, was born. It was June 1995. I was sixteen, and I hadn't seen his mother in months. I was in lockup again, so it was six weeks before I saw him for the first time. I actually went to his mother's house to say he wasn't mine, but when they put that baby in my arms, and his tiny fingers reached out, they tore right into that sunken place inside me, and I thought, *I got a son now. I got to be a father to this boy.*

That fall, I took custody of Darico, after the state took him from his mother. I gave up PCP. I got a job at a pool-supply store a few blocks from Mom's house. I worked forty hours a week, but at five dollars an hour I only made $150 a week after taxes, and Mom took most of it.

"What, you want the electricity cut off, Chris? Shut up and give me a hundred dollars for the bill." And the alcohol.

My sister had a new boyfriend who worked with her at UPS, a guy named Erick Wright. He was going to night school to be a sound tech, and he convinced me to tag along for my GED. He said I could study for a few years and get a real job.

This is it, I told myself. *We going straight for Darico.*

It was never going to happen. I can see that now. I didn't have my mind right. I wanted a different life, but I didn't want to do the work. I never tried on the job. I never read the books or did my homework for school. I never shopped for baby food or cleaned the house, and everything was filthy by then because it was just the two little kids, our two pit bulls crapping on the carpet, and Mom hollow-eyed on the couch like the ghost of our previous lives, with that half-patched living room ceiling hanging over her head.

Leslie had a plan. She was in ROTC, which guaranteed her acceptance into air force officer training after high school.

What was my plan? I didn't have one. I had a job and night classes, but that didn't mean I'd changed. I still carried a gun. I was still tied to that house. I was still trying to be the toughest guy in Temple Hills, like that meant something.

I shot up a dude's car a block from Mom's house while he was inside his mom's house cowering.

I robbed parked cars.

When I realized the father of a girl I was dating had an antique-rifle collection, I stole twenty, took them home, and sawed the barrels off with a metal file. Erick Wright and I went into a field that night and fired them. Erick panicked when the cops started chasing us and forgot he had a second shell in the chamber. That fool almost lost his foot.

"You were a mistake, Chris," Mom said one night when she found me smoking weed with Erick in the backyard. I didn't even know she was there. She snuck up on me, wrapped in a blanket with no shoes on, even though there was frost on the ground. "I wish you'd never been born."

Erick looked stunned. "Dang, that's cold, slim," he said as Mom stumbled off. "You good?"

"Yeah, man. Nah. I'm good. I don't care about that shit."

But I did. I gave everything to Mom. I built my life around her. Was I really the reason our lives had become so bad?

A few days later, Mom told me, "You should have died instead of your cousin, Chris, because you're no good."

Erick heard that, too. This time, he didn't say anything, because there was nothing to say. I believe to this day my mother loved me. I believe she knew how much I loved her. She was just in too much pain. She had to let it go because it was killing her. I had always been her favorite, her little man. I was the kid who took whatever she had to give, good and bad. So she laid her pain on me. At the time, though, I didn't see it that way. I thought: *If my own mother doesn't love me, who will? I guess I'm too awful to love.*

It was all slipping away. It was all just a big boulder of shit, rolling down on our heads. Big Daddy was dying. Mom was crying. The foreclosure notices were stuck to the front door. The party was long over, and only alcoholics and addicts were left to rifle through the last of our things. I fell into a depression and quit my job. What was the point? When Erick and my sister broke up, I dropped out of night school. I started robbing people in the neighborhood and giving most of the money to Mom. She never asked where it came from because she knew. She knew. But this was the only way. Big Daddy's money was gone. The electricity was on and off, and so was the water. I remember huddling up around the gas oven to stay warm and chipping ice out of the frozen pool for washing up.

We had a small Christmas that year for Korey and Darico, but I didn't have a birthday celebration. My birthday was three days after the holidays. I guess Mom forgot.

The next night, I went to my friend Butchie's house. Butchie had started selling crack in Southwest, and he was sitting on his mother's couch with his friends, showing off his cash.

I said, "Let me borrow three hundred dollars, Butchie. I wanna get my mom's electricity back on."

"Nah, slim," he said, laughing. "Who the fuck I look like?"

"A cornerman."

He smiled. "I earned this money, cuz. You want money, stand your ass on that block."

"I'm not gonna poison my people."

Butchie didn't like that. He got loud, we started going back and forth, and I pistol-whipped him.

"If I wanted it," I said, walking out the door, "I could have taken your bitch-ass cash."

Next time he saw me, Butchie and two of his friends pulled guns. So I pulled my .45, and we started firing at each other. It was right on Mom's block, in the middle of the day, but guns were such a part of our lives, we didn't think anything of it.

I let Butchie go, and that's the truth. I had him in my sights, and I missed on purpose. Butchie knew it, too. He'd tell you that now if he hadn't committed suicide. Butchie didn't make it to twenty-five.

Amazingly, he turned me to the cops. Butchie got me locked up for malicious gunfire. My journal says, when I called about bail,

Mom said it again: *Maybe it would have been better, Chris, if you'd never been born.* I don't think she said it angrily. I think she was tired.

She came through, though. Mom put her house up for bail. I came home on the bus, and a crooked cop who had hired me a few years before to destroy his ex-girlfriend's car but didn't pay me was sitting in the living room.

"You remember Rodney," Mom said with a sad smile. Like I was going to hug this bamma.

"Where's my money?" I said. "You owe me three hundred dollars."

Rodney's smile dropped. He stood up. "I don't owe you shit, nigga. Watch how you speak to me. I got ten years in on the force."

I punched him in the face. Then I jumped on him and kept punching, because once you start something like that, you got to finish it. Mom started screaming. Kenny heard it, blasted out, and started punching him, too. Then my friend, who was staying with us because of family trouble, joined in, and we tackled that bastard straight through Mom's glass table.

It shattered. Glass flew everywhere. Rodney was motionless, cut up and bleeding. Mom was yelling at me—*What have you done, Chris? You killed him! Oh my God! You killed a cop!*—but I didn't care. I grabbed his wallet. He had almost $500. I took the $300 he owed me and left.

A few days later, Rodney burst through the front door. Before I could jump, he lifted me off the couch and put a gun to my head.

"You think you're tough?" he said.

He had a friend with him, six-five and three hundred pounds. The man held my friend down, while Rodney pushed the barrel of the gun against my temple.

"Come on, Rodney," I said, "you don't have to do this. You owed me money."

"Look who's begging now." He pressed the gun hard against my skull.

"Please . . . Rodney, don't . . ."

"Give me a reason. I dare you."

His voice was trembling. His finger was shaking on the trigger.

"This ain't right," his friend said.

"Shut the fuck up, man."

"You told me three men jumped you."

"That's right. This the main one."

"That ain't a man," his friend snapped. "That's a kid."

Rodney kept his gun to my head, shaking and crying. I thought he was going to do it. He could have made up a story. Cops do it all the time. But he let me go.

A month later, I was standing outside Mom's house with Darico in his stroller when a green Lexus drove by. I had a friend with a green Lexus, so I waved.

The car stopped. A Jeep pulled up behind it. The passenger rolled down his window and pointed a gun at me. "Get in the car, nigga," he said. "Don't reach for nothing." These weren't my friends.

"Hey, you leaving Darico?" It was Kenny, in the driveway, washing his car.

Do something! I thought, but Kenny didn't get it. He thought I was going for a joyride.

"Take care of my son," I yelled as I got in the Jeep.

Three men were inside. One held a gun to my ribs. A pit bull was in the back, so close I could feel its breath on my neck.

"Where's my coke?" the man in the passenger seat said calmly.

"I don't know nothing about coke, cuz."

The man didn't turn around. "I'm not your cuz," he said.

Oh shit, this was serious. My legs started shaking. I'd been *playing* gangster. These guys were for real.

They took my gun, then took me to the basement of an empty house. They tied me up and beat me. They kept asking about the coke, but I didn't know anything about it.

"Someone's lying," I yelled. "Someone's lying! I swear!" It wasn't like the movies. I wasn't playing it cool. "Who said it was me?"

This was it. I was gonna die. It was gonna be like Mom kept wishing—like I'd never been born. Was that really what she wanted?

They were discussing where to dump my body: an abandoned house or the river. The pit bull watched, snapping at its chain. I yelled, *It ain't me, I don't even know y'all, I'm not a part of this*, but they were through with questions.

I thought, *It's just a day, like any day, and now it's my last. I won't wake up again. I won't see Mom again. I wanna tell her I'll be better, I'll change, I'll be a good son, she'll be proud of me, I swear, but it won't happen. I'm gonna die in this basement and they're going to throw my body in the Anacostia River, and I didn't do nothing. I didn't do nothing with my whole life.*

I was so scared I pissed my pants.

Then they hustled another kid down the stairs. I recognized him from around. He had a drug problem. Everyone knew it. I thought he'd deny everything, but he took one look at me, tied up and pissed on, and he copped. They didn't kill him. I don't know how he worked it off, but I saw the kid later, so he didn't die in that basement.

"No hard feelings," the main man said when he dropped me in front of Mom's house. "It's business. My money's important to me."

I walked inside, trembling and smelling like piss. Mom was on the couch with two of my friends, like it was just any other day. It had only been two hours since I'd left the driveway.

"Where you been, Chris?" Mom asked.

I told them the story. It was so traumatic, I started sniffling, then full-on crying. I never showed weakness, but at that moment I was weak. I broke down so bad, I couldn't say another word. I was like, *Give me a hug, Mom. Tell me this is all gonna be all right.*

And that's when my mom started laughing. She said, "You had a gun on you, Chris. A gun! How could you let yourself get kidnapped when you had a gun?"

Six Shots

MAYBE I WAS thinking of the kidnapping as I walked to the store that terrible night. Maybe I was thinking of all the things Mom had said to me—*I wish you'd never been born; you had a gun, Chris, a gun, and you let them kidnap you*—or of all my failures over the years. Maybe I was thinking, *I don't want to live this life anymore.* I don't know.

Here's what I remember: It was Darico's first birthday. My sister and I had planned to take him out, but when the time came, we didn't have the money. Everything was falling apart: no food, no money, and a last eviction notice sent by registered mail.

I smoked a little weed to calm my nerves and told my sister to watch Darico, who was asleep. I was going for a walk. It was 11:00 p.m., but it was summer in the city, and it was hot. I turned right at a four-lane, headed for the commercial intersection three blocks away. Nobody was out. A few cars passed, but they were gone in a second, red lights trailing away in the heat.

After a block, two men appeared behind me. They were hanging back, strolling, but I'd been around. I knew they were trouble.

I should have run. I had half a block on them. But I didn't. I kept strolling, my body calm but my mind racing. Were these the drug dealers who had kidnapped me? Butchie's friends? Rodney? The sick cop still stalking Mom? Ahead was a grocery store, a funeral home, and two gas stations. The grocery store and funeral home were closed, but the gas stations were lit. I figured I'd be safe if I made it to one of them.

So I stuck to the main road instead of taking my usual shortcut through an alley. I kept my pace so I wouldn't tip them off. When I was close to the first gas station, I checked over my shoulder. Still there. So I approached two guys I recognized from around the neighborhood at the pump and asked them for a ride back to Mom's house. They said, "Nah, man, we heading over the line," meaning the other way, toward DC. I didn't push because it was probably nothing, and I didn't want to seem paranoid.

But as soon as they drove off, the two men were there, pressing up on me. I didn't recognize them, but they were adults, in their thirties at least, and clearly from the streets.

"You Chris, right?" the first man said.

"Yeah, that's me. What up?"

"We been watching you. We know where you at, son. Don't think we can't find you."

"What the fuck you talking about?"

He said something about knowing where my mother lived. It was a threat, not just to me, but to my family. I tried to lock eyes, show I wasn't scared, but we were in the open, and his friend kept circling behind me. From back there, he could get the drop.

You had a gun, Chris. You had a gun and you let them . . .

I reached for the holster at my back.

"You ain't got a gun," the man said, laughing at me.

But I did. I had a .38, and by the time I pulled it, it was too late to do anything else. I fired six shots. I'd like to say I panicked. I'd like even more to say I was trying to miss. But I can't lie. I have to take responsibility for the things I've done.

I *thought* I missed because the men kept running. So I turned the other way and ran down the alley toward home. But I hadn't missed. I had hit one of the men with all six shots. He ran half a block to the grocery store, collapsed in the doorway, and died.

PART 2

The Middle Passage

You will not be punished for your anger . . .
you will be punished by your anger.

—THE BUDDHA

Upper Marlboro

I DID A year in Upper Marlboro, the Prince George's County lockup, awaiting trial. I was on the youth tier, but it was different than the youth facilities I'd been in before.

Hickey School and Boys' Village were violent and chaotic. You never knew what would happen, but you knew it was gonna be bad. At Upper Marlboro, everything was on a schedule. Most of the time you were in your cell. When you moved, they told you where and when. The yard was a cage. Everyone wore prison issue. There were no televisions, radios, or personal items in the cells. You can't strip a person down like that for long. Human beings without stimulation or a purpose will rebel. But Upper Marlboro was short-term. Almost everyone was there less than a year.

There were fights, of course. Drug deals. Beatdowns by guards. Inmates made homemade knives by scraping the hard plastic toothbrush handles on the concrete-block walls until they were sharp. That's prison therapy: a couple hours a day, every day, scraping a toothbrush on a wall. I saw toothbrush shivs pulled a dozen times, but I don't remember anyone being stabbed too bad.

Mostly, I sat in my cell, or I sat in the dayroom watching television. Maryland provided a Bible to every inmate and I tried to read it, but the Old Testament wasn't like Grandma's church, with its praise and hallelujahs. The Old Testament God was angry and violent. And everyone had slaves! Slavery wasn't a problem for God, apparently. He never said anything against it. So I figured the book wasn't for me.

Mom came to see me. She said, "Hang tight, Chris. Don't tell them nothing. We gonna take care of you."

I should have been apologizing to her. She was battling addiction while losing her house to foreclosure and her father to cancer. She didn't need a son in prison. But I just nodded. *Yeah, Mom, you gonna take care of me.*

Honestly, part of me was relieved to be in prison. For the first time in years, I felt safe. I had food. Not good food, but sort of edible. On the outside, I never slept. Even as a little boy, I laid awake on Grandma's floor, stressed out by the gunshots and squealing tires. At Upper Marlboro, I slept through the night.

I was facing a murder charge, but that wasn't unusual. Most guys on my tier had a serious charge. But nobody talked about that. We talked about the past: getting girls, getting a cheesesteak, hitting go-gos. It wasn't bragging. It was holding on. *We going back, son.* That was the message. That was our world, not the cage. Prison was nothing but a suspension of time, a break from our real lives, nothing to sweat. The only time we got heated was when Tupac died. Everybody loved Tupac. Guys were yelling and banging on their doors like we were a part of it. Like there was something we could do.

Every night, I thought about *that night*. Not the shooting itself, but the recoil of the pistol in my hand. I heard the shots, followed by the sound of my breathing as I ran. It was like a horror movie, running from the monsters. Then I'd wake up, and I was back in Temple Hills and it was all a dream. Except the wake-up bell was sounding and guys were yelling at the guards.

Mom got me a good lawyer. She didn't have any money, but she managed to hire Harry Trainor, one of the best lawyers in Maryland. She knew him somehow from the past, and he stepped in. Back when she was working and succeeding, everyone loved Mom. She was a funny, loving, good-hearted person.

I didn't take advantage of the opportunity. Most young black men had public defenders, and even though it wasn't true, every kid from Lincoln Heights believed public defenders worked with the cops to send you to jail. So I treated my lawyer like an enemy. I wouldn't tell him nothing except I didn't do it. I wouldn't discuss any strategy but innocence.

Greg, my stuttering friend from Hickey, was on my tier. He was facing murder for a drug deal gone bad. He copped a plea and got twenty years. I wouldn't consider copping a plea, because the truth, I told my lawyer, would set me free.

It was stupid. This was the summer of 1996, the height of "tough on crime," and prison terms were brutal. But I wanted to seem strong. That's what the old heads in Upper Marlboro told me, the ones who'd been through the system before. "Stay strong. Don't tell on yourself."

But those geniuses were locked up. Why was I looking up to them?

There was an older guy in Upper Marlboro, a bank robber from New York. It was rumored he had a million dollars stashed, so he wasn't sweating the possibility of ten years. He didn't sweat nothing. When guys argued or stepped to him, he smiled and shrugged it off. *Not worth it.*

That's how I wanted to be: with my lawyer, with the old heads, with the young guys talking about girls back home. Too cool to care. But that's not how it was. In reality, I was depressed. I was going down and I knew it. My family knew it, too. My mom visited less and less, and she started complaining about the money. She had to double-mortgage her house because of me. She had to pay for prison phone calls. *It's a burden*, she was saying, *having you for a son*.

She never even brought Darico, like I was a burden on him, too.

I called my father three months in. I don't know why. I needed something, I guess. The first thing he said to me was "How could you kill somebody, Chris?"

I said, "See, there you go. I didn't kill nobody. But you don't believe me, do you?"

"Then why are you locked up?"

"Why are you questioning me?"

We went back and forth on that, with me getting angrier every time he forced me to deny what I'd done. I was so angry. I thought it made me strong.

Finally, he gave up. "At least do something with your life. At least get your high school diploma."

"Fuck you." That's the last thing I said to him. "Fuck you."

And when I say "the last thing," I mean the very last, because my father's throat was slashed on November 11, 1996. Dad died slowly on his kitchen floor, in a pool of his own blood. Mom showed up, like before, with that empty look on her face. "Chris, I'm sorry, your father died yesterday."

He was trying to stop a fight between my brother Derrick, who was living with him, and a woman Derrick had brought home. The cops never even charged her.

That messed me up. That was the end of my relationship with Derrick. But the real pain only hit later. At the time, walking back to my cell, I felt numb. My father never loved me, I told myself, but I guess I always hoped to win his love one day and be his son.

My trial was long, three or four days. I know that doesn't sound long, given that my life was at stake, but I was worn down. Every day in Upper Marlboro, with its strict rules and long stretches of loneliness and boredom, wore me down. Thinking about my trial wore me down. Even getting to the courthouse was a burden, just like the state wanted. I was shackled at 4:00 in the morning, put in a holding cell, marched to a bus, then driven to a holding pen in the basement of the courthouse. By the time my lawyer brought my civilian clothes, I'd been in process for five hours. I had to wait another hour to be called. By the time the trial started every morning, I wanted it over. *Judge me already. Be done with it. Let me sleep.*

I didn't testify. I guess my lawyer didn't want me to lie, because that's what I would have done. Nobody spoke on the victim's behalf. The cops said he was a thirty-one-year-old with a long rap sheet, and that he lived on the other side of DC, but nobody spoke about him as a person. None of his family or friends were in the courtroom. The other man who threatened me never came forward. He disappeared, so there was no eyewitness to the crime.

They had the murder weapon. I had given it to a friend to dispose of, but he'd gone on a crime spree with it instead. When the cops caught him, he rolled on me. That's how they found me, seventeen days after the crime. But that was circumstantial. They knew I had possessed the gun, but they couldn't prove I had fired it.

It didn't matter; I was done. I was done the moment they charged me and I decided to plead not guilty and take the case to court. I was young; I was black; I had a record seventeen pages long.

And I did it. I did the crime. What did I think was going to happen?

I've never felt as alone as I did the moment I stood for my judgment. I couldn't look at the judge or jury, much less the family and friends who had come to support me.

I didn't react when they found me guilty. It hit like a hammer, but I didn't blink.

I knew I was going to get crushed at sentencing. Guys on my tier were pulling twenty years for handgun possession and a rock. They were pulling forty for robbery.

And these were teenagers. In the past, they would have gone to juvenile facilities. They would have received treatment and another chance. Now they were pulling life-destroying time.

I didn't want to spend decades in prison. I didn't want to lose my chance. But that was out of my hands. I'd given power to the state, and the state wasn't in the mood to coddle "super-predators" like me.

My family was there for the sentencing: Mom, Kenny, Leslie, my cousin Angie, and Darico, who was turning two in a couple weeks. My father was dead. Big Daddy was dying. Grandma never left her four-block world. The judge asked if I wanted to make a statement before he passed sentence. I'm not sure exactly what I said. I could find out from the official transcript, but I don't want to because I made a fool of myself.

I said I was innocent. I said it was a case of mistaken identity. I said they were making a terrible mistake. It was the stupidest, most cliché thing I could have said, and of course it was a lie.

I heard a gasp when the judge said, "I sentence you to spend the rest of your natural life in the prison system of the state of Maryland."

Bam. The gavel came down. The bailiffs grabbed me and pulled me roughly toward the exit. I turned to look at my family. Angie was screaming and crying, but Mom was sitting quietly, staring straight ahead with a blank look on her face, like nothing bothered her anymore. She'd cried her tears. Then the doorway blocked my view, and they were gone.

"What you get, Wilson?" guys were yelling up and down the tier. "What you get?"

"They crushed me, slim. I got life."

"Oh shit." That's it. Nothing more to say to someone with life.

My cell door banged open. It was two guards. "Let's go, Wilson."

"Where you taking me?"

"Five A."

The segregation unit. Apparently, it was standard practice for a life sentence. I was never getting out, so I had nothing to lose, and the state wasn't taking chances. They didn't want me to hurt myself or someone else.

So they shackled me and locked me in solitary, no belt, no shoelaces, just white walls, a cot, and a food slot in a metal door. I stared at my little room. What else could I do? I thought, *My life is over. I'm seventeen years old. I just got on this planet. I don't even have a mustache yet. And my life is over.*

I sat down on my bunk and everything fell away—everything but that cell—and I started to cry. No shame. I've witnessed a lot of young people dying, mostly from gunshot wounds. Ain't no bravery like in the movies. Everybody cries when they realize it's the end. Everybody.

Solitary

I HAD BEEN in tough places before. That basement, tied to a chair while drug dealers talked about dumping my body. Shoot-outs and arguments, the rape and beating of my mother, the murder of my cousin Eric. Cutting myself with staples, my grandfather's cancer, my mother's cruel words. But nothing was like sitting in solitary confinement, carrying that weight. The state gave me a death sentence. The slow kind, but death all the same. Then they put me in a room for a month, alone, with nothing to do but think about it.

There was no human contact. The guards were forbidden to talk to or touch us. I couldn't see or hear other inmates. I was given one hour of exercise a day, in a walled-off courtyard by myself. It was basically a bigger cell, but at least I could see the sky. There were no windows in my cell. No bars. I saw nothing, twenty-three hours a day, but walls.

I counted the concrete blocks. I studied the ceiling. I rubbed the concrete, just to feel the rough patches and cracks. I turned on my sink and watched the water. I did push-ups until my arms were dead. There was a slot in the metal door where they pass through meals. It was usually covered, but when the food arrived they unlocked the metal flap and folded it down to make a tray. If I left the food on the tray, they left the slot open. I left it the full hour so I could feel the air, smell whatever was outside, press the side of my face against the wall to catch a glimpse of the hall. There was nothing out there but solid metal doors.

I yelled "I'm here. Hello?" but nothing came back but an echo.

I had hated the sounds at Upper Marlboro: jangling keys, doors slamming, voices down the hall. Now I craved them. In solitary, sounds were a reminder I was part of the world.

I never thought about the future. Why bother? I had life with the possibility of parole, but parole had been dead since 1995, when a life inmate on work release murdered his girlfriend before killing himself. The story blew up in the press. In response, Governor Glendening, a Democrat with an 18 percent approval rating, gave a press conference outside the Maryland House of Correction Annex—the brutal maximum-security prison known as Castle Grayskull—and declared that no clemency or parole would be granted to any life prisoner in the state of Maryland.

"Life means life," he said. No exceptions.

His plan worked: his approval rating immediately increased to 32 percent. But the effect on prisoners was devastating. Elderly inmates were jerked back from the edge of freedom and put into cells for the rest of their lives. Men and women recently granted parole by the state board had their second chance vetoed by a governor who never learned their names, much less looked at their cases. Thousands of human beings who worked hard in prison saw their hope snatched away. For decades, Maryland had paroled fifty to ninety life prisoners a year. Then the governor, with one brutal policy shift for short-term political gain, snuffed out any chance that lifers, even teenagers like me, could be released.

All I had was the past, so that's what I thought about. I focused on moments—the night at the go-go when Eric said, "Go talk to her, Chris"; riding in Gwen's Corvette; Mom at her kitchen table explaining the Law of Scarcity with Blow-Pops. I thought of the first time I held Darico, when I promised to be his dad. I closed my eyes and tried to experience them like the man who had walked out of the cave: smell the colors, feel the sky, see the wind. I was never going to experience any of that again. The memories were all I had.

At night, I dreamt the same dream, over and over. A man was sitting in an old-fashioned prison cell, the ones with bars and sliding doors. He was turned away, slumped, rocking slightly. I watched him for a long time, although he wasn't doing anything, until I noticed that a young man was also in the cell, and he was holding something, and he said in a dead voice like he didn't care, "Hey, pops, here's your bowl." The man on the bunk turned, and it was me, and I was old.

I have a video from my sixteenth birthday where I say I'm gonna enjoy what I can, while I can, because I won't live to see twenty-one. I don't look upset. It's almost bragging. But it's cut through with sadness and fear. Back then, I was obsessed with dying, because I secretly wanted to live forever. Now my worst nightmare was growing old.

"Don't waste your life, Chris," Big Daddy told me. "You're young. You got time."

He was in the hospital, dying of cancer, so they let me talk to him one last time, near the end of my month. I remembered his voice as booming from on high, slow and deep. Big Daddy was a big man, especially to a child. Now he sounded small.

"I'm not gonna see you become a man, Chris," he said. "But promise me you'll be a good man. Get an education. Get a high school diploma. Learn a trade."

"I promise."

I didn't feel it. I didn't have a future. I had life. But what else could I say?

"I wish I could see you grown," he said, coughing. "I wish I could see the Redskins win another Super Bowl. It could happen. Maybe this year."

They took me back to my cell, back to those four walls. When Big Daddy died a few weeks later, I barely felt the pain. What did it matter? I had seventy, eighty years to go, but I had a death sentence, too.

Patuxent

FROM THE TRANSFER bus, the prison looked like a college, except for the razor wire and fences. The low buildings sat in the middle of wide grass fields—red brick with small barred windows that swung open to the outside. Inmates wandered the grounds. I saw a couple riding lawn mowers. Then I saw something even better: a line of women being marched somewhere. I had heard from inmates at the DOC transfer center that there were female inmates at the prison where I was headed, but I didn't know they mingled with the men. Some were nice looking, too: makeup, hair done, tight jeans. Guys on the bus were going crazy. They were yelling out the window like fools.

Okay, I thought. *Maybe I can live through this.*

I'd caught a break. My lawyer got me assigned to Patuxent, the only maximum-security prison in Maryland not run by the DOC. The DOC prisons were black holes; nothing came out of there. Patuxent was founded in the 1950s as a "rehabilitation facility," and it had the state's only youth program. Adult prison was a disaster for teens; everyone knew that, even the prosecutors who insisted on sending us there. The Patuxent program segregated young inmates and tried to rehab them for the streets.

I almost didn't get in. What was the point, after all, in rehabbing a lifer? I was never getting out, so who cared? Worse, I failed the evaluation. Mr. Mee, who administered the test and became my prison therapist, told me later I was so depressed, he almost put me on suicide watch.

Then he thought, *Why wouldn't this kid be depressed? He's seventeen with a life sentence.* He was testing a lot of young inmates who didn't seem to care about their crimes, or who didn't seem to understand the seriousness of what they had done. I was crushed by it. The youth program was only two years old and still in the experimental phase. Mr. Mee thought, *Let's see what happens to someone like that in a program like ours.*

In the end, even Mr. Mee's recommendation wasn't enough. I had to beg my judge to intervene. Thankfully, on July 26, 1997, he sent a letter requesting my admittance. I know the date because I keep a copy. It's short, just three lines, but it opened a door. It made me think, *Maybe this won't be hell after all. Maybe I really do have a chance.*

Then they stripped us down, right outside the transfer bus. I was used to dropping my drawers for inspection, but this time they took our boxers. They made us bend over and wait for the guards to come down the line.

"Spread those cheeks. Cough for me, inmate." I complied, but not enough. "Inmate, I said: Spread. Those. Cheeks. Don't make me say it again."

Somewhere behind me, people snickered. That's when I knew this was prison, because if there's one thing that defines prison, it's humiliation.

We stopped for our state-issued supplies: one blanket, two sheets, two pairs of socks, a pair of jeans with no pockets, a sweatshirt, and a small bag of hygiene products. Then we walked a long hallway, past the bulletproof observation booth, into the yard—sun shining, grass, a few inmates walking around—and straight back into the residence block.

It hit me in the doorway. First the smell, like bleach, sweat, and mold. Then the heat, heavy and rotten. And finally, the yelling, constant and loud: guards at prisoners, prisoners at guards, prisoners at each other. The walls were plastered with notices. NO THIS . . . YOU CAN NOT DO THAT. Guards stood at the metal detector, scowling.

My place was F-3, a barred hallway with thirty-four cells, seventeen to a side. Half had inmates standing in their doorways, watching us. Other inmates were on the floor, doing push-ups. I saw televisions, radios, even a potted plant. Heavy bass from the old-school song "Duck Down" by Boogie Down Productions was booming. A corrections officer (CO) yelled, "Turn that music down!" The inmate ignored her. She just sat back down at her desk inside a safety cage.

I walked into my cell: six by eight; bunk, sink, toilet, shelf. I put my clothes on the shelf and sat down on my bunk. This was it. My life.

An hour later they popped the door, and I hit the dayroom for the first time. It was like Hickey School: young men huddled in their corners, yelling over one another. Baltimore crew on one side, pants hanging low, playing Tupac's *Makaveli* loud. White guys in the corner, getting tattoos from a converted electric razor. White guys were always getting tattoos. On the other side, an inmate barber giving a haircut, because every tier has an inmate who cuts hair. A couple dudes at the ping-pong table. Bunch of brothers in front of the television, even though they couldn't hear it over the noise.

"Ca-ka . . . Ca-ka . . . Ca-ka . . . Chris!"

In the last corner was my homey Greg, playing cards with the DC crew. I'd never seen Greg on the outside. He was from Langley Park, about ten miles north of Lincoln Heights. It was an area of immigrants, mostly Latinos, and black dudes from Northeast rarely went up that way. But Greg and I had served time together in Hickey, Boys' Village, and Upper Marlboro. Every time I was inside, Greg was there. I couldn't believe it. He made the youth program, too.

"How much you g-g-get, Chris?" Greg asked. He knew I had a body charge. He'd copped to twenty on his own.

"Life," I said.

"Oh sh-sh-shit." He turned toward the door. "Yo, CO, put Wilson down by my cell," he yelled. "Cell twenty-one." He didn't have the power to assign cells, of course, but COs didn't mind putting crews together.

"It's g-g-g-good," he said, turning back to me. "Window works."

Suddenly, the guys watching television busted out. "That's my block! You see that shit, whore! You see that! That's how we do it, son! Ain't no one comin' up in our projects. They get they ass bodied! Baltimore, yo!"

The local news was the most popular show in prison because of the crimes. That's what everybody waited for. If an enemy died in their neighborhood, that was a celebration.

"Those my boys taking care of business!"

"I told you, yo, nobody hits harder than Latrobe Projects!"

If it was someone from their crew, they jumped on the phone. There were four pay phones on the wall in the dayroom, next to the guard station.

"Oh shit, we gonna get-back," they said, excited. "My crew not letting that shit slide! You watch."

We had group therapy for an hour on Wednesday and Friday

afternoons. I sat quietly that first Wednesday and listened as those same dudes said, "Yes, sir, Mr. Mee. Yes, sir, I'm sorry for what I done. I see the error of my ways."

I thought, *Fool, I saw you an hour ago talking all kind of murder.*

They were just telling the therapist what he wanted to hear. Everybody knew it, and everyone chuckled, nodding along. *Tell 'em, slim.* Nobody took therapy seriously.

I thought, *This isn't special. This isn't even a program.*

A few days later, I was in the yard with an older inmate named Ray-Ray, watching dudes in prison shorts made from stitched-together pieces of state-issued sweatshirts play basketball. Gangbangers were huddled up. Super-muscled monsters were lifting weights, slapping and yelling at each other. "Lift that shit up! Give me one more!" That was yard: slapping, yelling, huddling up in the dirt. We never went out on the lawn. We only saw female prisoners from a distance, walking their halls. I don't know what I'd seen from the bus window, because Patuxent wasn't like that at all.

"I thought this was a rehab program," I said.

Ray-Ray snorted. "Yeah, slim, they got rehab."

"I mean, I thought they chose us for therapy and education."

"Nah, man, this is prison. Maximum-security prison."

"But we can get out. We can pass the program and get released, right?" That's what my lawyer had told me. He said at Patuxent, because it wasn't DOC, I might make parole.

Ray-Ray laughed. "You believe that?"

I didn't say anything, just watched the basketball game degenerate into an argument.

"What you got?" he asked.

"Life."

He shook his head. "Look, slim," he said, "they tell everybody that. Act good. Do your work. Get out. But you see all these old heads?" I looked. There were a lot of men in their fifties and sixties in the yard. "Ain't no parole here, slim. That's just talk. Ain't nobody with life ever getting out of here."

I called Mom from the dayroom. I was desperate to stay attached to my old life. I said, "It bad here, Mom. It's not like the lawyer said. I'm gonna die in here."

"Uh-huh," she said. "Uh-huh, yeah." Like she wasn't listening. "I guess you shoulda thought of that, huh, Chris?"

Bammas

PEOPLE THINK THE worst part of prison is the danger. It's not. Gangs run prison, and they're pretty chill. They want law and order on the tiers so that they can keep their drug, loan-sharking, and contraband operations moving. They have their own phones, showers, and places to huddle up, and if you don't mess with them, they don't mess with you. There were wars, and those were bad, but the gangs were predictable. They acted for a reason.

The main problem with prison is the hassle. Guards at every door; guards walking the yard; four daily head counts, random cell searches, frequent pat downs. Most COs were cool, but enough were assholes that harassment occurred every day. Normal afternoon, nothing happening, until a CO in a bad mood comes on tier. "Something stinks." Looking right at you, like you're scum. *Here we go.* "There's contraband around and I know it."

He tears up your cell. "What's this?"

"That's a pen for my journal."

"Shut the fuck up, inmate. You want a write-up?"

You're passing through a door, minding your own business, and the guard stops you. "Hold on, inmate. Who told you to carry that bag?"

"That's my laundry."

"Stand over there. I ain't got time for that shit right now."

Sergeant Nick, ex-military, was always pressing me because I'd lost interest in my personal appearance. "Tuck in your shirt, inmate. Hitch up your pants. Where's your badge?" We had to wear an identity badge at all times. "Keep that badge high, inmate, or I'll write you a ticket."

Other sergeants terrorized for sport. They wanted you to get in your feelings and say something slick so they could search you, rough you up, and send you to lockup for a week.

Then there were the bammas, prisoners who were loud and obnoxious and couldn't chill. In prison, people are on edge. They're stressed out. And here comes a bamma, rapping his favorite song at volume ten, pants sagging, agitating everybody. Bammas had to be seen. That's how they survived the mental torture of prison. They were always shouting out what they used to do uptown or what they were going to do back home. If you showed weakness, they were on you. I saw a bamma named Skeeter stick his hand down the back of a new kid's pants. Kid objected. Skeeter pulled a prison knife. (That's when I stepped back.) Kid walked to the chow hall with Skeeter grabbing his ass, calling him a whore. It wasn't sexual. It was humiliation.

Every tier had a bamma, and every shift had an asshole CO. It was a grind, because they were always bumping heads: challenging each other, threatening, being loud, and the next thing you knew, the CO was yelling at you to clean up that mess or tuck in that shirt.

"Inmate! Where are you supposed to be?"

"Therapy, sir."

"Well, move faster! And comb that hair."

I tried to avoid it. I tried not to get drawn in by insults or frustration. I stayed above it, up in my head, like that bank robber in Upper Marlboro. *Not my problem. Everything important to me is in this net bag, and that don't include you.*

But I had two bammas near my cell, Skeeter and Omar. Skeeter was East Baltimore. He was serving five years, but he carried it like life. I've only met a few people as crazy as Skeeter; I think he was psychotic. Omar was just very small, very young, and very wild. He couldn't handle prison. He only had five years, too, but he hated it. He was always starting beefs, carrying a shank, robbing other inmates. Omar loved robbing. He told me once it was an addiction. I think he meant it was the only thing that kept him sane.

Mornings, before breakfast, were the worst. The COs weren't supposed to unlock our cell doors until we asked, but they were lazy; half the time they just popped them all. If they caught you unlocked and unprepared, Omar and Skeeter would run down on you. Steal your shoes, your radio, your food. Maybe rough you up, if they were in the mood.

That's why guys freaked when they heard the cell doors popping, *clink-clink-clink.* "Yo, bitch! Whore! Fuck you doing, yo?!"

Then we'd hear it, ringing out: "Rec time, y'all!"

"Oh shit, Omar running tier!"

Omar had brothers and cousins in the game real heavy in CBS— Calhoun, Baker, and Stricker; a tough Baltimore hood. He had two COs smuggling drugs for him. It only took a high school degree to be a prison guard, so some COs were barely older than us. Some were from our neighborhoods. Some were in gangs, or got initiated once they were hired so they could deliver messages and contraband.

Omar and the two COs were so tight, they played cards in the guards' security cage. One was a heroin addict. Omar supplied the dope, and the CO left him in charge when he went to shoot up. That's when we laid real low, because trouble was coming.

I saw my first stabbing when Omar was running tier. Dude was in his shower shoes standing in his cell door when two bammas walked past, peeked around, then doubled back and stuck him. The guy screamed, but a booming radio drowned him out. The bammas shoved him into his cell and slammed the door, locking him out of sight.

I just turned and walked to chow. *Not my problem*. He had a skin beef, meaning he was a rapist. Nobody liked skin beefs. And saying anything would get me stuck, too. That's prison. Sink in, sink down, and stay underground.

I saw my first truly messed-up thing a few weeks later. A new guy, maybe fifteen, was serving fifty for murder. Shortly after he arrived, the COs called him down for a phone call. That was unusual. We weren't allowed phone calls from the outside.

Kid came back crying. He was across the hall, so I could see into his cell enough to know he was on his bunk with his head down. Word got around his mom had been murdered. Her head was blown off with a shotgun. It was retaliation for the murder that put him inside.

"Don't do it," I heard someone whisper. "Whatever you planning, it ain't worth it."

The kid was crying and tearing his bedsheet into strips. A good prison knife is a six-inch piece of metal or ceramic, sharpened at one end. You make a fist and stick the sharpened end out about an inch between your middle fingers. The other five inches are against your palm and the inside of your arm. You take a strip of torn bedsheet and lash the blade around your wrist, then work your way up until you've wrapped your fist, like a boxer taping for a fight. Nobody can pry that knife out of your hand. They have to take you all the way down.

"Don't do it, slim." People were talking. Word was getting down the tier.

"Yo! Yo! Think on it, homey!"

I kept quiet, watching. Tears were streaming down the kid's face, and he was lashing that knife.

"COs coming!" someone yelled.

The kid kept lashing, crying so hard I could see him shaking. When the COs popped his door, he jumped out, swinging the knife. I'd never seen someone crazy like that before. When he found out what happened to his mom, he lost his mind. I think he wanted the COs to kill him.

They tackled him, but he wouldn't stop swinging. So they beat him bad. He was unconscious when they dragged him away, shackled and bloody. I turned back to my six-by-eight world. I thought, *At least he's getting out of here.*

Only a few weeks in, and I was already thinking like that.

What's the Point?

GREG HAD A PLAN. He said, "I t-t-told you my brother got deported back to H-H-Haiti, right?" Greg was born in Haiti and had come to America as a small child.

"Yeah," I said, checking my poker hand.

"Well, he was drinking at a b-b-bar over there, jumped in his car drunk, and killed someone. Now his dumb ass locked up. L-l-l-locked up in a Haitian jail, slim. You think it's hard here? You ain't seen n-n-nothing. They don't even feed you over there. Your people have to b-b-b-bring you food."

That hit home, because it had been two months since my conviction, and nobody had visited me. I called home every day, collect, but too often my family didn't pick up. If I was in Haiti, would they let me starve?

"That's rough, slim," I said.

"That's not the b-b-b-bad part."

In Haiti, Greg explained, they believed in blood feuds. If you killed someone, the family could retaliate. The victim's family was threatening to stack Greg's brother in tires, douse him with gasoline, and set him on fire. Their price was a 4x4 pickup and $2,500 American. Somehow, the responsibility to buy his brother's safety fell to Greg.

"I'm gonna smuggle weed," he said.

That was a bad idea. Weed sold for five times as much inside, but the gangs controlled the trade. It wasn't a good idea to cross the gangs. Greg had thought of that. He worked in an administrative office with some long-timers. He could use them to reach the older white inmates, he said, chill dudes who didn't mix with the gangs and just wanted to smoke off the stress of prison.

He'd been working on a CO, too. His name was Burchfield. He was tall and lanky with big feet. A real asshole. Burchfield wrote infractions for almost anything. That's the thing about tough COs: usually, they were dirty.

"I got him under my wing, young," Greg said, laughing. "No one will eh-eh-ever suspect that b-b-bastard to be my plug."

Greg had turned Burchfield with the Law of Reciprocity, where you give in order to get. For months, he had talked with Burchfield about music and women until they were friendly. Then he started loaning Burchfield CDs. When Burchfield said, "Damn, I wish I had that album," Greg said, "Keep it."

Before you knew it, Burchfield was bringing Greg CDs. Then the CDs turned into cheesesteaks. Greg thought weed was the next step. I thought Greg was taking a fool's risk. He could go down for another five at least. But Greg didn't feel like he had a choice. For his brother, this was life or death.

"Not interested, slim," I said when he offered to cut me in. "But good luck."

I wasn't interested in much, to be honest. The worst thing about prison, other than the hassle, was the boredom. Two hours of therapy a week, a couple hours of yard. Playing cards. Walking to chow, to the dayroom, to the shower. What was the point?

Some guys were working. There was a kid in the next dayroom over, for instance, always reading. I figured he was a short-timer, in for jaywalking or something, because he was neat, and his clothes looked rich. Then someone told me he had life.

I had known there was only one other lifer in the youth program. I assumed he was a bamma. *Are you kidding? This guy?*

I watched him after that, through the small barred window that separated our dayrooms, and out in the yard. No matter how much chaos swirled around him, the kid kept his head down, reading and taking notes.

I couldn't understand it. Why? If he was getting out, sure. Maybe. But he had life. No matter what we did, the two of us were stuck here until the day we died.

I turned away, half in confusion and half in disgust. *Screw that guy. What's he trying to prove?* I played poker with Greg and his friends every day, that was my routine, but half the time it felt like I wasn't there, like I was standing over my own shoulder watching my body throw cards. I didn't cut myself, but I stopped combing my hair. I stopped shaving, but I couldn't even grow a beard. It was nasty and patchy, like a kid's.

Every afternoon, I stared out the window, watching the COs change shift. I watched them pulling out of the parking lot and thought, *Damn, they're going home. They get to ride in cars.* I'm not talking about nice cars, like Gwen's Corvette. I would have done just about anything to ride in a Datsun, just once, with my shackles off.

That was the world. It was out there, beyond the walls. That's why I called Mom every day. Occasionally she picked up, and the conversation was good. Once, I remember, she was with my girlfriend, Star. They'd been talking about me, she said, looking at pictures.

They were talking about me! That made me happy for a week.

Most of the time, though, Mom didn't pick up the phone. I called at the same time every day. She knew it was me. Then one day:

"Yeah, I accept the charge."

Shit. It was Derrick. "Mom there?"

"Just me, nigga. I been going through your closet." I could hear the hate in his voice. He was loving this. "I'm wearing your favorite shirt. I guess it's my shirt now."

That was cold, but that's Derrick. I was gone for life, so I couldn't touch him.

"I ain't sweating that," I lied, but Derrick had been bullying me all my life. He knew how to hurt me.

"I saw your girl, Star, Chris. Star looking thick. You know we rap on the phone every now and then," he lied. "I think I'm going to hook up with her."

Star was the only person who always accepted my calls. She said she loved me, even though I'd been away fifteen months, including that year at Upper Marlboro. She said she wanted to be with me. But Star was a sophomore in high school. She was too young to understand what she was saying. I knew I should let her go, but I couldn't. She was all I had.

"Next time, little brother," Derrick said, laughing, and hung up.

A couple months later, my mom and sister finally visited. Leslie had graduated from high school about a month before my trial. She was in the air force. Mom lost the house in Temple Hills, but us children had inherited our father's home when he died. I signed over my portion to Mom so that she could live there. The house was less than thirty minutes from Patuxent. There was no reason she couldn't visit, but she needed someone to bring her, I guess, and Leslie had been away.

We talked about my case. Mom said she was working on an appeal. She said she hadn't forgotten me. "Make a list of what you need, Chris." I sent her the list, twice, but she never responded. Mom made a lot of promises she not only couldn't keep, she couldn't remember.

Leslie sent a box of supplies: Polo T-shirts, jeans, black Nike socks, and a pair of black Nike Air Max so that I wouldn't have to wear prison issue; a radio; and some of my favorite CDs (go-go, Tupac, Scarface, Jay Z). At the bottom was a GED study guide she had found at my father's house. He had bought it for me, she said, but didn't have a chance to send it before he died. It was the first and last gift my father ever gave me.

I held it in my hands, thinking about how I messed up. How I ruined my life. My hands started to shake as I wiped away tears. I thought about that lifer in the next dayroom, studying every day. I flipped through a few pages.

Then I threw the book on the shelf. *What the hell was wrong with that kid?*

Leslie sent me $60 in commissary credit a month. I made $35 a month from my job as a tier runner, passing messages between inmates and guards. Those credits were supposed to be for essentials and food, because you can't live on what they give you in chow, but I used them to buy cigarettes or a two-cup portion of ground coffee. Then I traded those to Greg for joints the size of toothpicks. He sold everything Burchfield supplied, usually in a day, but I didn't want anything to do with that business. I just wanted to smoke weed and play cards. Weed was the only way I knew to make it through the day.

That and calling home, which I did twice a day, each time I was in the dayroom. What else could I do? Mom hadn't answered since her visit, but calling home was like my prayer. It was the only thing that brought me peace and made me believe that—

"Hello?"

I caught my breath. "Mom?"

It had been a month, at least.

"Mom, it's me! It's Chris."

No response.

"What's up, Mom? You good? I miss you. I love you."

I waited. I could hear her breathing.

"You ain't got no rap for me, Mom?"

I wanted to reach through the phone. I wanted to hug her. In prison, you need contact. You need someone to say they care and that they haven't forgotten you. Instead, my mother said, as cold as the grave: "I don't have anything to say to you, Chris. You got life. What's the point? You're never coming home."

Decisions

I TALKED TO my sister on the phone a few days later. I was a broken kid trying to hold himself together. My mom had crushed me. She hung up on me, and she never took my call again. Those wounds are a part of me I can't trade. I've learned to live with them. I've learned to *use* them. Right then, though, I needed comfort. I needed my sister to have my back.

She gave me my medicine instead.

"Look, Chris, these calls are expensive," she said. "We spent eight hundred dollars talking to you."

Dang, I didn't know it cost that much. I knew calling collect from prison was a scam. It was like five times the normal rate. With the $60 commissary deposits, the clothes, and the radio, my family had probably spent $1,500 on me. And that didn't include the lawyer. But I needed them. Surely I was worth the price?

"Then come visit me, Leslie. It's free. I'm half an hour away."

Leslie was quiet. I was hoping . . . hoping hard . . .

"You did what you did, Chris," she said. "That's on you." She sounded sad, but determined. "I told you to stop being so hot, little brother. I said you were headed for trouble. But you didn't listen."

Leslie was getting married. She was being posted to the Middle East. "I've got my own family I have to focus on. I'm sorry, but you can't keep calling us."

Then she laid it straight: "We don't owe you, Chris. You're eighteen. You're a man now. You're not our responsibility anymore."

I went back to the picnic table in the corner of the dayroom. Wu-Tang was blaring, and five guys were yelling at the television, happy their neighborhood caught a murder that day. My sister had told the truth: I was a burden. It was better for everyone if I was out of the picture.

The next time I talked to Star, I told her, "I can't see you anymore. You're young and beautiful. You got to live your life, and I'm only going to hold you back."

It was heartbreaking. She cried and begged me to change my mind, and I wanted to, because I was throwing away the only thing I had left, but it had to be done. When I hung up, I knew that was the end, not just of our relationship, but of the outside world.

I was stripped bare. I was at the bottom of the ocean, with nothing but my journal, my CDs, the clothes on my back, and my name. They tried to take that in prison, too: they called me by my number, 265–975. But I was Chris Wilson.

It was time for me to decide if that name meant anything at all.

PART 3

The Master Plan

Faith is taking the first step even when
you don't see the staircase.

—MARTIN LUTHER KING JR.

Giving Water

THEY CALL IT rock bottom, like it's a hard floor you go crashing into and stop. But here's the thing: There's no floor. You only see it that way later, because rock bottom isn't a place. You can *always* go lower. Rock bottom is a decision. It's the moment you decide to stop falling and take control of your life.

I could have kept falling. Honestly, I almost did. For weeks after my family broke it off with me, I was so depressed I could barely get out of my bunk. I couldn't see anything but the cave, and I couldn't see a point in living that way.

It was fear, and only fear, that got me on my feet. The youth program had a six-month probation period. After that, they sent you on to the next tier, or sent you into the regular population at the black hole prison known as the Annex. Patuxent was bad, it was a meaningless and painful life, but the Annex was worse. The Annex was dangerous. And I was a lifer. They never wanted me in the program in the first place. Most people thought my place was over there.

Every path starts with a step. Here's some advice: take the easiest one first. At Patuxent, that meant getting a high school equivalency diploma (GED). Mom always said, "Get your diploma." I had promised Big Daddy I would get my diploma. That's what my father wanted, too. That's why he bought me the study guide. That's all anyone from the outside ever said: "Get that diploma, Chris."

Patuxent had a GED certificate program. I figured getting that GED would prove I belonged.

So I took my father's study guide down from my shelf and tried to read it. After a few days, I quit. It was too hard, sitting in my cell, to stay motivated and focused. I needed help.

I enrolled in the GED school. I was shocked to discover, on the first morning, that it was coed. The female inmates had their own residence building and yard, but they took classes with the men. For many male inmates, that was the draw. The school at Patuxent was barely more organized than the dayroom or the therapy sessions. It was mostly the bammas from the yard, lounging, lying, and cutting up. There were inmates who had been in "high school" for twelve years. They didn't want to graduate, because then they wouldn't see the women.

I was there to learn. I listened. I read. I tried . . . But I struggled, especially at math. My education had essentially ended in the eighth grade. Now I had to pass geometry and algebra.

"You need help, Chris?" the teacher asked.

"Yeah, I don't understand."

"Steve," she yelled across the room, "help him out."

I looked over, and here comes the lifer always reading in his dayroom. His name was Steve Edwards, and he was smart. He scored so high on his GED, the administration made him take it again to prove he hadn't cheated. That time, he made a perfect score. So they offered him a teaching assistant job making the highest level of pay in the prison, $38 a month.

"What you need help with?" Steve said.

I thought about playing it cool, but I knew that would hurt me in the end. "Everything," I admitted.

"That's cool. That's what I'm here for. What you working on today?"

He sat down and started explaining concepts: history, nouns and verbs, scientific principles. Math was hard for me, but easy for Steve. He had a way of breaking math problems down step-by-step, until equations that looked impossible became manageable parts. That's a good lesson: Don't get overwhelmed. Don't try to get it all at once.

I liked the work. Reading the GED study guide had frustrated me, but when I practiced with other inmates, I learned, and it felt good. I started to see Steve with new eyes. I had looked down on him at first. He had nice clothes. Good manners. Every week, he got his hair trimmed by the inmate barber. He wasn't like the rest of us, I had figured. He was middle class. He had someone on the outside taking care of him. What did he know about my problems?

Now I wanted what he had. Not just knowledge, but confidence. A purpose. The determination to better himself, no matter what everyone else was doing or saying. I made myself flash cards so I could study at chow and in my cell. I worked my dad's GED study guide, remembering the tips Steve had given me. Skeeter and Omar laughed at me. Greg shook his head. "J-j-just play this hand of poker, man."

"No," I said, "this is what I need to do."

Steve ran a tutoring center outside of class, and I started going. The last six weeks of my evaluation period were intense, like training camp. I was Rocky training for his big fight against Apollo Creed (or Adonis Creed getting ready for his big fight in Ryan Coogler's movie years later), except instead of an old man throwing practice punches, Steve threw math word problems. I was terrible at word problems.

"Break them down, Chris."

"Twenty-six?"

"Remember the shortcuts."

"Oh, yeah. I forgot to subtract the distance the basketball is thrown!"

"Now what about the points? Come on. You got this."

If I didn't get the problem right, I had to chug a full glass of water, or I had to get on the floor for twenty-five push-ups. I loved it. I missed so many problems, I could feel myself getting strong.

I challenged myself. Didn't matter how many problems I missed, I kept going. If I started getting too many problems right, I pushed to the next level. "Harder, Steve. Next lesson."

Or: "Time me on this one. I think I can do it in ten seconds."

Even in the tutoring center, inmates thought I was crazy. They weren't used to hearing a guy talk trash about math.

"Time's up, Chris."

"Nah, I got this, Steve, come on. I'm almost there."

"Get on the floor, Chris," Steve said, smiling. "You got to get the floor pregnant!"

"All right," I said, knocking out the push-ups, thinking about the problem. "The train's going thirty miles an hour!"

"Show me your work!" he barked like a drill sergeant in the army. He was enjoying it, too.

Pretty soon, guys stopped to watch, and about two seconds after that, they had to start commenting. This was prison, after all. "I don't think you got it, Chris. That's a hard one."

"Oh, I got it. Don't sleep on me!"

"Bet you two cigarettes he's got it," someone said. They watched me work the equation, looked at Steve to see if my answer was right.

"He's got it," Steve said, nodding with pride.

"Yo, let me try one of those," the bet loser said.

"All right," I said, laughing, "but you got to take the penalties if you fail."

Pretty soon, there were three or four guys watching every day, pushing me to get better. If I couldn't get a concept, Steve kept hammering. Numerator. Denominator. Add. Multiply. Like jabs and uppercuts, jumping rope and shadowboxing. Sometimes, I missed the same problem six or seven times. It didn't bother me. I'd get there. All failure cost me was water or push-ups. Soon, my state-issued T-shirts were fitting tighter. My muscles were coming in.

I took the GED exam in December 1997, seven months after my conviction. The test took most of the day, but my boys were waiting in the tutoring room when I got back. "Did you pass?"

I gave them a smile. "Of course I passed." I wouldn't get the official results for a month, but I knew.

"Was it easy?"

My smile got bigger. I flexed my biceps. "I was prepared, homey, and I knocked it out!"

I received my high school diploma on February 27, 1998, in a ceremony in the prison auditorium. There were fifteen graduates that day from the different prison programs—GED, carpentry, plumbing, et cetera—and every single one had family there to support him, except me. I had written my mother, inviting her to the ceremony. My therapist, Mr. Mee, reached out to her. We never received a response. Not even "Congrats, son, but I can't." It was obvious, in hindsight, that she wouldn't come, but I was a sucker. Even that morning, as I dressed in my best shirt for the ceremony, I thought she would come. All through that decade of silence, whenever I accomplished something, I thought, *She'll come. Mom will come this time.*

She never did.

It hurt. But I wasn't the old Chris Wilson. I *felt* that hurt, but it didn't overwhelm me, because it wasn't about my mom anymore.

It was about me. I had taken charge of my life. And I had a plan.

What's Your Endgame?

WHAT'S YOUR ENDGAME?

That's the question I ask people when I think they're ready to make a move. It's the question I want everyone to ask themselves— and *keep* asking: "What's my endgame?"

Why are you here on planet earth? Where do you want your life to go? Okay, you got your high school degree, that's good, but why? Where is it taking you? How can it help you get there?

And most important: What's your legacy? How do you want to be remembered, slim, when you're dead and gone?

That last question hit me hard. It was something I struggled with for a long time, because in prison they take your humanity. At most, I was my last name: "Wilson! Against the wall!"

Usually, I was a number: "Squat and cough, 265–975! Shakedown!"

Sometimes I was my sentence: Life. That's what defined me inside, the length of time I was serving. It was more important to my identity than my crime. People in the yard would nod their head in my direction. "What he got?"

"He got a body." Then they'd sum it up: "He's a lifer."

I didn't want to be defined that way. I didn't want to be known just for my crime or my punishment. But what else had I done? It was December 1997. I was turning nineteen. Nineteen! What had I accomplished?

What good things could people say about me? That I loved my mother? That was true, but she wouldn't even answer my calls. And so what? Everybody loves their mother.

What else?

The only thing people on the outside would say about me, I realized, sitting in my cold concrete cell, was that I had taken a life.

But I was only a teenager. I had time, as Big Daddy had said. And I had already taken the first steps to turning my life around:

I had accepted my reality (prison), and my responsibility for it.
I wanted to change.
I was doing work.

Now: What was my endgame? I was working, but what was I working toward?

Getting out. That was obvious.

But why? What did I want to get out for?

I decided to stay in my cell until I figured it out. I thought it would take a few hours. How hard could it be, right? I ended up staying down three days.

I started with a handwritten list of everything I wanted. The things I dreamt when I wasn't having my nightmare about being an old man. First on the list: *Grow a big-ass beard.*

Sounds crazy, I know, but as I told you, I couldn't even grow a real mustache on the day I was sentenced to life. I might as well have written *Become a man.*

The list continued:

Run a marathon
Learn Spanish
Skydiving
Buy a Corvette

That was my dream since I was nine years old. I *had* to have that car. Owning a Corvette, for me, was the perfect symbol of success.

But what about *experiences*, like:

Party on a cigarette boat
Go to a bullfight
Party in Barcelona, Spain
Party in Vegas at the Wynn
Horseback riding
Snorkeling
Join the mile-high club

What can I say? I was a young man in a concrete cage, dreaming about another life. A life I had never experienced, with money, dope music, and women.

I put that list away. I didn't *throw* it away. I still have it today, because I try to keep everything so I can remember where I used to be.

Now that I'm looking, twenty years later . . . it's not bad. I've done half the stuff on the list; I'll probably do most of the rest. But a list like that is not the way to accomplish anything in life. Those are rewards. They're for later, when the money's made and the freedom's earned. Right now, I needed to do the work.

I pulled out another piece of paper. I had a belief in my soul: I was

my
[Bucket List]

1. Grow a Big-ass Beard
2. Run a marathon
3. Earn 3 college Degree
4. Learn Spanish
5. Learn mandrin
6. Learn Italian
7. Sky Diving
8. Buy a corvette
9. Party on a cigarette boat
10. Publish my memoir
11. Paint growing Patrick Party
12. Go Bungee Jumping
13. Go Rock climbing
14. Go to a Bull Fight
15. Go to Lake Tahoe
16. Take a cooking class
17. Go to the Detroit car Show
18. Stand above the Oggenheimr Octillo well
19. Ride Dune Buggies thru the Desert
20. Hike thru the swiss ALPS
21. Party in Barcelona, Spain
22. Go to the Picasso museum, Spain
23. See the La Grada Familia, SPAIN
24. Party in vegas at the WYNN
25. Go White water rafting

26. Horse Back Riding
27. Go Roller skating
28. Go to the Audubon Penisula
29. Helicopter Ride
30. go camping
31. learn archery
32. Climb a mountain
33. Join the mile High club
34. Go to Africa
35. Party in Sunset Beach for a week
36. Go Trail Running
37. Sky Diving
38. Triathlon 50
39. Go skeet Shooting
40. Party in LA for a week
41. Party in the DR for a week
42. Go Snow Barely in Aspen skiing
43. Go Kyaking
44. Oversley BBQ Pool me
45. Have a Boat BBQ
46. Start my own Business self-employed.
47. Go to 1804 of muscle make it to
48. Go snorkeling
49. Go mountain Biking
50. go to the Lorve in France

First thoughts on a new life

convinced, if I handled myself the right way, I could get out of prison and lead a good life. Maybe it was a one-in-a-million shot, but I was going to be the one. So I asked myself: What do I need to do today, tomorrow, and for the rest of my life to get a second chance?

Once I thought about it, I knew the first step: *Stop calling home every day.*

My family had abandoned me. They never visited. They had blocked my calls. It was time to let them go.

Forget about my fake-ass friends, meaning my so-called homeys back home that never visited, either. This was my life now.

Get my high school diploma (done)
Work out six days a week (gain thirty pounds of muscle)
Attend weekly therapy and resolve my issues
Identify my faults that led me to prison
Always seek advice
Remain a lifelong learner

That last one was important. I needed to keep pushing myself like I'd pushed for my GED. I had to devote myself to the struggle.

Then I thought of the bad habits I'd developed over the years. Not just committing crimes, but taking shortcuts, wasting time. I needed to get rid of those, too:

No gambling
No horseplay in public
No sex jokes
No junk food

The list wasn't perfect, by any means. At the very bottom of the first page, I wrote: *Pay my brother back*. I didn't mean for a loan. I meant for the abuse.

Derrick deserved it, but revenge was self-defeating. How could I stop my family from hurting me if I was still angry and wanting revenge?

The second page was rewards: world travel, a cool leather jacket, a fresh pair of Prada sneakers, a black Corvette convertible with nice rims and a kicking sound system . . . the mile-high club. Sex on an airplane, y'all! Think how glamorous that was for a kid from inner-city DC who hadn't even been to Baltimore, an hour away, except when sentenced to the Hickey School.

And then, at the very bottom of page two: *Meet a smart, beautiful woman that's business savvy*.

It took me two days to make the list because I was focused. This wasn't just a bunch of things that popped into my head. This was real. If it was on the list, it was law. I wouldn't stop until it was done.

On the third morning, I went to the typing center, a room provided so that inmates could type letters to lawyers, appeals to politicians, self-made legal briefs, and even (I guess) letters home. I typed my notes. The first draft was three pages long. I went over the list again and again until I'd condensed it to one page. In the end, I had thirty-five things I needed to do to live the life I wanted. I titled it: *My Master Plan*.

I made three copies.

I sent the first to Judge Wood, the man who had convicted me, with a note explaining that I was working hard to turn my life around. I told him I would update him on my progress. Judge Wood couldn't parole me, but he had the power to reduce my sentence. When I

spoke to him again—if I ever had the chance to speak to him again—
I wanted a record of my work.

I sent the second copy to Grandma, because she was the only
person I had on the outside. I knew I'd never hear from her, because
she hadn't communicated with me since my arrest, but I could use
that silence. I knew Grandma was in her house on Division Avenue.
I knew she studied her mail like it was from God Himself, so I could
assume she was reading my notes and following my progress, and that
would keep me honest.

I took the last copy and taped it to the wall beside my bunk. That
way it would be the first thing I saw in the morning, and the last
thing I saw at night. I wanted it to haunt my dreams, because my
Master Plan was only a tool.

It was *following* my Master Plan that truly mattered.

My Master Plan

By Chris Wilson

December 1997

Stop calling home every day

Forget about my fake-ass friends

Get my high school diploma (done)

Work out six days a week (gain thirty pounds of muscle)

Attend weekly therapy and resolve my issues

Identify my faults that led me to prison

Always seek advice

Remain a lifelong learner

No gambling

No horseplay in public

No sex jokes

Always dress neat

Mind my own business

Learn how to speak real English

No junk food

Graduate from carpentry vocational shop

Pay my brother back

Start my own business

Travel the world

Get an apartment in a nice neighborhood

Get a black Corvette convertible

Get a pair of cool Prada gloves to wear in the convertible

Get a cool-ass leather jacket

Go skydiving

Party on a cigarette boat

Get a fresh pair of Prada sneakers

Join the mile-high club

Lay out on the beach

Drive dune buggies through the desert

Party in South Beach

Go on a helicopter ride

Go to New Orleans

Go fishing

Meet a smart, beautiful woman that's business savvy

Workout

I WOKE UP AT 8:00 the next morning, looked at my Master Plan, got my door popped, and went to the yard. There's no privacy in prison, but a rec session in the early morning, when everyone is sleeping in, comes close. It was December, so it was dark. And cold. I could see my breath, and I could feel it, too.

In the middle of the day, the yard looked small, because it was filled with ballers, loafers, huddled-up gang members, and cigarette smoke. There was no room to maneuver. Everyone was on watch. But that morning, it felt huge. The basketball courts were empty. The picnic tables were quiet. The weight pit was empty. The sun was below the wall, and the sky was a shadow, so dark I couldn't see the razor wire.

I put on my headphones. I breathed deep, nodded to the beat, and started jogging. I could feel the frozen ground through my thin rubber prison sneakers, but the rocks didn't stop me. I did five laps. Occasionally I passed someone, but Kurt Cobain was screaming in my ears. I pounded harder, faster. It hurt. And the more I ran, the stronger I felt.

I stopped at the free weights, bobbing like a boxer to the music to keep my mind sharp. The bench padding was torn and the bar rusted. I switched to Jay Z, with that slow heavy beat, and started pumping, performing a routine I'd worked through in my mind the night before: bench, curls, lifts, squats. The sky was lightening. Other inmates were moving. But even when they were beside me, working their own reps, they were in the background. When you're focused on your work, you can find privacy, even in the yard.

I worked until the sweat was coming off my shoulders like steam. I nodded along to Project Pat, feeling the burn. The clouds were high and thin, turning the morning sky white, but the yard was gray. Nobody was at the picnic tables, but the weights were clanging, getting worked. The weights were the most popular spot in the yard.

I wanted a shower, but I had to wait for the afternoon. Showers were limited to ten-minute blocks, seven people at a time for three showerheads. You stepped aside to soap and let your buddy in, then stepped back in to rinse. Everyone wore boxers in the shower. I owned only two pairs. So after every shower, I hung the wet pair in front of the vent in my cell to dry and put the other pair on.

I went back to my cell. I took off my shoes and brushed them clean. I had been letting my hair grow since my sentencing, but that morning, I shaved my head. I trimmed the goatee I had been working on since Upper Marlboro. Grow a big-ass beard hadn't made my final list; I could be a man without it.

I brushed my teeth, checked my fingernails. Pride is in the details.

I flexed, checking for those thirty pounds of muscle in the bolted metal plate that was my mirror. Nothing yet. But it's not one day that changes your life. It's every day.

Book Crusher

THERE WERE FOUR LEVELS IN the youth program, each with its own tier. Each level had more perks than the one below it. On tier two, the dayroom had hot plates and pans and spatulas to cook a meal. We had time with our cell door popped. Tier three increased the freedom and added a pool table. On tier four, up top, you could move around as you pleased, as long as the prison wasn't on count (meaning head count) or lockdown. This was the heart of the program, a system that gave you more benefits the more you achieved.

I'd been promoted to tier two, but that didn't mean life was better. Inmates on two had huddled up and formed friendships, which helped avoid the chaotic sorting out of tier one, but they were still wild. Skeeter never made it to two, but Omar was there. Greg was there, running his drug empire. He always had extra food from commissary, so he often cooked on the hot plates in the dayroom.

He said, "You want a sausage, Chris?"

"Nah, I'm all right."

"You want a hat?"

"No thanks."

"It's c-c-c-cool. I got, like, fifty hats!"

Cash wasn't allowed in Patuxent. Since it was contraband, it was worth twice face value—the Law of Scarcity—and had two main purposes. The first was buying drugs. The second was buying sex from female COs. People outside are surprised by that, but it's fairly common in the prison system. The going rate for CO sex at Patuxent was $500. Some guys hoarded cash for months, even years, until they had enough. They got robbed of that cash, too, especially if they talked too much.

Even with the limited amount of cash around, Greg paid his brother's blood ransom in six months. But he didn't want to give up the business. He bartered his weed for anything he could get his hands on: cash, commissary tickets, food, shoes, hats (fifty of them!), and especially burner phones, which were illegal inside. Prison was awash in contraband, along with an elaborate system to hide and distribute it. There was straight bribery, of course, involving COs like Burchfield, but most of the action was underground. Inmates made quarter-inch-long screwdrivers by sharpening the metal clasps on pens, then unscrewed the ceiling light in their cell. They used the screwdrivers to take apart their radios and televisions to hide cell phones, drugs, and knives. If you wanted to get high, no problem. If you wanted to make a private phone call, it was available. It was prison: everything was available for a price.

I fell into it at first. Anything to escape my world. But once I started on my Master Plan, I avoided everything. I didn't get high. I didn't smoke cigarettes. I never drank toilet liquor. I never hid contraband. I didn't even take gifts from Greg, like the hats, because that might lead to the Law of Reciprocity, and I didn't want to be in his debt. Once, he came to my cell with a full bottle of Rémy Martin. That was gold in prison: good high-quality liquor. I turned him down.

"What's your p-p-p-problem, slim?" Greg asked, confused and insulted. "You got life. You got to take advantage of y-y-your opportunities."

I was having another recurring dream. I was a child, in my childhood bedroom at Grandma's house. Just like in real life, the bed had a wooden base with four drawers, one each for me, my two brothers, and my sister. I wanted to explore those drawers. I knew there was something inside, and I wanted to play with it. So I walked toward the bed. I bent down, looking around to make sure I was alone. Then, slowly, I stuck my hand into one of the drawers. A snake bit me, I jerked back, and I woke up in my cell.

It wasn't a complicated message. My brain was saying: Don't give in to temptation, not even once. Don't cut corners or do anything that could lead to trouble, even if I could get away with it. One mistake, and I'd be living my other nightmare: the helpless old man in a prison cell.

I was out of school by then, because Patuxent offered classes only until you got your GED. That's a dangerous time: when you have nothing scheduled. That's when you have to focus and use your freedom productively. For the first time in my life, that's what I did. I worked out. I ate right. No more sugar. Limited carbs. At meals, I traded my dessert for vegetables. I spent my commissary on peppers, onions, and things like that.

The prison had a library. It's not easy to read, honestly, especially if you're out of practice. I asked other inmates for recommendations, but sometimes the books were boring, or pointless, or not to my taste. I finished them anyway. I read for ninety minutes, then took an hour break, often to watch *Seinfeld*, then read another ninety. That's a skill everyone needs: the determination to finish disappointing tasks.

The first book that stayed with me was Robert Greene's *The 48*

Laws of Power, a guide to getting over and defeating your enemies. It's a real Machiavellian worldview, where every action is about getting ahead. You have to break others, Greene suggests, using real strength, but also lies and misdirection.

That's not me. I believe in honesty. If I beat you, I want it to be because I worked harder and smarter. And I don't want to beat you, anyway. Unless you're standing against me, I want to bring you up, too.

But life is a hustle, especially in prison, and *The 48 Laws of Power* helped me understand the game. I didn't talk much back then. I watched, and I started to see the ways people around me lied and manipulated, like the way the gangs operated or Greg brought CO Burchfield into his weed operation. Once I understood their methods, I understood their priorities, and I could combat them. Even though I was playing the game straight, that gave me power.

Robert Greene also said this: *Your greatest accomplishment is molding yourself.*

I took my pen and wrote that down in my notebook, because I believe in taking notes. I go back and study my notes from time to time so I don't forget what's important. Molding myself: that's what I was doing with my diet, my exercise, my reading.

I also read *Rich Dad, Poor Dad*. The rat race, the book said, was working for others and spending your money as soon as you received it. Live like that, and you would always be poor, even if you made a lot of money. That spoke to me. When I made my Master Plan, it didn't say be a lawyer or a doctor. It said, "Start my own business."

Rich Dad, Poor Dad pushed me further. A lawyer could start his own business, working out of his own office, but that wouldn't make him rich. You can't truly become wealthy using your own labor. True wealth was built by creating a system with specific roles for employees and investments. Then, everyone's labor made you money.

That's what I had done when I convinced my friends to help me sell Blow Pops at school. That's what Greg did with his weed business. He had CO Burchfield, runners, spies, and the older white inmates, who helped him distribute. In fact, the drug business run by crews in rough neighborhoods was a classic wealth-building business. I tell those guys, when I talk to them now, "You're great businessmen. You built a corporation. You have dozens of employees. You don't have to do this. You could take what you've learned and do something legal that helps your community."

I tell leaders in the community, "If we could tap the brainpower and business expertise here right now—if we could turn all our efforts to the positive—we wouldn't need anyone's help, which is good, because they don't want to help us. We're poor, but we have the potential, right now, to overcome."

That was in the future, though. Back then, at nineteen, as an inmate, I needed to study and learn. So that's what I did. Steve wasn't on my tier. I only saw him in the yard. But I had two friends on tier I met weight lifting—Sean and David, two white dudes—and they were readers, too. We started a group to trade books and talk about what we read. We called ourselves the Book Crushers.

It wasn't a competition, but we kept track of what we read. Even when we grew to twenty Book Crushers, we still kept track. And I am proud to say that I was the number one Book Crusher at the Patuxent Institution fifteen years in a row.

Positive Delusions

I WAS PROUD to be the number one Book Crusher, but let's be honest, at Patuxent that title (which I made up, obviously) didn't come with respect. Guys gave me funny looks when I read in the dayroom. They laughed when they saw me eating with one hand, holding open my book with the other. They didn't trust my new behavior. "You got life, slim. Who you fooling?"

For most inmates at Patuxent, prison was marking time: playing basketball, lifting weights, blasting music, telling stories from the wars. They were still living the street life, starting beefs, stabbing over minor insults, smoking weed and playing cards and being too loud. It grinds on you, being in that environment.

So I wasn't happy when another crazy bamma was promoted to two. He was young, and he couldn't shut up. Every time it got quiet on tier, he had something stupid to yell or hip-hop lyrics to shout. He didn't mean anything by it; he was making noise to fill the empty space. Emptiness is scary, especially inside.

I told him, "Look, you can't be like that in here. You got to be respectful, slim."

He wasn't a bad kid, but he was putting everyone on edge. Even I couldn't concentrate on my books, because he was on my nerves. So I knew it was trouble when two wild young dudes from down the tier came at him. "They want you down the hall, Wilson," they told me.

I knew what that meant, so I walked away, and they threw scalding baby oil in the bamma's face. Stabbings were the preferred method of retribution, but hot baby oil was second. Guys bought it at commissary and heated it in their hot pots, which were like kettles. They could bring a pot past unsuspecting guards, saying it was soup or that they needed to wash up. After the attack, they could pass it back to guys on the tier and the COs couldn't identify it as the weapon, since hot pots weren't contraband.

Usually, the consequences weren't bad: a few days in the infirmary, a week of painful blistering, a lesson learned. But these bammas were sick. They put sand in the oil. The kid's face was melting. His eyes were burning. His natural reaction was to reach up and wipe the oil away. But when he did, the sand became abrasive. It tore his skin off.

He served, I think, five more years. It took all that time for his skin to grow back. For five years, he was a scar. No color on his nose. No lips. Skin slick like plastic. Like his old face had melted off.

Is that a metaphor? Prison burns your old face off? I guess everything is a metaphor if it doesn't happen to you. But the kid was real. I saw him every day. He lived with that pain and embarrassment until the day they set him free.

I justified walking away. *I warned him. All he had to do was cool down.*

But it grinds on you, that kind of violence. The humiliation, the disrespect, the routine.

I can't spend my life in here, I thought. *I'll go crazy.* I figured I could work hard for seven years, maybe eight. After that, I wasn't sure. Prison can break you in a thousand ways.

Then I thought of a book I'd read. It wasn't anything special, just a cheap paperback with a black-and-white cover I'd picked up at the DOC processing center after coming out of solitary. The subject was the Hanoi Hilton, the brutal Vietcong prison where John McCain and hundreds of other captured soldiers were tortured during the Vietnam War.

I remember the line drawings of torture positions. Arms wrenched backward by poles for so long they locked in place. Men hung by their wrists until they collapsed like Jesus on the cross. Bamboo shoved under fingernails. I was in isolation for a month and it almost broke me. Some men in that book were isolated for years. Their only human contact was tapping on the walls, praying someone was on the other side to hear.

I'll never forget one man, although I don't know his name. The Vietcong were going after him, beating him savagely, but he wouldn't crack. He'd be thrown back to his fellow prisoners unconscious and barely alive, and they'd give him water, rub the blood from his wounds, and he'd finally open his eyes, see the hell they were living in, and whisper through broken teeth, "We'll be home by Christmas."

The other prisoners thought he was crazy. *We ain't going home for Christmas. We're never going home. None of us are making it out of here. Especially not you.*

Nobody thought he would survive a week, but he kept saying they'd be home by Christmas, they'd be home by Christmas, so everyone started to play along, *Yes, yes, we're going home*, and eventually, they started to believe it. Not that they would be with their families for Christmas, but that they'd make it out.

And the more I thought about those men—most of whom did

make it out—the more I believed. At my worst moments, I would think of them, and tell myself, *If they can endure their imprisonment, so can I.*

Everyone needs something to hold on to. That was part of the reason for my Master Plan: giving myself a goal to believe in. But I needed more. So I started collecting pictures. I cut them out of old magazines with prison-issue scissors, which are worse than the plastic safety scissors in kindergarten. I couldn't have cut my throat if I tried.

At first, the pictures were straightforward: A beach. A pretty girl. A nice watch. A slick apartment with a city view. It's not wrong to want nice things. After all, these were on my Master Plan. The author of *Rich Dad, Poor Dad* disagreed about money buying happiness, but *Rich Dad, Poor Dad* had never been desperately inner-city, life-in-prison poor. My take is this: If you put in the work, dream the rewards.

I called the pictures my Positive Delusions.

They gave me strength. I mean that: dreaming about beaches and women made me strong, in the same way "home for Christmas" kept that man in the Hanoi Hilton alive. Instead of worrying about the CO tearing up my bunk, I took out my photos and thought, *It's not always going to be like this, Chris. This is the life you're going to have.*

I started pasting the photos into my notebooks to make collages. I'd take a beach, add a few pretty girls in bikinis. Maybe a Corvette parked on the side. I loved art when I was a kid. Back on Division Avenue, I used to draw all the time. But I hadn't made anything beautiful since I was twelve years old. Now I was noticing colors again, working shapes off each other, and figuring out compositions. It wasn't long before those girls weren't just sex objects but design elements in elaborate abstract scenes.

"Keep dreaming, brother," inmates said, laughing, when they saw those bikinis and Corvettes. *We ain't going home for Christmas. Especially not you.*

"I'll be there one day, slim. You watch."

"You'll be making your pictures, fool, but you ain't going near a woman like that."

The more the other inmates joked about my dreams, though, the more real they felt. I could hold them in my hands. I could see them. This was why I was putting in the work. Why I was learning. Growing. I was going to be on the beach. I was going to have the Corvette, the watch, the penthouse.

But I was also going to be working with my hands, creating, making beautiful collages out of the broken, cutup pieces around me. Yes, the picture was the dream. That's where my Positive Delusions started. But *making* the picture was the dream, too.

It's the action, not just the reward. It's being the artist, not just admiring the view. That's the endgame. Do you understand?

I didn't understand it myself, not at the time. All I knew was that the more time I spent working on my Positive Delusions, the better I felt. And the more convinced I was that I would get there—to that happy life—one day. All I had to do was keep going.

Tooky

I ENROLLED IN carpentry at the vocational shop. Carpentry was more popular than the GED program because inmates thought, *What will a GED do? It won't get me a job. But if I master a skill, I can find work.*

I took it to the next level. If I understood woodworking, I figured I could own a carpentry shop. That's not just a job, it's a business. And besides, I wanted to *learn*. To me, with my new mind-set, learning was valuable, even if I never used the knowledge directly.

Wood shop was also popular because you owned your projects. If you built a shelf or a box, you could use it in your cell, or you could sell it to another inmate. There were old heads who had done carpentry for decades, and they built cabinets that looked store-bought. Some had secret drawers. The guards would check them, but you had to know the code. Take out a drawer, press the bottom of the drawer above, turn another drawer around, reconfigure something else, and, *bang*, hidden compartment.

That was the ingenuity developed inside: inmates could hide items in the smallest cracks. (No, not there, although that happened, too.)

I've seen inmates reach inside slots I had never noticed, grab hidden strings, and pull up entire bags of contraband—from cell phones to porn to candy bars. Guys could disassemble an electric razor and turn it into a tattoo gun in less than twenty seconds—and put it back again just as fast if the wrong CO walked on the tier. It was the rose growing in a crack in the concrete, the prodigy rising up from the tenement floor. The system will never break the urge to find a way.

It wasn't just about money and contraband, though. These old heads were craftsmen. They had pride. They were making puzzles, testing themselves with new techniques and better methods. A man can do incredible things with time, patience, and desire. For old heads like my friend Geronimo, who'd been in for twenty years, carpentry was a lifestyle. They were making art.

I just wanted to build a CD rack.

There was another reason the wood shop was popular: the women. The shop, like the school, was a rare point of contact. If you lived your life without women—not seeing them, not smelling them, not hearing their voices—even staring at them across a wood shop was dope. Guys in the dayroom went nuts for the female news reporters on TV. If they interviewed a pretty girl, especially a neighborhood girl, lewd comments would fly. That's how starved we were.

No physical contact was allowed, of course. Everything was monitored and segregated. But like I said, the urge was unstoppable. And COs were greedy.

So there was flirting. There was touching. There was sex. I saw girls give hand jobs and blow jobs and quickies for cigarettes. I saw a woman have sex with six men in a row.

The other inmates were like, "You got to get some of this, Chris."

I remembered the snake in the drawer. "Nah, man, I'm good."

"You got life, fool. What you waiting for?"

It was tempting, and that tells you the loneliness of prison, because this was dirty. No condoms, no privacy, no eye contact. There were diseases. Women were getting pregnant. Pregnant women were giving it up for cigarettes or heroin, or maybe just to feel like they weren't alone and unloved.

"I can't do it," I said.

"I like how you carry yourself," an old head said as I was sanding down my wood for a rack.

His name was Tooky.

I'd seen him around. He mentored young inmates. When guys were beefing, he came on tier to be a peace maker. COs did that a lot. They used respected inmates to resolve problems.

Me and Tooky (left) (Howard Ware)

Tooky was laid-back, like that bank robber in Upper Marlboro. He was quiet, but not inside his own head like Ray-Ray. He was talented, too. He could build a cabinet with rosewood inlay and beveled edges. He took his time, made sure everything was right. Tooky always took his time. He was carrying life, so what was the hurry?

Everybody loved him, even the women. He was good-looking and smart. They laughed at his jokes. They flirted. But I never saw Tooky with an inmate. I thought he was a monk, but I later heard rumors he was getting action with a few COs. When you put men and women together in a prison environment, there's a sexual charge. I told you female COs slept with inmates for money, but some were in relationships with inmates, too. Tooky was rumored to be a favorite. That was another reason the inmates respected him.

Above all, he was comfortable with himself. And that's not easy. It's hard, in hell, to find peace.

"I like how you carry yourself, too," I told him, because I did.

"Let me give you some advice," he said. He took my CD rack and showed me how to make it stronger, cooler, smoother.

"You're pretty good. You going into the next class?" he asked me.

"I'm trying, but they say it's full."

"Go see the CO on Wednesday with cigarettes. Gonna take five packs." Everything in prison cost cigarettes. "Tell him Tooky sent you, and I said you all right."

I did what Tooky said, and it worked. I was accepted into the next level. Somebody got bumped, I guess, but not my concern. He had his chance. Now I had mine.

After that, I started hanging with Tooky and his friends in the shop. I filled whole afternoons scraping and sanding, dovetailing drawers, listening to Tooky talk about life.

"I met this girl at the go-go, she was looking fine. She had on her Fila tracksuit . . ."

"Fila tracksuit?" I said. "What year was that, Tooky, 1989?"

Turns out it was 1989! Tooky had been in ten years, and a lot changes in ten years. He would be like, "I love that boxy Range Rover . . ."

"Boxy Range Rover? You serious? Nobody drives a Range Rover like that anymore."

Tooky laughed. He never took it the wrong way.

"Why you hanging with those guys?" some bamma asked me, running his mouth. Inmates had to question every social interaction because they had nothing better to do. It was the same way guys watched crews on the outside, or those prisoners in the cave watched shadows on the wall. It was their world.

"They cool, slim. They been through the wars."

"They old, man."

It's funny. Tooky was only twenty-six, but he came before the super-predator panic of the 1990s started stacking young black bodies in prison cells. That, and his cool attitude, and his knowledge of the way prison worked, made him a respected old head before his time—even though he still looked sixteen.

"Careful, slim. You'll be old one day," I said.

"Nah, not if I can help it, cuz."

I laughed. These young fools didn't know what they were saying. They were getting out in a few years, and all they talked about was running their old streets with their old crews. I figured they'd be back.

And I'd still be here. Maybe I'd be an old head like Tooky, working off my years in the carpentry shop. Maybe that wasn't the brutal death sentence I had thought it was.

But I didn't want to get comfortable like Tooky. I wanted to get out.

Master Plan

Chris Wilson

January 2000

Stop calling home every day (done)

Forget about my fake-ass friends (done)

Get my high school diploma (done)

Work out six days a week (gain thirty pounds of muscle) (done—
almost)

Attend weekly therapy and resolve my issues

Identify my faults that led me to prison

Always seek advice (done)

Remain a lifelong learner

Never go against the grain

No gambling (done)

No horseplay in public (done)

No sex jokes (done)

Always dress neat (done)

Mind my own business

Learn how to speak real English

No junk food (done)

Graduate from carpentry vocational shop (soon)

Get a tailored suit
Learn to tie a tie
~~Pay my brother back~~
Complete all the therapeutic models at Patuxent
Start my own business
Travel the world
Get an apartment in a nice neighborhood
Get a black Corvette convertible with nice rims and a sound
  system
Get a pair of cool Prada gloves to wear in the convertible
Get a cool-ass leather jacket
Go skydiving
Party on a cigarette boat
Get a fresh pair of Prada sneakers
Join the mile-high club
Lay out on the beach
Drive dune buggies through the desert
Party in South Beach
Go on a helicopter ride
Go to New Orleans
Go fishing
Meet a smart, beautiful woman that's business savvy

I taped the list to my cell wall. Then I sent a copy with a letter to Judge Wood, telling him my progress on the Master Plan. I wrote to my grandma. I wrote to my lawyer. The only thing I received back was a form letter from the judge's office saying, "Your letter has been received and placed in your file." I kept at it, though. Persistence was part of my Positive Delusions.

Tier Three

I WAS PROMOTED to tier three, where we had a pool table in the dayroom. We also had important things, like access to the library and more free time with our cell doors popped. There was no more Omar, who was stuck on two, but Greg was there, still building his weed empire.

"I made eight hundred dollars today, s-s-s-slim," he told me.

We were allowed a limited number of items in our cells, so Greg had people in other cells holding extra clothes, CDs, and food for him. There was a commissary catalog, but we could order only a few things every couple months, so Greg had people ordering him Nikes.

Greg was small; he wore size six. These guys were six-four with giant feet. "They're for my little cousin. I'm just holding them until his birthday," they told the COs in the mail shop when the shoes arrived.

"Yeah, okay, sure," the COs said. They didn't argue, but they knew something was up.

"You got to get out of the game, Greg," I told him. "There's no future in it."

"Nah, cuz, the g-g-g-getting is good."

Greg had a plan. He had a system and employees, just like *Rich Dad, Poor Dad* advised. I watched him grow his business; watched his clothes, his diet, and his status change. But was he really making it? What was his endgame? How could this possibly work out?

No, Greg wasn't my role model.

My role model was Steve Edwards, the guy who tutored me for the GED. We hadn't seen much of each other in the past year, because I wasn't allowed in the school after I graduated, and Steve was a level ahead of me in the program. I tried to talk when I saw him in the yard, but he was guarded. You had to be that way in prison, but Steve was extra tight.

I worked on him, though. We were both from DC, so we had common ground. We talked about the city. After a few months, he said, "Hold on, your sister's Leslie? Leslie Wilson?"

He knew my sister. He was from across town, but she used to hang in that area. I hadn't even known that, and Leslie and I were close.

Still, Steve was cautious. He didn't like how close I was with Greg's crew. "They're cool," I said. "They're from our part of town."

"So?"

I looked at him like, *You know how this works.*

"Just because you come from the same place," he said, "doesn't mean you have to be friends."

"It don't matter," I said. "I'm not involved in what they're doing."

"It does matter."

He had a point. You had to be careful. People judged you by the company you kept. Just huddling up with a loud bamma or a drug dealer could get you a reputation, and that could get you sent to solitary . . . and there goes your one-in-a-million chance.

"What you reading?" He had a big textbook. Steve was always reading textbooks.

"It's nothing."

I looked over his shoulder. "Is that even English?"

"It's computer code," he said, closing the book like I was being nosy.

I probably laughed, because he was missing the most important part. "You don't even have a computer," I said. There wasn't a computer inmates could access in the whole prison.

"I will one day."

"Oh yeah? How's that?"

"I'm getting out. I'm going to start a software company."

I know I laughed then. "Man, you tripping." *Software company!*

He shrugged and turned away like I always did when bammas said that kind of thing to me.

But I admired him, you know? Steve was the only guy working as hard as me. So when I was promoted to three, I snagged the cell across the hall from him. When I saw what he had—a shelf full of books, nice clothes, a hot pot, a television, and stacks of newspapers and magazines—I was impressed. He had people on the outside keeping him supplied.

I had nobody. My sister had stopped sending me extra commissary, so I was holding tight to my few possessions: two old shirts, two pairs of pants, a pair of Nikes wrapped in a shower cap to keep them clean. I had a radio and a small black-and-white television, a last gift when Leslie cut me off. Everything else I owned fit in a blue plastic bin: my journals and photo collages; old CDs; a few books, since most of what I read I had traded for or gotten from the library; some photos from back in the day; copies of the Master Plan updates I sent to my judge, my lawyer, and my grandma; and all the letters I ever received. I hadn't spoken to my mother in years, but she wrote to me on and off. The letters were usually about money and how she didn't have any. She rarely mentioned my son, Darico, who was still in her care.

So Steve was more than an inspiration, he was an opportunity. He had stacks of reading material, more than I could read in a year—and more coming all the time.

He wouldn't share. Steve didn't like loaning his stuff or giving it away. He cooked in the dayroom, but even after we became friends he wouldn't share food with me. And I was *hungry*. When you don't have extra commissary in prison, you are starving, especially since I was working out every day, putting on that thirty pounds of muscle from my Master Plan. Steve would be frying a big pile of sausage and peppers, more than enough for one person, and I'd ask him for a few bites.

"Nah, man, sorry."

"What?"

"I don't do that, Chris. Sorry."

Steve almost never ate in the chow hall. He looked down on guys like me that had to. He looked down on sardines, ramen, and the other cheap food we could afford from commissary.

"I'm not going to eat that," he said about sardines, like he was insulted. Guys didn't like him for that. They said he was too smart for his own good.

"Don't hang with him, Chris. He's not one of us."

They were right, Steve was smart. But I liked him for it. He didn't have a "man of the people" vibe, that's true, but that was his personality—and his protection. So what if he didn't eat with us? So what if he was cold to bammas and guys from the street? I still hung with him in the dayroom, the yard, or on tier with Sean and David, my book-crushing buddies. The tiers had barred doors to break them into sections, and one happened to be between Steve's cell and mine, so we started pulling up milk crates and sitting on opposite sides to talk.

He finally started loaning me his magazines and newspapers. They were mostly about business and computers—*Fast Company*, *Forbes*, *Wired*, *BusinessWeek*, *Fortune*—although he also had a subscription to *Car and Driver* and a magazine about boats. Steve had his Positive Delusions, too.

He had a subscription to *The Wall Street Journal*, and we read it cover to cover. After, I asked Steve questions. What is the stock market? Why do they keep writing about this company? How can one person be worth a billion dollars? That's a thousand million dollars. That's crazy!

That's what we did for a year. Steve and I pulled up our milk crates, leaned on our cell doors, and discussed everything: technology, corporate structure, the Middle East, the European monetary system, the Bush–Gore election that was going on. I had never cared about an election before. When I was sentenced to life, I wasn't old enough to vote.

I was a sponge. I couldn't learn enough. There was an Italian American guy down the tier. His parents wanted him to learn Italian, so they sent him study guides and books. He never used them, so I asked if I could have them, and I started teaching myself Italian. I studied until 11:30, when a 1980s Italian-language television show, *La Piovra* (*The Octopus*), came on. I had to move my antenna around to get it, and the picture was fuzzy, but I loved that show. It was about a detective investigating the Mafia in southern Italy, so not only did it help with my Italian, it taught me about their culture.

I also watched *Sex and the City*. Man, I was addicted to *Sex and the City*. Beautiful rich women in New York, fancy restaurants and clubs, fashionable clothes, all that sex. Guys laughed at me so much, I sat on the edge of my bunk and flipped the channel whenever someone walked by, but, come on—that show lit me up! That was another foreign culture I loved learning about: New York City. It was my Positive Delusions on-screen.

What I learned most that year, though, was what it took to be successful. Steve knew *everything* about computers. He studied magazines and newspapers. He wrote code in his cell. He knew all the players in the industry and why they failed or succeeded. He understood things I had never considered, like intellectual property rights, financing, investors and "angels" and "unicorns," and all kinds of business speak. I had laughed at him, but he was for real.

If I wanted to be a businessman, I needed to get real. So I studied Steve's business magazines. I read about Mark Cuban, Steve Jobs, and Donald Trump, who was popular with African Americans back then. Trump made me think about living that *Sex and the City* life. That's what I talked about with Steve: getting out and getting mine.

I graduated from vocational woodworking at the end of the year. It took me fifteen months, even though it was a two-year course. I was proud of that, because it showed my work ethic and dedication. I was a carpenter now, my first marketable skill. I had a certificate and everything. I could work construction, make furniture, run a repair shop. I could own a company doing all three.

There was a ceremony, just like for the GED. My family wasn't there, of course, but Steve's family was, since he was a teacher. I talked with his parents, who were smart and successful professionals, and I played chess with his little brother. I was happy. That's what accomplishments give you, beyond the cigarette boats: they make you proud.

I went back to the tier, and it was coffee and chicken wraps, hip-hop, high fives. That was the way we celebrated in prison, with coffee and wraps. For half an hour, it was a party . . . and then it was back to locked doors, barked orders, and four blank walls.

"That's nothing," Steve said the next day.

He had moods. He never got too happy, but he was prone to feeling down. I knew what he was thinking because I was thinking it too: What had I really achieved?

"Come on, man," I said. "Don't be like that. Carpentry is important."

"All this is nothing," Steve said again.

"I'm making progress. I'm making a case for release."

He shook his head. "You're just doing for yourself, Chris."

Steve looked away down the tier, like he hadn't dropped a bomb.

"You're always thinking about what you're going to do out there," he said, looking back at me. "Your business. Your money. But look around you, Chris. Look around. Think of all the good you could be doing for people in here."

Steve's Story

STEVE DIDN'T TELL me his story, at least not right away. He was closed off about his past, even after we became friends. I pieced this together over the years as I got to know him and his family. His life was different from mine but, as I soon realized, it had the same basic shape. I guess that's true of so many kids that end up inside.

Steve came from an accomplished family. Both his parents were professionals with demanding jobs. They were committed Christians and attended a strict church. Steve and his four brothers were schooled in the church; played only with children from the church; and lived in an apartment building that was 90 percent church members. The church dissuaded its members from contact with the outside world, including television, radio, and video games.

When he was ten, Steve's life was shattered. His parents abruptly left the church and their apartment building, in part because they discovered the church was a cult and not teaching the principles of true Christianity. Steve was thrust into a new majority-white neighborhood in one of the nicest areas of Northwest. Most of the other black kids in his school were bused from the inner city, including some of the roughest neighborhoods in DC. This was in the late 1980s, and Steve had never heard of Michael Jackson, much less N.W.A. He wasn't prepared.

He tested into the gifted program, but when that led to being picked on, he dropped out. He tried to act and dress like his classmates, but he didn't understand their style. He didn't know the neighborhoods, and in those schools, everything revolved around knowing those alliances. He was eleven years old, and he was lost.

Worse, his older brother was a bully. Michael had belittled Steve for years. He had punched him, insulted him, and burned the bottom of his feet with a curling iron. Steve hated him, but craved his respect. It's an odd feeling, but because of Derrick, I knew it well.

Michael acted out at the new school, threatening people and getting into fights. "Trying to beat his way to the top," as Steve put it. As the younger brother, Steve was pulled in. The more enemies Michael made, the more dangerous it was for Steve, and the more he needed his brother's protection. By the time he was a freshman in high school, Steve was part of Michael's crew.

Then one of Michael's friends got in an argument with his girlfriend over a necklace. That's how things can start in the hood. You hear tragic stories, and the trigger is so unimportant it's laughable— a necklace?—until you remember lives were destroyed.

The problem was straightforward: The friend had given his girl the necklace. When they broke up, he wanted it back. She said no. He got heated, said some things. She wouldn't give in.

The next night, she called him and said come get it. He thought they might get back together. Instead, when the door opened, the girl's new boyfriend sucker punched him in the face. He was a teenager in high school; the new boyfriend was twenty-seven. The man hit him so hard, he knocked out the kid's front teeth.

Steve got the call from Michael. He threw on his shoes and headed out. He didn't know anything except their boy was in trouble, and in the hood, you answer the call. Steve didn't even throw a punch. He came around the corner and somebody blind-sided him with a crowbar, knocking him out cold. When he woke up, five or six grown men were standing over him, beer bottles in hand.

They were laughing. That's one of the last images Steve remembered: grown men standing over him laughing. Then one smashed a beer bottle into Steve's head, knocking him cold again.

He woke up one more time. The men were pounding him with metal bars, kicking him, hitting him with bottles. He put up his hands to defend himself. They broke his arm. He passed out for the last time. The men might have killed him if a passerby hadn't convinced them to stop. By then, Steve was battered and almost naked. They had dragged his body half a block, leaving a trail of torn and bloody clothes behind. He was fourteen.

He was airlifted to a suburban hospital where the doctors stabilized him. The next morning, they sent him home. They never told his parents he might have permanent damage. This was before anybody understood PTSD or traumatic brain injury. The doctors said he didn't have a fractured skull or swelling on the brain. His life wasn't in immediate danger, so there was nothing else they could do. Unspoken, but surely a factor: Steve was a black kid beaten on the wrong block. They could have done more, but it wasn't required, so they turned him loose.

Steve wasn't right. He couldn't remember what happened, but he could feel the pain in his bones, muscles, and head. Paranoia sank in so fast and so deep, he couldn't find a way around it. He couldn't sleep. If he nodded off, he awoke in a panic, unable to recognize his room. The beating was his first fight. Now he felt on the edge of violence every day.

He walked the streets in erratic patterns in case someone was following him. He skipped school because it felt unsafe. He'd get on the Metro, get off at the next station, walk to the other platform, get on, and ride back to the original station. He started carrying a gun. Next thing he knew, he was carrying a duffel bag full of guns.

"I felt like I was attached to a bungee cord, and I was being ripped through life in the wrong direction, not a good direction at all, but it was out of my control," he told me years later. "There was nothing I could do about it."

He was maced. He was chased. He was shot at point-blank, and barely avoided a drive-by not intended for him. His grades plummeted. His parents enrolled him in a magnet school. They sent him to counseling. His father signed him up for boxing lessons.

Everyone knew he was heading the wrong way, but nobody considered that he might have trauma from the beating. Nobody asked, "What's the matter with Steve?"

If they did, Steve wouldn't—or couldn't—answer.

Eventually, he found himself in a situation. "He was six years older than me. A knucklehead from the neighborhood. All I ever knew him to do was robbery and killing. I knew it then, and I know it now. I don't have a doubt. It was him or me."

The state tried him for murder as an adult, even though he was barely sixteen. He had fallen into dealing drugs in his last weeks outside, and the prosecutor claimed the killing was a drug deal gone bad. It wasn't, but it fit the stereotype. The jury on the first trial didn't reach a verdict. At the second, Steve was found guilty and sentenced to life plus twenty years. I hate those sentences. Like they think they can imprison your soul even after you're gone.

Steve couldn't take the weight. His lawyer said he'd get out, that he'd be paroled, because everybody—even the prosecutor and the judge who gave it to him—thought the sentence was too harsh. Eleven years. That was the promise. You'll only serve eleven. It was no comfort. Depressed and paranoid, only sixteen, Steve wanted to die. But he had a strong religious belief. It was against his morals to commit suicide. He'd find the worst person in the yard, he decided, and goad the man into murdering him.

The state sent him to isolation, then to the DOC for standard medical testing before transfer. In the infirmary, he wound up sitting next to Shaft, a kid he knew from boxing lessons. Shaft said, "Where you going, Steve?"

"Grayskull." The Maryland House of Correction was legendarily rough.

"My dad's in there," Shaft said.

The next day, Shaft tracked Steve down. He had a sealed letter. "Can you give this to my dad?" he said. "His name is Hal-el."

Steve thought, *Yeah, I can do that. One last good deed. Then I'll find a way to die.*

His unit at Grayskull was a five-story wall of cages. Steve stood at the bottom with his hands shackled, looked up, looked right, looked left—that's all he could see: black men in cages. And everyone seemed to be yelling. Everybody wanted to get their hooks in the new kid. Steve sat in his first-floor cage, locked in, depressed, and ready to die. After a while, he realized one inmate wasn't yelling. He was quietly sweeping the hallway in front of the cages, ignoring the chaos around him.

Steve watched the man work his way toward him. He had a white skullcap with tassels, so Steve thought he might be Muslim, and a Muslim might know someone named Hal-el. When the man reached his cell, Steve said, "Hey, you know Hal-el?"

The man stopped and leaned on his broom. "Who's asking?"

"I have a letter for him."

The man stared at him calmly. "Who are you?"

"I have a letter from his son."

"Who is his son?"

"I don't know. Shaft."

The man didn't move from his broom. "I'm Hal-el," he said.

Steve was like, *No way.*

The sweeper called up to a man on the third tier, who was also sweeping. "Butter," he said, "what's my name?"

Butter laughed.

"What's my name, Butter?"

"Come on, Hal-el, everybody knows you."

Steve handed him the letter. Hal-el took it back to his cell, the only one left unlocked by the guards. When he came back a few minutes later, he was wet around the eyes.

"Anybody my son talks about like that is family to me. You have no idea what that means right now, but you'll learn."

Steve was like, *Sure. Whatever. I won't be here long, but I guess that's all right.*

When Steve went to breakfast the next morning, Hal-el's crew had the table in the back, and they had saved him a chair. They didn't go through the line. An inmate brought them eggs, sausages, and pancakes. The cafeteria wasn't even serving those things that morning.

Hal-el said, "Your cellmate has double-life for murder. The parents of the victim put a twenty-thousand-dollar hit on him. So you'll be moving to a new cell before lunch."

Steve moved into a cell near Hal-el and his crew. They were from all over the country, every race, all walks of life, and they ran the tier.

Steve had no idea how Hal-el got to that position. It was probably for the wrong reasons, but the Hal-el Steve knew was kind. He was calm. His attitude soothed Steve's mind. He thought, *If God set this up for me, He must have a plan. It must not be my time.*

After a year, he was separated from his friends and transferred across the street to the Annex, another maximum-security unit. The Annex was bad. Gangs went cell to cell, cleaning house. Guns were smuggled inside. Three guards were stabbed in coordinated attacks. Steve was watching television in the dayroom when Governor Glendening stood on a hill outside the prison and said, "Life means life." Suddenly, Steve's future had gone from "Even the judge wants you paroled" to a guaranteed death inside. It was like that all over the prison. A lot of inmates in the Annex were serving life.

"It was quiet," Steve said. "Nobody said a thing. They were quiet as church."

Prison is never quiet like that. Never.

About a year later, Steve was in the first group transferred to the new Patuxent youth rehabilitation program. He was nineteen, and he'd already been inside for three years. His parents had given him the computer-coding books by then. They had given him nice clothes, a Walkman, and commissary. He believed he was getting out. The state wanted to keep him inside under the "Life means life" policy. They wanted to throw away the key.

But Steve wasn't worried. God hadn't abandoned him. God would open a door.

Mentor

THINK OF ALL *the good you could be doing for people in here.* Those words really stuck with me.

Steve wanted me to be a tutor. In his five years at Patuxent, he had tutored almost two hundred inmates, and most had passed their GED. He had founded a tutoring center, where he oversaw several other student teachers. That, he said, could be my prison job, instead of wasting my time running messages on tier. But tutoring was Steve's purpose, not mine.

He was right, though. If I wanted to get out of prison and be a successful person, I had to stop thinking only of myself.

I had been a slow starter in therapy. I told myself it was stupid, but really, I had too much pain. I knew if I was honest about my mother, my cousin Eric, my son, the dam would break and I would fall apart. I didn't want to cry in group, in front of all those bammas. Word would get around, and Patuxent would eat me alive.

I had a private session with Mr. Mee every other Friday, and I didn't want to open up there, either. But I had to do it. It was on my

Master Plan—*Attend weekly therapy and resolve my issues. Identify my faults that led me to prison.*

That's the power of the Plan. I had to complete every step, even the ones I hated.

We only talked about my crime once a year, at my review, because it was required. Otherwise, we stuck to my life. I had realized something important by then: Nobody was going to look down on me for my childhood, because almost everybody in prison had gone through a similar experience. We were all abused, neglected, or forgotten. We had all lost friends. Most of us witnessed at least one violent death at a young age. That helped put us here.

But it wasn't an excuse. That's the biggest thing I had to accept: Yes, I was traumatized, and I had PTSD, and I was lost and depressed and young as hell—but I'd still made those decisions. All my wounds and all that anger: They were part of me. And if I was going to be a better man, I had to take responsibility for what that part of me had done.

I can't even recall the moment I realized that. I think, like a lot of things, it happened so slowly I never saw it coming. I only remember Mr. Mee taking me aside and asking me to become a mentor. He wanted me to talk to bammas about taking responsibility and making a Master Plan. For a year, I turned him down. "I'm young, Mr. Mee," I said. "I'm barely twenty. I don't know anything. How could I help somebody?"

Tooky was a mentor. He never talked about his life, that's one thing I had noticed. Tooky was very quiet on what he had done. But people felt comfortable talking with him about their own lives, and he always had good advice. I talked with Tooky almost every day. I watched what he did, and how he treated people with respect, from the lowest skin-beef to the worst guards. If I had problems, he laid out solutions. *Talk to this CO. Take this class. This dude in the yard, he's tough, but he's fair. He's got what you need.*

To me, a mentor should be like Tooky: a cool old head who knew the ins and outs of prison. Someone calm who knew how to open your mind and change your perspective. A man with connections who could get you into wood shop or whatever else you wanted. I was young. I was messed up. How could I possibly be like that to someone else when I was still learning to take care of myself?

So I took a job in the yard instead. I wasn't sure how it would help anyone, but the yard was my happy place. Yard was where everyone mixed: old heads, young dudes, inmates from different places with different stories. I liked watching the gladiator types crushing weights with their beats blasting. I *loved* watching the female COs in their tight uniforms.

I brought my books, but I listened to the old heads telling stories. Gun battles in Baltimore over dope, big gold chains, and trips to New York. These guys could *take you there*. It was like reading books, except these were stories about my world. And the moral was always the same: "Yeah, I thought I was slick, son, until I got caught."

My job was grunt work—setting up equipment, digging ditches, cleaning—but it was worth it for the stories. I worked so hard, the CO in charge called me Heavy Duty.

"If I had two more like Heavy Duty," he barked, "I wouldn't need the rest of you."

I had been studying communication, especially Leil Lowndes's book *How to Talk to Anyone*. Guys laughed when they saw the title. "What? You don't know how to talk?"

"What?" I said. "You think you know everything there is to know about communicating? Is that how you ended up in here?"

They waved me off. "Whatever, slick."

Lowndes's book gave me confidence. Most guys just said whatever was on their minds; I was studying how to engage people with a strong opener, how to read body language, how to talk with a purpose.

I used that knowledge in the yard. I was from one of the worst neighborhoods in DC and I carried that with pride. I read books, sure, but I still walked and talked like a kid from Lincoln Heights. Bammas could see I understood them, but they could see I was different, too. I had confidence. When I talked, it wasn't loudmouth opinions. I was informed. If I didn't have the information, I said so. Then I researched and got back to them. I didn't say it out loud, but Leil Lowndes taught me to say it with body language: *You like what I have? You can have it, too.*

Once they were comfortable, I hit them with my money question. "What's your passion?"

What do you care about, slim? If you could choose to do anything with your time, what would it be?

"My passion is starting businesses," I told them. "That's why I'm studying these books. What's yours?"

Pretty soon, we were talking about cars, music, building houses, or just having a fine girl and being a good father. Then I'd maneuver them, slowly, to what I really wanted them to think about: *What can you do in here to make that passion a reality?*

I got young guys to enroll in GED school. I got guys into carpentry and other trade programs. I got guys to start working out, stop smoking dope, write letters to their moms. It was mentoring, but unofficial, outside Mr. Mee's program. It was finding my own way to what I needed to do.

Then Greg went down. It was a sting operation. The authorities must have been working on it for quite some time. They swept in and got everybody: Greg, Burchfield, all his dealers and distributors and customers. Greg was sent to immigration prison. Eventually, he was deported to Haiti. I still talk to him. He calls to ask if I have any old shoes or cell phones. There are a lot of things we throw away here in America that are worth money in Haiti. That's Greg's hustle now.

Greg's fall made me think of those words I had heard in the yard: *I thought I was slick, son, until I got caught.* That's what they all say when they're operating on the wrong side of the law.

That's what happens to everybody, I realized, when they've only thought halfway. When they say, *This is how I'll make some money, this is how I'll impress that girl, this is how I'll get my car.*

You got fifty hats? You got a gold chain? So what? That's not a plan. A plan always starts at the end. What's your endgame? That's not just a question. It's the only question that matters. Because if you're heading in the wrong direction, it doesn't matter how many steps you take. You're already lost.

So let me ask you again, like I asked so many young men in the yard: What's your passion? What do you really want to do with your life? What do you want people to say about you when you're gone?

Now tell me: What's your Master Plan to get there?

IAC

I JOINED the Inmate Advisory Council, the group of inmates chosen to address problems and advocate for prisoners' rights. IACs exist at most prisons. Some have the support of the administration and get things done. Many are a waste of time. At Patuxent, the IAC was dominated by the older inmates. There were fifteen of them, compared to two representatives for the youth program—Steve and me. It was clear, right away, nobody liked us. The prison had been running fine, in the opinion of the COs and the older inmates, until the youth program came along.

"The kitchen is a mess," an old head complained at my first IAC meeting. "These youth guys are lazy."

"Hold on," Steve said. "You're dealing with young individuals, some fifteen or sixteen, who have never held a job, and you're asking them to do something critical, like serve a thousand people three meals a day. Did you think about a training program?"

There was grumbling, but eventually they agreed. Training was the solution.

I looked at Steve. *Impressive.*

It was the same dynamic for everything: discipline, programs, the yard. The youth were blamed for all the problems. Steve stood up for us. He kept pointing out the same thing: Yes, we were young. We were loud and abusive. *So we needed help.*

"I meet with the majors twice a month," Steve told me after the meeting. A major ran each guard shift. "We talk about problems and find solutions. I have, like, an eighty percent success rate. They're starting to see our side of things."

I was shocked. "Why you keeping this a secret?"

"I'm not," he replied. "I'm just working."

Steve wanted to meet with each tier in the youth program (there were eight, on four levels) to discuss concerns, then bring those issues to the IAC. Unfortunately, a lot of inmates didn't trust him. Some even called him Uncle Tom. There are always people like that: sitting on the sidelines, not participating in the struggle, criticizing those trying to make a difference. Sadly, in our communities, both inside and outside, those people too often hold sway. I tried to debate them in the yard, to show them the error of their ways, but it was no use. People like that don't want to change; they want to complain.

Most people aren't like that, though. They go along, laugh with the loudmouths, but they want a voice. They want life to be better. So I started going around the youth tiers, using the kids I mentored in the yard to get with the bammas. It was all communication, just rapping and watching and figuring out what could be done.

"Yo, why they have a pool table up there? We need a pool table down here."

"That's tier three," I explained. "The pool table is an incentive for you to accomplish things and progress in the program."

"Nah, but I want a pool table, slim."

"But that's a reward . . ."

Shaking his head, like, *Nah, what you good for, then?* There were guys in Patuxent who couldn't grasp the system.

"Look, okay, I can't get you a pool table, but I noticed the hot plate in your dayroom doesn't work. What if I get you a new hot pot so you can heat up your ramen and soup?"

"Yeah, yeah, all right, that sounds good."

Steve and I started holding regular meetings on the tiers, listening to requests and complaints. Afterward, Steve typed up notes and distributed them for feedback. That's how we focused, for instance, on staggering the mealtimes. Patuxent was bringing all two hundred youth to eat at once, so chow was loud, violent, and hot. In the summer, it was more than a hundred degrees. We convinced the administration to split our meals into four shifts. We even convinced them, after the shifts created a major drop in violence, to bring in fans during the hottest months.

Steve was opening my eyes. There was a system. Instead of fighting it, he was working it. That's not being an Uncle Tom, because he was doing it for our benefit. That's being smart.

"I'm writing a proposal," Steve said. "I think the youth should have their own board. Why should inmates not in the program have a say in what we do?"

Writing a proposal was new for me, but I was learning through my Master Plan the power of writing. It can focus the mind and make an argument. A proposal says: Here's what we want; here's how we want it; here's the evidence it will work.

The old heads didn't like Steve's idea. They were used to speaking for the inmate population, and that's a hard thing to take away from guys on thirty-, forty-year rides. For many, the IAC was all they had. Plus, they kind of hated the young generation. There were too many of us, with too much attitude. They called it a coup.

So we talked to Tooky, who—of course—was president of the IAC. Tooky was skeptical of the plan, but he was a calm, methodical dude. He didn't care about territory or power; he wanted to get things done.

"It's not a coup," Steve said. "I want to work together. You got a problem with fights in the yard? You got a problem with noise? Let me know. I'll talk to my guys. We'll get these bammas under control. But you have to let us run our things our way."

Tooky, Steve, and I reached a compromise. The two boards would act separately, but coordinate priorities before talking to the administration. That way, we would come organized, with an agenda. Tooky went to his people and got them in line, and then he went to the administration. With their blessing, we formed the Youth Planning Committee, with Steve as president and me as vice president.

I took matters into my own hands, too. For instance, there was a fight on first tier, someone got thrown, and the ping-pong table broke. There wasn't money in the youth fund to buy a new one, but I didn't let that stop me. I was reading a book, in Italian, on Leonardo da Vinci. I was inspired by the way Leonardo invented to solve problems; he designed tanks, machine guns, helicopters, everything. His mind was always looking for a better way.

So I designed a stronger ping-pong table, one that could withstand the abuse of prison. I calculated supplies, priced them, and ordered them through the carpentry shop account. It wasn't just about function. When the material came in, my guys and gals in the carpentry shop spent weeks cutting, sanding, and oiling to bring out the beauty in the wood. It was more than we needed to do. It was more than the bammas on tier one would ever notice. But I was also reading W. E. B. DuBois, one of the greatest African American thinkers of the early 1900s, and his thoughts on craft. DuBois talked about the "aristocracy" of labor, and the importance of doing simple jobs right. We would raise ourselves with our labor, he said, African American and white alike, when we found the beauty in everyday work.

Prison was a hassle. It was stabbings, beefing, bad food, and looking away, every day, when COs and inmates broke the rules. But in shop, in the late afternoon, life was calm. It was just the smell of the wood, the sound of the sandpaper, and the perfect smoothness of a ping-pong table the inmates would be able to use for the next twenty years.

"Yo," someone said when we brought the table to the tier. "They got a pool table on three."

"Hey, yo, chill," someone yelled back. "Chris made that for you."

"That's good. That's nice. I'm just saying, you know, why can't *we* have a pool table, that's all."

Leonardo worked for a prince, and that's how it went for him, too: his customer was never satisfied. But W. E. B. DuBois was right; it's the craftsmanship that counts. Building something beautiful, and building it right, gives you a sense of purpose and accomplishment nobody can take away, no matter how hard they try.

Progress

STEVE'S LARGEST TRIUMPH came soon after: the creation of a college degree program at Patuxent. This was around the turn of the century, so there weren't online colleges. And besides, Patuxent didn't have computers for inmates. All we had was the GED program. Once you got your high school diploma, you were done with education for the rest of your life. That didn't make sense. Steve wanted a college degree, and he believed the chance would inspire other inmates to further their education, too.

It took years of planning and coordinating. Steve wrote hundreds of letters and a dozen proposals. He had that kind of patience. He believed, with consistent effort, that he'd get there. And he was right. Thanks to Steve, Patuxent launched a pilot college program in 2001 with a local school, Anne Arundel Community College. There were twenty slots. About 150 inmates applied, all high school graduates, most tutored by Steve. I was desperate for one of those slots. I wanted to prove to my judge I could excel at difficult work, because every inmate asking for a second chance had a GED, but how many had a college degree?

But I also wanted to learn.

I knew it would be tough. There were a lot of smart inmates at Patuxent. So I outworked them, studying for questions that might be on the entrance exam, figuring out what to say in an interview to convince a professor to take a chance on me. That's called doing your homework. It's the simplest but most effective thing you can do. Never go to an interview unprepared.

They took me. There were twenty slots, and I was the very last person to make it—lucky number twenty! Technically, I wasn't qualified. I had to take remedial math. Realistically, I wasn't ready. I was kicked out of school after the eighth grade. Now, after only two months of formal study for my GED, I was in college. And I was going to succeed. I was going to make sure of that.

It was shortly after the college was announced but before classes began that Steve got his sentence reduced. He was quiet about the process, but I knew his lawyers had been working on it for years. He had to sue the state of Maryland in federal court because they wouldn't grant him a hearing, but he won. Steve got his chance.

He was lucky, because his original judge presided at his modification hearing. The judge had intended for him to serve only eleven years with good behavior. He had told Steve that at sentencing. His lawyer marked it down. Then "Life means life" happened, and Steve got trapped. He had already served six years, and his behavior couldn't have been better. Mr. Mee, our therapist, testified on his behalf. The judge reduced Steve's sentence . . . to forty-five years.

I can't find statistics on sentence modifications for life prisoners, because the state of Maryland doesn't publish them. I've spoken with several organizations that study the matter, and they can't find the numbers, either. Nobody knows for sure what happens inside the system. But I know modifications for life prisoners *based on their behavior in prison* are rare. During the first ten years I was incarcerated, I suspect Steve Edwards was the only one.

Forty years plus five. That's what Steve got. He was supposed to serve eleven years, but he ended up with forty plus five.

He committed his crime at fifteen. He'd be out at sixty. That's tough. What can a man do for the world when he's starting from scratch at sixty?

But he'd be out. Steve wouldn't die inside.

He showed me the way. Or rather, he showed me there *was* a way. I sat down and wrote to my judge, my lawyer, and my grandma. I told them I was on the youth advisory board, I was starting college, I had built a ping-pong table, I mentored youth. I'm a good person, I said. I have a Master Plan. Just give me a chance.

I never heard back.

Family

It was cold, so it was probably February 2001, when Steve received the care package. We could receive packages during only two months each year, but they always came for Steve. If he needed something, within reason, his parents provided. They sent shirts, pants, shoes, even ties. Looking good was part of Steve's Positive Delusion. It kept him believing in his path.

"Here," he said when the cell doors popped. "Take these."

It was two pairs of socks. Steve was my best friend, but he never shared his belongings with me. He loaned me magazines and newspapers, but he still wouldn't give me a bite of food when I was hungry.

"No, man," I said, "I can't take your stuff."

"Please," he said. "You need these."

It was embarrassing, but he was right. I owned only two pairs of socks. They were the same two pairs my sister had given me back in 1997. They were so torn up, they weren't even socks anymore. They were more like holes outlined with string.

Just because I needed, though, didn't mean I should take.

"I can't," I said. "Your parents sent those to you." *That makes them special.*

A few days later, I received a care package. It was from Steve's parents. Inside were socks, T-shirts, and an electric toothbrush.

"I told my parents about you," Steve said. "They want to meet you. Put them on your visitors' list."

Only people on your list could visit. There was a limit, and you could change your list only every six months, but that wasn't a concern for me. There was nobody on my list. When I came in, I put my whole family on, my girlfriend, my cousins, and friends. When I decided I wasn't going to beg my family to talk to me anymore, I took everyone off.

It was an empty gesture. If Mom showed up at Patuxent, and they turned her away because of my list, I would have dug a tunnel to see her. I would have ripped straight through the concrete with my bare hands. But it made me feel better to know I wasn't expecting them. It made them not visiting feel more like a mutual decision.

"Okay," I said, "I'll put them on."

Maybe they'd come, maybe not; the care package was more than enough. You would not believe how nice it was to wear new socks after not having any for so long.

The very next weekend, I got the call.

"Inmate 265–975. Wilson. Visitor."

I jumped out of my skin from shock. I hadn't been to the visitors' room since Mom told me to send her a list, she was working on my appeal, then disappeared from my life. When they buzzed me through the door, it was like coming into the light after six months in a hole. I was shielding my eyes and turning away, it was so bright.

Then I saw Steve, sitting with a well-dressed, middle-aged couple.

"This is Chris Wilson, the friend I've been telling you about," he said. "Chris, this is my mom and dad."

I sat down. "Um . . . Thank you for the socks."

I didn't know what to expect. I figured, at the least, I'd have to explain my crime. That's what I had to do with Mr. Mee. That's what I had to with my family, back when they were still in my life. To my family, I was bad. It was "Why'd you do that? What's your problem? Where did I go wrong?"

It wasn't like that with Mr. and Mrs. Edwards. It was like, "So, I hear you like books."

Now I see why. They had a son serving life for murder. They knew he was a good person who had made a terrible mistake, and they believed in him. So they weren't going to judge a person based only on his crime.

And that feeling of not being judged, of being spoken to like a person after so long as a number? Powerful. Very powerful.

Steve had clearly told them good things about me: how hard I worked, how I was changing the way I spoke and carried myself, how I gave to other inmates. Looking back, I suspect he had never spoken that way about anyone else. I had never put myself in Steve's place before, but he must have been lonely. I think, after five years, I was his first real friend inside.

Mr. and Mrs. Edwards asked about my studies. I told them about my Master Plan. They asked about my past, but only in a "We hear you're from DC" way, not like, "So you killed somebody, huh?" It was like someone on the outside actually wanted to know me.

They asked if I needed anything.

I told them no. I needed a lot of things, but I didn't want to push. At the end, Mrs. Edwards gave me a pat on the shoulder, and Mr. Edwards shook my hand.

"They liked you," Steve told me.

I got the call again the next week. "Inmate Wilson. Visitor."

Honestly, the second visit touched me more than the first. Mr. and Mrs. Edwards had met me. They'd put a face to my name. They still wanted to spend time with me?

They visited the week after that, too, and the next week. Usually it was Steve and me, but then one week it wasn't. It was just me. They wanted to give me a chance to talk privately, if there was anything I needed to get off my chest. You have to understand: they were given an hour a week to spend with their son, and they were giving part of that time, with Steve's blessing, to me.

They said, "Chris, we know you don't have any family coming to see you, but if you're interested, we'd like to have a relationship with you."

Me (right), *Stephen* (second from left), and Mr. and Mrs. Edwards (Arthur Miles)

Are you serious?

It was overwhelming. It was *shattering*. It was the first evidence, really, that molding myself could really change the way I was.

So I stood up, leaned over the table, and gave Mrs. Edwards a hug. I remember because I hadn't hugged anyone in years and, you know, you weren't supposed to have that kind of physical contact, even in the visitors' room. But I didn't care. That was somebody I loved over there. And she and Mr. Edwards loved me back.

"Thank you," I said. "I want that. I want it very much."

Master Plan

Chris Wilson

2001

Stop calling home every day (done)

Forget about my fake-ass friends (done)

Get my high school diploma (done)

Work out six days a week (gain thirty pounds of muscle) (done)

Attend weekly therapy and resolve my issues

Identify my faults that led me to prison (done)

Always seek advice (done)

Remain a lifelong learner

Never go against the grain

No gambling (done)

No horseplay in public (done)

No sex jokes (done)

Always dress neat (done)

Mind my own business

Learn how to speak real English

No junk food (done)

Graduate from carpentry vocational shop (done)

Get a tailored suit
Learn to tie a tie
~~Pay my brother back~~
Earn my AA degree
Start my own business **that makes people's lives better . . .**
Meet a smart, beautiful woman that's business savvy

Showstack

I HAD ANOTHER visitor that year: Erick Wright. You probably don't remember him. He had a minor role in my life, and I hadn't seen him since I was sixteen. That's the point: of all the people from back in the day to step forward, it still amazes me it was Erick Wright.

He was my sister's boyfriend back in 1995, the chill dude who encouraged me to go to night school and almost shot his foot off with a shotgun during that last year when our lives were falling apart. After he and my sister broke up, Erick finished night school for audio engineering. He got a good job, then made a mistake. A few days before he started, he got popped for a low-level crime. He spent a year in jail. He kept in touch with his boss, though, and they took him back. He'd been straight ever since, working as a sound technician for a local television station. Erick was making it.

Erick wasn't from my neighborhood. As it turned out, he was from Steve Edwards's neighborhood, and they had been friends for years. That's how Steve knew my sister. When Erick heard from Steve's brother I was in prison for life, he told me later, he knew my family wouldn't support me. I guess my path was obvious to an outsider, even if I never saw it. So Erick came to visit.

"You're different, Chris," he said within the first five minutes.

"Yeah, I am. I been working on myself. I'm not angry anymore."

"I hear that."

"I got a plan. I got things I want to do."

He nodded. "I can see it." Other people who knew me back in the day have said that, too: my face is different. The change on the inside is so great it shows up there.

A few weeks later, I got another call: "Inmate Wilson! Legal visit!"

Three visitors in one year? Suddenly, I was a popular dude.

I hadn't spoken to my lawyer in a long time. He had kept in touch after the trial, but then a serious health issue—I think it was cancer—forced him to take a leave of absence. I still sent my letters. I called his office every few months to check in. His paralegal was nice. She always told me, *Don't lose hope, Mr. Wilson, keep working. Mr. Trainor hasn't forgotten you.* I loved the sound of her voice. For about two years, her voice on the phone was my only connection to the outside world.

If Mr. Trainor was here now, though, he must have good news. Right?

But when I walked into the privacy booth for legal visits, it wasn't Harry Trainor at the table. It was a different white guy. And he was young. Pale, like he didn't get much sun. Sweaty. But confident. I could tell that right away. He had the swagger and charisma of Robert Downey Jr., but with more gel in his slicked-back hair.

"Mr. Wilson?" he said, extending his hand.

"Yeah, that's me."

"I'm Keith Showstack."

He had an accent so thick I could barely understand him. He told me it was South Boston. Working-class.

"I read your letters," he said, but it was like, *Ahredya-lettuce*.

What?

"They were *inya* file."

It took a bit, but I finally figured the situation out. This Showstack character was a newly hired associate at Harry Trainor's law firm, and he had somehow gotten hold of my case file. He'd read the updates I'd been sending on my Master Plan. Being an ambitious young lawyer, he saw an opportunity nobody else gave a damn about. So he came to Patuxent to eyeball me.

He saw exactly what he wanted to see: a confident young man with good manners in a nice button-down shirt and pressed slacks. I had my head shaved and my goatee tight. I was ripped, too. The Edwardses had set up a commissary fund for me, and I spent it on protein powders. I told them books I wanted, and they bought them for me, up to $30 a month. We had a maximum wardrobe in prison—eight shirts, four pants. Steve gave me old clothes he could no longer keep, so at this point I even dressed like I was Mr. and Mrs. Edwards's son.

I told Mr. Showstack about my GED, my carpentry certificate, and my B-plus average in college. I mentioned my readings in history, communication, and business. I told him about the IAC, the youth council, being a mentor, and helping young guys navigate prison the right way.

What's your endgame, Chris?

"I want my life to mean something," I said. "I don't want people to see a murderer. I want them to see someone who did good with his time. I'm a hard worker. I'm a lifelong learner. I'm going to keep reading, studying, and improving my mind until the day I die. I just want that day to be a long time from now, on the outside. Maybe Paris, right?"

He laughed. "Why not?"

One thing I didn't study in prison was the law. I wasn't one of those prison-lawyer types who figured out how to get a new trial. I took a different approach. I figured if I actually became a good person, and proved it every day, they had to let me out. That was my greatest Positive Delusion: thinking the universe was fair.

Showstack explained my legal situation.

I would not get paroled. No lifer had been paroled in Maryland since Governor Glendening's declaration in 1995. Even after a new governor was elected in 2002, nothing had changed.

I would not get a new trial. I was guilty, and the state had proved it. There were no issues with my conviction.

I had one chance: a reduction of sentence hearing. This wasn't amnesty or a reconsideration of evidence. It was reconsideration for *a guilty person* based on subsequent behavior in prison. Mr. Trainor had applied for the right at my sentencing, as required, and the judge had granted the application because I was so young. The teenage brain is not fully formed and, scientifically speaking, no person is the same at seventeen as they are as an adult. That's why the Supreme Court recently made life without parole illegal for children like me who had committed their crime under the age of eighteen.

There was a catch: I had the *possibility* of a hearing, but the judge still had to grant the motion. As I knew from my life surrounded by prison-lawyer types, judges rarely granted motions. After all, Steve had to sue the state of Maryland in federal court to get his hearing.

And when they did get a hearing, few people succeeded. That's one thing my lawyer stressed: this was a long shot. What happened to Steve was like someone rising from the projects to the NBA. It happened, but it was rare. For a lifer? It was next to impossible.

In Maryland, sentence modifications were mostly used to correct errors. In 2012, for instance, Maryland jury instructions from before 1981, which said presumption of innocence and reasonable doubt were advisory only, were ruled unconstitutional. There were 250 people in prison still affected by the ruling—90 percent African American, and all but one a man—and the state used sentence modification hearings to slowly release them on supervised probation. When NPR checked on them in 2016, not a single one had reoffended. They had been in prison for at least thirty-one years, after all; most were in their sixties or older. If it hadn't been for the court ruling, though, none would have been released, even though they were no longer a danger to society. They would have served out their full sentences on the state's dime.

"We can't rush it, Chris," Keith told me. "Your record is impressive. It's incredible, actually. But the political climate isn't right."

It wasn't just about me, my lawyer explained. It was also about the mood in society. If a judge let a life prisoner out and that person committed a crime, the judge would be blamed. If the crime was famous or gruesome enough, it could destroy her career.

On the other hand, nobody celebrated the judge if the person went on to a remarkable life. Almost nobody would know. So my best chance was catching the right judge, at the right moment, when the heat was low.

"Judge Wood wrote a letter recommending Patuxent," I said. "He mentioned my age and background. He said he would give me another chance."

Keith leaned toward me. We were both wearing button-downs, but Keith had rolled up his sleeves. There were sweat stains on his collar.

"I'm with you, Chris," he said, looking me in the eye. "I'll do it pro bono. It won't cost you anything. The firm has agreed. You just have to trust me."

It wasn't a matter of trust. I wasn't Steve Edwards, with his large legal team. I had no money, no family, no contacts on the outside. I was a penniless young man on a life sentence. I had to go with Keith Showstack. If he had been a raving lunatic in a fuzzy bear costume, I would have gone with him. He was all I had.

"What do I have to do?"

"Exactly what you've been doing."

I smiled. "I can do better than that."

Business

STARTING A BUSINESS isn't about a sudden great idea. It's about seeing opportunities. When you're an entrepreneur, you are always looking for openings. *What's missing? What could make this better?* It's a skill you develop. I've started multiple businesses now, and every one has grown out of work I was already doing, because you have to know the market to understand the opportunity. It's a little like Leonardo with an idea: you sketch it in your free time; you test it; you see what's working, then take another step. You might eventually become a master of your craft, but it's the mind-set that triggers the change.

My first business grew out of my work on the youth board with Steve. I loved the graduation ceremonies, where families came and celebrated with a picnic on the grounds. My family never came, of course, but I knew a picnic with loved ones was the perfect reward because I could see it on the faces of the other inmates. Maybe I valued it so much because, outside of freedom, it was what I wanted most.

So I proposed a yearly family picnic. Every inmate who received no infractions for a whole year could come, with five guests from the outside. The number of qualified inmates turned out to be small—COs at Patuxent were toughs, they wrote tickets for nothing—but the picnic was crowded because everybody but me had five guests. We had grills firing, barbecue cooking, plates of home-cooked food brought in by moms and grandmas. The Edwardses came with Steve's brother David; Erick Wright was there; we had a great time laughing and eating. It felt like one of the large family reunions I had seen back in the park in Temple Hills.

Not long after, in Steve's new issue of *Popular Science*, I saw an article about digital cameras. This was before smartphones; I had never owned a cell; and I had barely used a computer. I couldn't believe it when I read that cameras could preserve photos electronically. You could take hundreds of pictures, look at them on the camera, then print only the ones you wanted.

"We could do that," I said to Steve. "We could have photographed all those families at the picnic."

We could have sold the photos and not only made money, but preserved those memories. I had been reading about social entrepreneurship: starting businesses that made money by doing good. And here it was. An opportunity to be a social entrepreneur in prison.

I couldn't afford a digital camera, of course. Even if I could, taking photos in prison wasn't allowed. I had to go through the system.

So, with Steve's help, I wrote a business proposal. For an entrepreneur, writing a business proposal may be the most important skill you ever learn, because a proposal gets you the money to start your business. It's called seed capital.

I had one source for my seed capital: the prison administration. I needed them to provide supplies, especially the camera. So, the first question: Why would they want to do that for me?

Answer: Because it was good for prison morale for inmates to feel connected to their families. When people were reminded of the children and loved ones waiting for them, they worked harder to improve their prospects and avoid infractions. It was when they felt they had nothing that guys stabbed, robbed, and started trouble.

What about the money? How would the prison get back its investment?

The youth program had a pool of money for things like library books (a basic need), replacing broken dayroom televisions (a common problem), and backed-up toilets (a constant issue, which was why Tooky, who was the prison plumber, was around so much). When Steve and I founded the youth council, the fund was $800. That was nothing. We spent almost all of it on new hot pots and other small items requested by the tiers.

I proposed that the profit from the photo business would go into the youth fund. This would stabilize our finances and generate funds that could be used for, say, new ping-pong tables or computer learning tools, since the Anne Arundel college program had forced the prison, finally, to provide a few computers for inmates. Meanwhile, the prison could use its funds for its other priorities.

Made sense for the prison, right? They were making money while encouraging good behavior.

What was I getting out of it?

I asked for three things:

First, that taking photos become my prison job, and that I get paid double. Seventy dollars a month!

Second, that the youth council be allowed to decide how the money in the account was spent. We'd done the work, so that was only fair.

Third, I wanted access to the whole prison.

That was the sticking point. I had to sit down with the administration, because access was a safety issue. Inmates weren't allowed to roam the prison. We had a schedule, and everything was monitored.

I needed access, though. I needed to be on the tiers and in the yards. I had to be in the visitors' room to get family shots, and family shots were important. An inmate could put a family photo in his cell. His young daughter could put it in her bedroom. It would be the last thing they each saw every night, before the lights went out.

Everybody needs a reminder of what's important.

Like my Master Plan taped beside my bunk.

Like a picture of a child who loves you and wants you home.

The administration agreed to my terms. The prison rarely granted requests, but it didn't surprise me. It was a great idea with a smart financial structure. I'd proven myself as a mentor, a college student, and an IAC member. I'd put in the work for years. That's key: Before you ask, prove yourself. Put in the work.

"Sergeant Nick will monitor you," they said. "He'll go everywhere you go."

Sergeant Nick was tough. He'd been through the Tet Offensive in Vietnam. He didn't like bullshit—and he thought *everything* was bullshit. He was the CO who had pressed me when I first came in. "Tuck in your shirt! Where's your ID? Pull up your pants!"

Looking back, Sergeant Nick was right. In those first months, before my plan, I was slumped over, sloppy, with taped-up shoes and my shirt hanging out. I wasn't even shaving. I looked like what I was: a prisoner who had lost his will. Since then, though, I had turned my life around. Sergeant Nick knew I was crushing books, and he appreciated that I kept my clothes neat, my bunk made with military corners, and my badge high.

He was still a hard-ass.

"Why you stopping, inmate?"

"I just want to say hi, Sergeant Nick."

He whipped out his book. "You know you can't stop by the door. That's a ticket."

"Whoa, whoa. I'm just chatting with you, Sergeant Nick. I thought we were friendly."

He laughed, because he knew how much I valued my perfect disciplinary record. "I'm messing with you, Wilson. Now move along."

When it came to the photo program, though, Sergeant Nick was serious. He didn't like an inmate having access, or he hated the idea of following me around, or both. He didn't think it would last, but in the meantime, he told me, he was going to make sure I didn't step out of line.

I wasn't worried. I knew I wouldn't cause problems, and I was confident the business would work.

I was wrong, though. The business didn't "work." It exploded. I didn't even have to do marketing. I had so many inmates wanting photos, I couldn't handle the volume. The first six months, my photo business made a profit of almost $4,000. Not bad when your product sells for $1.50 and your clients make less than $40 a month.

Ethics

THAT FALL, I took college courses in ethics and modern American history, including the civil rights movement. I knew of Dr. King, of course, but I'd never considered that my mother was born when blacks weren't allowed to attend public schools in many states. I didn't know blacks were kept from voting through taxes, "citizenship" tests, and lack of polling places. I learned about redlining, when the U.S. government decided not to offer assistance to the poorest neighborhoods, deeming them beyond help—a practice that continued for decades and was still the policy in some areas when I was born in 1978.

The government hadn't put me in prison. It didn't make me acquire a gun or force me to pull the trigger. I made those decisions, and I took responsibility.

But it was true that Lincoln Heights had been redlined into poverty, on purpose, because it was black. Big Daddy and Grandma had seen the middle-class life they had worked so hard to build undermined, *on purpose*, when the government bulldozed proud working black blocks in the 1960s to build a massive housing project—along with that alley where Eric died.

Knowing that history awakened something in me. I could no longer look at the way the world was and think of it as an accident. I couldn't see success and failure on a community level as nothing more than the sum total of individual effort. Whether by bad people or by good people who didn't comprehend the consequences of their actions, black poverty was planned.

Society didn't put me in prison; I would never say it did. But society created the cave. Society put obstacles in the way of black people—slavery, lynchings, redlining, job discrimination, voter discrimination, and all manner of segregation, official and otherwise—then criticized us when we didn't rise above it. Imagine applying for an apartment and having someone put a C on your application, meaning "colored," meaning, "Sorry, whites only, go back where you came from." Imagine working for decades and investing your life savings in a house, then having your white neighbors *burn it down* because of your race. That happened to black Americans—*in my mother's lifetime*. She had to live with that.

My photo business was booming, so I hired three inmates to help me. Steve constructed frames for an additional fee. I asked Sergeant Nick for a monthly sales report. He said no. Inmates didn't get paperwork. We lived in a world without records of what was said and done. Or at least without records we ever saw.

"I need to know where and when I'm selling the most photos," I argued. "If I analyze my sales data, I can adjust my business model better and offer better service."

Sergeant Nick nodded. "That's smart, Wilson. I'll see what I can do."

In the end, I was allowed to look at my sales data. I couldn't keep copies, but I could study my numbers while Sergeant Nick watched. With that information, I planned my routes around the best times to be in certain locations. I made sure I went to every corner of the prison except the off-limits women's areas: every yard, every tier, the grounds, the chow hall, the classrooms, the visitors' room, even "behind the red door," as inmates called the building for the mentally ill.

Everyone knew me, old heads and young. "Picture man on the tier!" they shouted when they saw me coming. They crowded around to see what I'd brought, even if they knew the photos weren't for them.

And everywhere I went, I saw the same thing: black men. So many black men. Young men with years ahead of them. Old heads who had come in young, at the end of the civil rights era, and had done forty years, in their sixties now, their bodies already breaking down.

There were white guys, too. This was *Patuxent*, after all, the fanciest and least punishing maximum-security facility in the state of Maryland. Prisoners were chosen to serve here, so it was disproportionately white. Some people in the system even called it "the white prison." The hardest prisons, like ECI and Castle Grayskull, were almost entirely minority. Even so, most of the inmates I was serving with were black.

It was impossible not to see that as a choice—two, actually. Our choice to commit crimes. But society's choice, too.

It would have been easy to come out of my ethics and modern American history classes angry, especially when I was living the practical effect of hundreds of years of racist policy. And I did feel frustration, I can't lie on that. But what I took away, more than anything, was the fire of Frederick Douglass.

This great black American was born a slave in Maryland. He was taken from his mother when he was an infant. He was sent to Baltimore, where his new master's wife taught him his letters. The master caught her, and twelve-year-old Frederick overheard him scold her.

"Don't teach them to read. We won't be able to control them if they can read."

From that day on, Frederick Douglass had one goal: to learn to read. He found a way by watching the white people write messages to each other. He read everything he could. He taught other slaves to read until he was discovered and sent to a "slave breaker" to learn his place. Instead, he beat the slave breaker half to death with his own fists. He escaped to the North and became a leading abolitionist.

When slavery finally ended, at least as official law, Frederick Douglass had a new mission: he wanted to teach every black American to read. He helped found schools. He ran a newspaper. He wrote some of the most important books and essays in the history of the United States, particularly his autobiography, *Narrative of the Life of Frederick Douglass: An American Slave.*

Knowledge, he believed, *is the pathway from slavery to freedom.*

This dude was dope. He came from the lowest place imaginable, a slave shack on the eastern shore. He raised himself through education. And when he became rich and famous, he turned around and tried to lift his entire race up with him.

That was what Steve and I were trying to do at Patuxent, I realized. We were raising ourselves with education. We were trying to raise others with us. It was hard. By the summer of 2003, I had been in for seven years. I was twenty-four years old. What did I have to show for it?

I was raising myself, molding my mind and body, but was I any closer to getting out? Was any of it making a difference?

The answer came one afternoon, when DD walked up to Steve and me in the yard.

Now, DD was a big dude with a big reputation. Right before I arrived at Patuxent, there had been a monthlong war in the youth program between DC and Baltimore, and DD was at the center of it. He was loud. He carried knives. He could do what he wanted, when he wanted, and mostly he wanted to ball. He didn't so much play basketball, though, as argue. Everyone argued back, but not for long, because DD was the hardest dude in the yard. The only time I ever saw Steve in a physical fight, it was with DD on third tier. I think it had something to do with the television in the dayroom.

So when DD approached us, I didn't know what to expect. He stalked toward us, like a gladiator, then hunched in close and sort of whispered, "Yo, Steve, can you help me with the GED?"

When Steve took him on, I thought, *Good luck*. DD was in his thirties. He had ADHD. I doubt he'd ever read a book. I never suspected he wanted to. But Steve was a genius at explaining concepts, and he was patient.

"Man, I don't know," DD would say, pushing away his math problems.

Steve would answer in a calm voice, "Let's think about it this way, DD. You have two basketballs, right? You take one and cut it in half, then toss away one of those halves. How many do you have now?"

"Man, I don't know."

"Yes you do."

DD would glower. "One and a half."

"Right. Now I take the whole basketball away. How many do you have?"

"Half."

"That's right. Now, say I've got six basketballs . . ."

DD loved Steve, like you love your annoying little brother. He called him Study Buddy, a nickname Steve hated, so of course we all called him that for years. DD and Study Buddy worked together for months, and DD passed his GED. I remember his smile when he got the results. That was one of my best moments in prison, seeing that smile on DD's face.

After that, the floodgates opened. If DD could get his GED—if he thought it was cool to get an education—then anybody could. Steve's tutoring sessions grew. The GED program expanded. For fourteen years, I looked back on DD as the turning point. He was the guy who gave education credibility in Patuxent with the hard cases, the ballers, the street kids who dropped out of school in the fifth grade.

When I talked to Mr. Mee for this book, he disagreed. He said there was another hard case before DD, a guy from the streets with a heavy charge who never talked, who never smiled, who hated everybody and hung with the wrong people and wasted every opportunity and seemed destined to become an old head muttering and licking mush from the bottom of his bowl, lost in his own angry world. When Steve tutored that guy, and *that guy* turned his life around, it proved that anyone could succeed.

Yeah, yeah: he meant me.

I was offended, at first, because I never thought of myself that way. I was never impossible. I had problems, sure. But I was never *that guy*.

But now I see it's true. At one point in my life, I was so messed up that nobody—not even my own mother—could see my potential. I was as low as a human being could be. And I lifted myself up. I became a good man. And I'm going to keep lifting, every day, until they put me in the ground.

What better legacy could I create for my people—for all people—than that?

The Rosetta Stone

MR. AND MRS. EDWARDS moved overseas for a job transfer. That was tough, because they'd been visiting Steve and me every week, and now we wouldn't see them on a regular basis anymore. But that's what happens after almost a decade inside: life moves on without you. Erick Wright had a girlfriend. I knew it was serious because why else would you bring a girl to meet your friend serving a life sentence, unless you were thinking of locking her down for a life sentence, too? Mom moved to South Dakota to be with Leslie, who was stationed there in the air force. I got a letter about it, I'm not sure why; it wasn't like she ever came to see me. She had abandoned me long ago.

I was down when I first heard about Steve's parents' move. But it only took me a few hours, at most, to realize . . . I was okay. I loved seeing the Edwardses; it was the best part of my week. I *wanted* to see them, but I didn't *need* to see them anymore.

Back in 2001, when I first met them, I was the butt of jokes for striving. But since then, Steve and I had carved out a world and created a place for ourselves. Now when new guys said, "Who this bookworm? What up with Uncle Tom?" old guys stepped in: "That's Chris, yo. That's Steve. They doing their thing."

I wasn't on the level of Tooky. Inmates *accepted* me. They *admired* him. But together, Steve and Tooky and me, we were able to do a lot of good.

And we had wood shop. We had college. There was a computer lab in the prison now, so Steve had proposed coding classes, and the administration let him lead the program. The prison had no way to organize its own data, so Steve analyzed and optimized their systems. Patuxent got a hundred thousand dollars worth of computer programming for nothing. Steve got an even better deal: after years of reading books, he was writing real code.

I was crushing my books: Thomas Cleary's *Classics of Strategy and Counsel*, a thousand-page, multivolume set of the most important texts on strategy and success, including those by Sun Tzu and Machiavelli. Business books like Jim Collins's *Good to Great*. My brother Kenny, who was in the air force and stationed in San Antonio, sent me books about real estate. The housing market was booming, so I was studying that, too. I even started a discussion group about investing.

My new passion, though, was Spanish. There were a lot of Spanish speakers in prison, and I wanted to communicate with them. I dreamed of going to Cuba, Puerto Rico, and Spain. It's hard to see the world these days without knowing Spanish. When you get down to it, it's pretty hard to understand America, too.

It took a year of study just to get competent. I was fluent in Italian, but learning Spanish required more than a thousand hours on vocabulary alone. People often ask what my favorite book in prison was, and they're surprised by my answer: *501 Spanish Verbs*. For years,

I carried that book everywhere. I made flash cards out of it and studied them in the chow hall, the dayroom, the yard. When I see the book on the shelf in my house now, it makes me so happy because it reminds me of the work I put in to get where I am today.

As a going-away gift, Mrs. Edwards gave me the Spanish Rosetta Stone software so I could learn by listening to people speak. I wasn't allowed to own software, so I donated it to the prison school. That way it was available to everyone. I was friendly with Mr. Shipe, the head of the school, so he let me use it whenever I wanted—and I wanted it all the time.

You have to lift everyone up, though, right? That's what Frederick Douglass believed—and what Steve counseled. You have to do for everyone as you do for yourself.

So I created a Spanish study group. We met twice a week for class work, and we quizzed each other every afternoon on vocabulary and pronunciation. Push-ups, as always, were the punishment. A right answer meant you asked the next question.

Through Spanish, I became close with Brian Carter. Brian was from Charles County in the DC suburbs, so he was more rural than most of us. One night, a friend of Brian's said he needed to pick up some money before hitting the clubs. They stopped at a house, the friend went in and shot somebody. Brian said he had no idea that was going to happen, and I believe him. Brian could be a jerk, he made fun of people too much, but he wasn't a killer. He wasn't violent. They don't tolerate that kind of thing in the suburbs, though, even if you were only waiting in the car. Brian got forty years.

He approached me in the yard, which I appreciated. Stepping forward is a good skill to learn. "I like the way you carry yourself," he said. "I want to learn, too. Can you help me?"

He tried to program computers with Steve, but hated it. Steve was knocking out professional-level code. If you didn't understand computers, you couldn't work with Steve.

So Brian Carter switched to Spanish, and for a while we were inseparable. We drank coffee and grilled each other on Spanish vocabulary. That's what work means: not occasionally, not when you feel like it, but every day.

"'Airplane'?" we said, throwing words over meals.

"*Avión*. Past tense of 'run'?"

"*Corrió*. How you say 'runny eggs in my mush'? Really, I want to know. 'Cuz it's happening right now."

At first, people thought we were crazy, yelling back and forth in nonsense Spanish. Eventually, they stopped noticing. New people started asking to join. After a while, my Spanish study group was so large, Mr. Shipe let us meet in the auditorium.

Rise up, Frederick Douglass had said.

Okay, he didn't say it like that, because it was in the 1800s. He said it better than I could, even though I believe it to my core: "Knowledge is the pathway from slavery to freedom."

In other words: Study. Read. And rise.

"GOOD NEWS," Keith Showstack said, throwing his briefcase on the table. He came to see me every three or four months, but he never had good news. Every time he filed for a hearing, Judge Wood put my case into abeyance, meaning he wouldn't schedule a hearing but he kept the possibility open. Don't worry, Keith would explain. Judges always turned down the first three requests. It's the wrong political climate. There was always an excuse.

Until now. "Judge Wood granted my hearing!" I exclaimed. *Finally.*

"What? No. Judge Wood is retiring."

"So?"

Showstack smiled. "I'm going to make your case the last on his docket," he said. "There's a lot of pressure not to release. The career damage of a wrong decision. The political situation, as you know. But I know Judge Wood, Chris. Helping someone like you is exactly what he'd want for his last case."

Master Plan

Chris Wilson

2004

DAILY GOALS

Stop calling home every day (done)

Forget about my fake-ass friends (done)

Work out six days a week (gain thirty pounds of muscle) (done)

Attend weekly therapy and resolve my issues

Identify my faults that led me to prison (done)

Always seek advice (done)

Help guys embrace self-improvement through mentorship (done)

Remain a lifelong learner

Never go against the grain/learn to work the system (done)

No gambling, no horseplay, no sex jokes (done)

Always dress neat (done)

Mind my own business (done)

Learn how to speak real English

Learn to tie a tie (done)

Prison Goals

Get my high school diploma (done)

Graduate from carpentry vocational shop (done)

Earn my AA degree (working on it)

Complete all the therapeutic models at Patuxent (working on it)

Learn to speak Italian (done)

Learn to speak Spanish

Learn to write résumés

Get my sentence modified to twenty years

Life Goals

Get a tailored suit

Start my own business that makes a difference in people's lives

Travel the world

Get an apartment in a nice neighborhood

Get a black Corvette convertible with nice rims and a sound system

Get a pair of cool Prada gloves to wear in the convertible

Get a cool-ass leather jacket

Go skydiving

Party on a cigarette boat

Join the mile-high club

Lay out on the beach

Drive dune buggies through the desert

Party in South Beach

Go on a helicopter ride

Go to New Orleans
Go fishing
Meet Mark Cuban
Meet a smart, beautiful woman that's business savvy
~~Pay my brother back~~

Perseverance

THANKS TO my photo business, we had more than $20,000 in the youth fund. So I did my research. It was enough to wire the prison for cable TV, and my business revenue would pay for the subscription fees going forward. Guys freaked out when Steve and I asked if that was something they wanted.

"You mean we can have cable in the dayroom?" We had only four fuzzy channels.

"You can have cable in your cell, slim!"

Everybody was excited. Morale was high. We were even going to have money left over for new weight equipment. That's the power of social entrepreneurship: not only do you offer a valuable service, you invest the money back into the community.

When we went to the administration, though, they shook their heads. "There's no money," they said.

I smiled like, *Nah, come on now.* "There's twenty thousand dollars."

"That money's gone."

I wasn't smiling anymore. "What do you mean?"

"You bought our new security cameras."

I couldn't believe it. They stole the money from the youth fund. And they used it on *security*. They said the new system was for our own good. That the cameras would cut down on violence, which was *bullshit*. (I'd given up cussing, but this called for it.) The last thing we wanted was to be watched even more. Steve and I had worked for years to earn that money. We wanted it to make inmates' lives better. Instead, the administration used our profits to make our lives worse.

Understand: I wasn't a fool. I knew how it worked. The system was cruel. Every rule, every physical space, every interaction with staff was designed to humiliate. Their goal, every day, was to prove that we were nothing, and that by being in here we'd given up, in the name of discipline and punishment, every right—privacy, respect, property, safety from physical harm—except the basic rights to not be starved, murdered, or left outside to die.

"Drop your pants," the COs would say.

There was nothing to do but drop them.

"Turn around. Spread your cheeks."

I had to do it. There was no choice. I stood bent over and naked for ten seconds, thirty, what felt like an hour. And what did the guards do? They laughed.

"Pull your pants up, inmate. You disgust me."

They didn't even search. All they wanted was to prove their power.

But still, it crushed me when the administration betrayed me, and it wasn't just the money. It was the trust and respect I thought I'd earned. I never thought I was equal. I never thought I was free. But I thought there was an understanding. If I lived by their rules, I would be rewarded. But now I saw that no matter what I did, they would never stop knocking me down.

"I'm quitting the business," I told Steve. "I'm shutting it down."

"Stay focused, Chris," he said calmly. "Don't make a decision out of anger."

I was pacing the tier. I *was* angry. But I pushed my mind back to the big question: *What's your endgame?*

That's what I had to ask myself. *Why are you doing this, Chris?*

It wasn't for the money. It wasn't for cable TV and weights. It was for the experience. I wanted to be a businessman, so I needed to learn to run a business.

It was to show the people in charge I was a good, talented, creative, hardworking man they should release to the outside world.

It was to help my fellow prisoners. I wanted to make them happier, more connected, and more focused on self-improvement. I knew that part was working. I saw the proof when inmates smiled in the family room for portraits, pulling their children tight. I saw it when everyone crowded around on the tiers to see photos of other people's families, not just their own. I saw it, especially, when I walked that tier a week later and saw a photo I had taken taped to the wall beside a man's bunk, or when an inmate approached Steve and said, "I want to send this picture to my little girl. Can you help me write a letter to tell her how much it meant to see her, and that her daddy is going to find a way home?"

We kept the business, but we lowered the price to fifty cents, our break-even point. The inmates would get their photos, but the prison would get no money.

The administration called us to a meeting a few weeks later. "You're not lowering the price, boys," they said. "You're raising it. We're thinking a dollar seventy-five."

I breathed deep, trying to stay calm. *What's your endgame, Chris? Is it this business—or is this a stepping-stone? What are you really trying to achieve?*

"Judge Wood pushed the request again," Keith Showstack said the next time I saw him. "I'm sorry, Chris. He won't hear your case. He retired last month."

That was devastating, because I was a sucker. All those years, I believed in Judge Wood. He said in 1997 he'd give me a chance if I earned it. Instead, he denied me three times.

"The good news," Showstack said, "is that your new judge, Cathy Serrette, is great. She's from family court. She's recently promoted. I met her, Chris, and I like her. She is exactly the kind of judge who will respond to a case like yours."

"Do you trust him?" Steve asked.

We were painting. If you want to know how to pass time in an institution where nothing changes, try painting it. That's what Steve and I did. We wrote a proposal to the administration to paint Patuxent, and they accepted our offer. (We were "charging" them $38 a month in commissary credits, so it was a pretty good deal for them.) We worked a few hours after lights-out, usually 11:00 to 2:00, five days a week. The job took us three years.

We weren't just applying a brighter, less filthy coat of paint. We created murals. There was one of Steve Francis, a popular basketball player at the time. There was one of a white neighborhood next to a grubby, trash-strewn minority neighborhood, with the word *gentrification*. My favorite was two dung beetles pushing an enormous ball of feces up a hill while two other beetles lounged around watching. People don't respect dung beetles because they spend their lives rolling poop, but dung beetles are grinders. They're the hardest workers in the animal kingdom. And they're strong. They can lift 1,141 times their body weight, the most of any animal. That's like a grown man lifting 120,000 pounds.

It was no secret: that's how the world saw us inmates, as dung beetles, the filthy bottom of the food chain. Steve and I wanted to show the work dung beetles do. Inmates were Sisyphus, always pushing that rock uphill. We didn't tell anybody those two beetles were pushing balls of crap. Tell them that, and that's all the bammas would ever see.

"I trust him," I said, thinking about Showstack pushing this ball of crap forward for me, year after year. He didn't have to show up every few months, but he did, and that proved he was grinding, too.

And besides, what choice did I have?

We applied for a hearing. It didn't take long to hear back. Judge Serrette pushed my case into abeyance, just like Judge Wood had.

Victims

I DON'T WANT to paint a pretty picture, because prison wasn't pretty. Prison was ugly. Every day in Patuxent sucked rocks, but some days were worse than that. One day, in group therapy, a teenage inmate started saying how he was arguing with his best friend, it got heated, and he blew the kid's head off with a shotgun while he was sitting a few feet away on the sofa. It was shocking to hear, even in the therapy room, where so many terrible, abusive stories were told.

But what scared me was the way the kid laughed. It wasn't evil. It was crazy. It was clear the shooting was basically an accident, but after it happened, and he sat there in his mom's den looking at his best friend's corpse with his head blown off, the kid lost his mind.

I was like, *What's he doing here? This kid don't need prison. He needs help. You got to at least put him in psych.*

Then I went "behind the red door" on my photo rounds, and I knew that psych wasn't the answer, because it was terrible behind the red door. It was an old, crumbling building, and even the air was bad. It smelled like a mouth full of rotting teeth.

The first cell inside, a man was eating the flesh off his own arm.

They tried to restrain him with a straitjacket, but it wouldn't hold him. I saw a man with visible sores strapped spread-eagle to his bed. Men covered themselves in their own feces so the COs wouldn't touch them. I gagged every time I passed their cells. The dayroom had no windows and plexiglass over the television, and several men were naked. One was jerking his dick every time I came by. The COs yelled at him to stop and he'd yell back, "Yes, boss. I hear you, boss," and kept going.

"You have my pictures, boss? You have my pictures?" the naked guy asked every visit.

"Yeah, I just gave them to you."

"No you didn't, boss. I haven't seen them."

"They're in your hand."

It was the worst place I've ever seen. They had special COs that served only in that unit, and they were saints. It would have driven a normal person crazy to be near those men, much less inside with them.

So I don't know what to do with a kid like that, except don't send him to prison, because prison is a violent place. People in prison are damaged. We have PTSD from our childhoods. We have traumatic brain injuries from abuse and neglect. I don't think I'd have killed a man without all the abuse I'd seen: the beatings, the rape of my mother, the kidnapping. I had hypervigilance: a constant feeling of danger. I had a voice in my head saying, *Act first or die.* That voice, that fear, urged me to pull my gun.

It doesn't stop once you enter prison, because the violence in prison causes PTSD, too. Take a fight on third tier—nothing special, at least at first. Reggie and a dude from Park Heights got into an argument, and the punches flew. Sausage was simmering on the dayroom stove, and Park Heights grabbed the frying pan and swung. He missed. Reggie took the pan off him and beat the kid half to death. Worst beating I'd ever seen. Park Heights's face was split almost in two. His cell was across from mine, so I watched as his friend took a regular needle and thread and put ten stitches in his face. No anesthetic, but Park Heights didn't flinch. He spent his recovery in his cell, doing push-ups.

Finally, he saw his chance. He snuck out to the pool table. Reggie was taking a nap with his cell door open, so he never saw it coming. Park Heights beat him unconscious with three pool balls in a net bag.

Reggie didn't go to medical, either. Nobody went to medical for fights, because they put you in protective custody. That ruined your reputation inside. You were a rat and a coward the minute they sent you to protective custody. As long as you could stand on your feet twice a day for count, you stayed out of medical.

So Reggie bought three Motrin off a kid down the tier and stayed in his cell for a few weeks, getting out of his bed only for count. His whole face was swollen and bruised. He couldn't move, he was in so much pain. I visited him often, brought him ramen and soup, since he couldn't eat solid food. I tried to talk to him, but Reggie didn't say anything until finally he muttered, more to himself than me, "I'm going to kill 'im next time."

He was serious. I could see it in his eyes. Reggie got quiet, even after he healed. Never said anything to anyone, never took part in any activities. I'd seen it before: the victim becomes the victimizer. It happened to Steve after the beating he took. It happened to me after the kidnapping. Maybe Reggie started the first fight, I can't remember, but it doesn't matter. Reggie had been knocked unconscious; his mind wouldn't let him become helpless again.

Then one day Jimmy started barking in the dayroom. He was a good kid, but he could get agitated. He started cussing at Reggie about something, working himself up until he finally said, "I'm gonna kill you, whore. I'm gonna put a knife in you."

Reggie didn't say anything, but the look on his face—everybody knew. Jimmy was in serious trouble.

I tried to get him to apologize, but Jimmy wouldn't do it. He wasn't scared, because he'd seen Reggie's look, too, but he was stubborn.

The next morning, I saw Reggie putting on his battle gear: dark pants, black shirt, gray hat pulled low over his eyes. He was wearing weight-lifting gloves, but he wasn't going to the yard. I tried to talk to him, but he walked away.

Ten minutes later, I left for the wood shop. There was a long hallway, and toward the end was a stairwell. As I got close, I saw Reggie in the shadows under the stairs. He was tying a blade to his hand. It was long, about ten inches, and looked like a Christmas tree. The barbs on the side were for maximum damage.

I knew Jimmy was coming, because he always came this way. He was probably a minute behind me.

I started to say something—"Don't do it," or something like that— but it was no good. Reggie had that blank look, like his mind was gone. Reggie was going to get blood, one way or another.

Maybe I should have turned back and warned Jimmy. Maybe I should have told a CO. But the golden rule of prison is *Don't get involved*.

Don't. Get. Involved.

I walked to wood shop and sat down. Ten seconds later, the alarm sounded and locked us in place. I heard COs running, screaming into their walkie-talkies. I knew what that meant.

People say, "Oh my God. You're so different now, Chris. You would never do that now. Do you feel bad for not stopping it?"

What I feel is conflicted. I don't feel good about what happened.

But I don't regret my decision, because I didn't make a decision. If I had done anything but walk on, Reggie would have stabbed me. If I'd warned a CO, Reggie would have hit me as soon as he got out of solitary, and Jimmy, too. Jimmy was going down the moment he spoke like that to a haunted man. If I had helped him, I would have gone down, too.

Mr. Mee was upset. He was so angry during our next group therapy session. "How could you let this happen?" he said. "How could you all sit there while this happened? Jimmy didn't deserve this. Why didn't you stop this tragedy from happening?"

He didn't even know I'd seen Reggie behind the stairwell. He was talking about the argument, and Reggie, and his state of mind. But I *tried*, that's what he couldn't see. I tried to talk Reggie out of his anger for weeks. Once he made his decision, it was too late.

If I had intervened in that hallway, I'd have been in it. You understand? I would have been in the middle of retaliations, threats, violence, and infractions. It would have gone on for months. And no matter how I handled it, it would have gone on my record. And I'd still be in prison right now.

That's a 100 percent guarantee: if I had stepped in, I would have never gotten out.

That's prison. That's the neighborhoods. Staying quiet isn't about protecting bad people or sticking with our own, it's self-preservation. It's the only way to get out. If you don't understand that, then you don't understand our world.

It's not all bad news, though. Jimmy survived. Reggie stabbed that Christmas tree so deep into his neck, blood splattered the ceiling. The COs ran to the scene, then stood around staring at Jimmy while he bled. That's what they always did. But Jimmy got lucky. One CO was from his neighborhood and knew his people. She jammed three fingers into the hole in his neck and kept him from bleeding out. He was airlifted to the hospital. I saw the helicopter from lockdown in the shop. Jimmy came back a few weeks later with a huge scar on his neck.

He never caused problems after that. He was an ideal inmate. But he had terrible nightmares. He was a haunted man, like Reggie before him. He thrashed in his bed and screamed every night.

New guys always freaked out, but we told them, "Don't worry. That's just Jimmy. Jimmy's like that."

Opportunity

IT WAS TOUGH, grinding so long through that violence and pain. Most of the teens in the youth program were on short sentences, so almost everyone I came in with, including bammas like Omar, were out. The next wave, the guys I mentored, were reaching the end of their sentences, too. No one had worked harder than me. Most had done nothing but play cards, watch television, and talk. And yet I kept hugging them good-bye, wishing them luck, and walking back to my cell.

I never did anything wrong. I never smoked. Never drank. Barely cussed. Avoided sugar. I never reached into the box, not once. One night, a female CO said, "You want me to leave your door open after count tonight, Chris?"

I knew what that meant, and oh, man: that was the snake in the garden right there.

"I got to study," I said.

"You sure you don't want to keep me company?"

She was fine, too. And clean. I hadn't touched a woman since I was seventeen. I was dying to touch a woman. But I wanted my freedom even more.

"No thanks," I said. "I'm sorry."

I had life in prison, slim . . . *and I turned down sex!*

I talked about my frustration with Mr. Mee. Even after I started officially mentoring in Mr. Mee's program, there had been a distance between us. Mr. Mee wasn't one of us; he was one of *them*. Men who looked like Mr. Mee *victimize* young men like me. I didn't think that directly, but I felt it instinctively, in my bones, because kids like me learn it through our encounters with white authority figures. Aggressive cops, backstabbing school counselors, racist strangers—they broke our trust.

Nine years of therapy was a long time, though, and Mr. Mee and I had earned each other's respect. I told him hard things about my mom, my depression, my drug use, my disappointment with myself, and he never betrayed me. He tried to give me what I needed, and I returned the favor by speaking in group, mentoring new inmates, and trying to set a positive example. I even came to him for advice on how to handle issues on the tier or approach the administration about changes. The best thing I can say about Mr. Mee is that he cared about inmates more than the rules. He's the only person at Patuxent I can say that about.

"What's the problem, Chris?" he kept asking. "What's different?" He knew I was becoming angry and depressed.

It was the time, that's all. I had told myself, when I developed my Master Plan, that I could do seven or eight years. After that, I wasn't sure I could hold up. Now I was on year nine.

"I want to be promoted to tier four," I said. "It's been six years since I was promoted to three. There are inmates up there who weren't even inside when I was last promoted, and they haven't done anything. They just play cards and smoke."

"Well . . ."

"They aren't working the program, Mr. Mee. I'm working it. I'm creating my own program. I have a real estate club. I have a Spanish club. I run a business. I'm on the youth board. Why are they moving ahead of me?"

Mr. Mee knew I was right. He had watched me change from an angry teenager into a leader, and he took pride in that. I didn't realize it at the time, but he had a deep personal interest in the success of the youth program. He had worked in the prison system for almost thirty years. His life's work was rehabilitating young offenders, but this was the first time in his life that idea had been taken seriously.

"I'm sorry, Chris," he said. "The program isn't designed for people like you and Steve. Tier four is only for prisoners in their last year before release."

The system, as always. "Are you saying I'll never get there?"

He looked away, so yeah, he was.

"Let me think about it," he said.

"We need to change the way group works," I snapped, hoping to at least salvage that.

Group was twelve inmates in a room with one therapist. We were supposed to discuss our problems, but it didn't work like that. You couldn't admit to being scared, angry, or unhappy in front of inmates you didn't trust.

I had a group I trusted. Ten of us on longer sentences had come in together, and we were supporting one another. We had the makings of a great therapy support group.

But in Mr. Mee's sessions, the other two guys were always new inmates. These dudes were young, often fifteen or sixteen, and they didn't want to be in therapy. They cut up and made jokes. They laughed when we tried to speak honestly. In theory, ten old heads could set a good example, but that's what the mentor program was for. I didn't want to deal with bammas when I was trying to fix myself.

"We need our own space, Mr. Mee," I said. "Those of us working the program need respect and peace."

"I hear you, Chris," Mr. Mee said. "I hadn't thought about that."

He got that done, at least. We got our own therapy group, with no bammas, and we started getting somewhere.

"Good news," Keith Showstack said at his regular three-month visit. He was wearing a nicer suit, but he still had the Robert-Downey-Jr.-gone-to-seed hair. I've always loved that my attorney looked like Robert Downey Jr. "I've been talking with other attorneys in the office. They think I have a shot at reducing your sentence to thirty years."

Thirty years! I was reeling. I'd still be alive in thirty years. I'd leave Patuxent, and not in a box. But thirty years was a long time. Thirty years meant twenty-one years to go.

"I can't do thirty," I said.

"What?"

"I can't do thirty, Keith. I'll lose my mind."

"Well, Chris, thirty would be a miracle. Thirty is a lot better than—"

"I want twenty."

That was the number in my Master Plan. Twenty years. And what I put in my Master Plan was law. It had to be. I couldn't start cutting corners, or that snake would bite.

Showstack scoffed. "To get twenty years," he said, "you're going to have to cure cancer."

"Then I better get started."

Part of the reason I was so stubborn, sadly, was ignorance. I had only one chance at freedom, given the parole situation in Maryland, and that was a sentence modification. As a life prisoner, I was entitled to a modification hearing—*but only one* in my entire life. I was twenty-five. If I served fifty, sixty, seventy more years, it didn't matter. If I was granted a hearing, and I failed, I was done. And so far, I couldn't even get the hearing!

Steve chewed me out when I told him I'd pissed off my attorney over ten years. "You could get out, Chris! With thirty years, you could get out!"

But one of the reasons I didn't like thirty was Steve. "Are you satisfied with forty-five?" I asked.

That stopped him, because he knew the answer. Steve had been so happy when his sentence was reduced, but now he hated it. His attorney and judge had promised eleven, but he was going to be inside until he was an old man.

"I'm working on it," he said. "I got options."

That was the problem with taking a deal. Everybody would see you'd hit the lottery, so nobody would give you more. No parole. No more hearings.

Steve's family had money. He had, I think, almost twenty lawyers working on his case at one point. Maybe he had a shot. But me? No. If I got thirty, I'd do thirty.

But thirty is better than life, right? Anything is better than life, right?

I was delusional. Positively Delusional. I had faith I was getting out. Partly, that was self-preservation. I couldn't work this hard forever. It was wearing me down. But for the other part, in a way, I blame therapy.

Remorse

I HATED TALKING about my crime. What I did will always be a stain. Talking about it, though, was a mandatory part of therapy. We had to explore the act that put us in prison, and that started with a program called Victim Impact, where the victims of crimes would come and talk to our therapy group about their experience. This was early on, after only a few years inside, and nothing made me angrier than Victim Impact.

What does this have to do with me? I thought. *I didn't hurt these people.*

One week, the victim was an older African American woman. She was probably in her late sixties, and she was beaten down, the way my mother often looked. She started talking in this real sad voice about how her car had been stolen, and I was like, *So what?*

"Didn't you have insurance?" I snapped.

"I didn't pay the premium," she said sadly.

"Well, why not?"

"I didn't have the money."

"Why not?" I was in a bad mood that day. I didn't like the way this woman slumped, like all the fight was out of her. It hit too close to home.

"Well, Chris, I was raising my granddaughter on a minimum-wage salary. Do you want to see a picture of her?"

She took out a photograph and passed it around. Her granddaughter was about sixteen, and she looked good. Guys were nodding *Hell, yeah.* We didn't see many pictures of clean women in prison.

"She's pretty, right?"

"Yeah," I said, "she's pretty."

"Well, a couple of grown men thought so, too. They grabbed her off the street."

Oh no.

"They took her to an abandoned building, and they raped her. They raped my grandbaby five or six times." She was looking right at me.

"I'm sorry," I said.

"Then they strangled her."

Oh no.

"They killed my baby."

She looked away, wiping tears.

"They cut my granddaughter's body into pieces. They put the pieces in a barrel, and they burned her. They burned my baby until there was nothing left for me to bury."

That shook me. I felt bad for this woman; I felt bad that I had looked down on her for looking beat. And beneath that sadness, I felt anger. I felt angry that someone could do that to another human being. Those men were monsters.

But they weren't us. That was part of my anger, too. We weren't monsters—*I wasn't a monster*—so why was this woman acting like we were?

Then something else happened. The woman left, and the bammas in group started laughing. They made jokes about her dead
granddaughter, like, "I'd rape that, son. She fine."

Then *everyone* started making jokes: about the grandmom's hair,
and her shabby appearance—even though she had clearly put on her
best outfit—and how she was beat like a hooptie car.

Then they went back to the dayroom and acted the same as always: arguing over music, eating chili, yelling at the television and
celebrating murders on the news. I couldn't believe it. They didn't
care. They heard that story, and they didn't care. There *was* a little
monster in them after all.

And if that hardness was in them, then maybe a piece of it was
inside me, too.

I can't be like them, I thought. *I have to be honest with myself. I
have to face what I've done.*

I wasn't a monster. But I did do something monstrous. I took a
life. The hardest part was acknowledging that, if I wasn't a monster,
despite what I'd done, then neither was the man I had killed.

That's how I had made him out in my mind. I told myself it was
him or me, he was a straight killer, and he was gonna gun me down
if I didn't defend myself. *Act first or die.*

In other words, I blamed him. He was a criminal, I told myself.
He caused his own death by threatening me and pushing me to the
edge. Even now, I'm not fully willing to say the killing was my fault.
Maybe you find that disappointing, but then again, you don't know
how hard it is to sit with that kind of sin. I believe his aggression
caused the crime, but the broken things inside me, my anger and
helplessness, caused him to die.

That took me years of therapy to acknowledge. Even after Victim
Impact, I fought it every step. I think I risked a life sentence, pro-

claiming my innocence instead of taking a plea, because I didn't want to face what I'd done. I never really saw the victim because he was circling behind me. He died half a block away. I had no image of him, alive or dead. I knew his name from the trial, but that was all. None of his family or friends testified. No one spoke for him at my sentencing.

By the time I began researching him in 2005, I couldn't find more than the basic facts of his life. He was in his early thirties. He came from a housing project in Southwest DC, a long way from Prince George's County, where I took his life. He had a criminal record. It told a story of constant legal trouble dating back to his early teens.

He had a mother, of course. I knew her name, but I couldn't find her. She had moved from a public-assistance apartment without a forwarding address. I don't know if he had siblings. He must have had friends, but they must have known him the way I knew Little Anthony and Jay Jah and Butchie, because they walked away when he died.

They were in the cave. The man I shot, he must have been living there, too.

I suppose that could have been a comfort. I could have told myself he was a bad person. He was in the streets. He was committing crimes. I could have lied to myself and said I didn't take much from the world.

But that wasn't true. The more I researched him and found nothing, the more real he became to me. I knew only the outline, but I could fill in the details because I had lived them: bad childhood, poverty, struggles in school—or maybe struggles at home that bled into school. Drop out. Get lost. He was living in the streets for fifteen years. He was a grown man but still kicking with his crew, getting by as best he could, and if someone offered him $300—or $30, or whatever—to drive across town and threaten a teenager he didn't know, he wouldn't think anything of it.

He wouldn't think it was wrong. He definitely wouldn't think it would end his life.

That's what brought it home to me: the long chain of events that led us to that place. All the choices we made. All the people who had to abandon him for him to bleed out alone in that grocery store doorway, far from the world he knew.

And when I finally pictured him there, scared and bleeding, probably crying for his mom, I felt a powerful and freeing thing: remorse.

Remorse isn't feeling bad about what you have done. It's not "accepting responsibility." I had done that years before. Remorse is bigger. It is acknowledging that you did something irrevocably wrong, followed by the overwhelming feeling that *you need to dedicate your life to making up for that sin.*

It's powerful. It's wonderful. It's the only thing that will free you from the hate you feel inside. Remorse is what held me up during times of stress and depression. It's what helped me through those long crushing years. It's a purpose, lifting you up. You can see true remorse in a person, because it changes them. I saw true remorse in the men who became deeply religious in prison, the ones who studied their Bibles or Korans every day. I saw true remorse in Steve, who found himself through tutoring. Maybe Hal-el, who saved Steve's life in Castle Grayskull, was motivated by remorse. That's one of the ways it works: reaching out to save others.

But it's not the only way. I saw true remorse in Tooky, too, who created peace on the tiers by staying calm and being comfortable with himself. He didn't define himself as a killer or a criminal but as a fallen man redeemed. He was a *prisoner*, but only in the physical sense. He made this world his own, and in a way that set him free.

I felt that, too. After finding my remorse, I spent the years working, every day, to be the man the world needed me to be.

I thought the administrators, the judges, the magistrates—whoever made the decisions in the system—would see that. I thought it was so obvious I was a changed man that they would grant my release. Talk about a delusion—and not a positive one. There were hundreds of prisoners in Maryland who felt genuine life-changing remorse. I knew dozens in Patuxent. None were getting out. Not for that, anyway.

So, I fought my lawyer over the idea of asking for thirty years . . . because I felt good about myself? Because I felt I would be rewarded for my genuine rehabilitation? I laugh about it now, because that was baller. That has to be the dumbest thing I've ever done.

And yet, if I'd been given thirty years, I'd still be in prison today.

Tier Four

"I CAN'T MOVE you to tier four," Mr. Mee told me. I wasn't surprised. Prison had rules, and they don't change the rules for the likes of me. "But I think we've come up with something better."

Instead of promoting our group to fourth tier, the administration gave us our own tier. We had our own dayroom, with a kitchen, and we had all-day open-cell privileges with no guards on patrol. That meant, inside the locked metal doors at the end of our tier, we policed ourselves. We were still subject to midnight count, afternoon count, and inspections, but by that point, inspections were easy. The COs knew Steve and me so well, they wouldn't even toss our rooms.

They'd look around to see if anyone was watching, then nod toward our televisions. "Turn on the game." They might sit five minutes, chatting, before moving on.

Even better than the freedom of movement, though, Study Buddy and I were allowed to choose the inmates who would share the tier with us.

That's trust. The administration was not only willing to try something new for us, they invested in our judgment. I guess they *had* been watching. They could see the change in us—the remorse—and they rewarded it, finally, just when I needed it.

The men we chose were all serving hard times for hard crimes. Brian Carter, my Spanish-language study partner, was an accessory to murder. So was Juan, one of my weight-lifting partners.

Bingo had committed a notorious crime. For gang initiation, he and another wannabe lured a rival's little sister to a garbage-strewn lot and stabbed her. She didn't die, so they kept stabbing her. When she still wouldn't die, they picked up a broken toilet and smashed her skull. She was fifteen.

I heard his first years at Patuxent were bad. Nobody talked to him. He was slashed by other inmates, but nobody stood up for him, not even COs. They hated him inside, until Steve took him in. Bingo was Cambodian, and he was smart. He found his place as a tutor, and he found his remorse. He was getting out. He got only twenty years. I don't know how. Maybe he rolled on the other kid.

Getting Tooky to move over was a big deal. He'd been in his cell for fifteen years. He had a fish tank and potted plants. He'd painted the walls. He brought his fish with him, of course, but it's still hard, moving out of your home. He didn't want to do it, because comfort is the hardest commodity to acquire in prison. But he did it for us. He knew how much we looked up to him.

Tooky was serving life on murder. His friend Geronimo was a skin-beef. When I found out, I couldn't believe it. Geronimo seemed so peaceful. I couldn't see a violent predator in him. Finally, I asked him about it.

Geronimo looked away. "It's true," he said. "I was young. I was with my girl in a car. We were kissing and rubbing, you know, and I got excited. She told me to stop, but I didn't. I don't know why. I knew she didn't want it, but I kept going until, next thing you know, I'm having sex with her, you know, against her will."

He was quiet. I could tell he was ashamed.

"I paid for it, you know what I'm saying, Wilson? I paid a heavy price."

Rapists can be dangerous. They talk a good game, but they're cold inside. Geronimo wasn't like that. He had been a young guy who made a mistake, and now he was an old guy redeemed. That was a good lesson for me on never judging a man by his charge. It probably helped me see my way past Bingo's crime, too.

We also took seven guys from carpentry shop, all white. We wanted to mix races, and these guys had skills. Kevin, the one I knew best, built ingenious padded wooden seats to fit over the toilets. It was almost like having a chair. As a thank-you for taking him on, he built one for my cell. I'm not above a little bribery, I guess.

The last, but definitely not least, of the guys on tier was Scar. Scar was everybody's little brother. He was fifteen when he came in on a ten-year charge, but even then he was enormous. I worked out with him for years, and he crushed those weights. Never studied. I couldn't get him to crack a book. But Scar was funny. Never hurt anybody, never took anything seriously. He had problems, though. At midnight roll call, we had to stand by our bunks until the CO shone a flashlight and confirmed we were present. Scar thought it was hilarious, every other week or so, to stand there naked.

There was a gorgeous CO. All the inmates had a crush on her. Once, when Scar saw her coming down the tier for count, he stripped butt-naked. When she shone her light into his cell, Scar did a little dance, his dick flopping. He got solitary for that one.

I was like, "Scar, you can't do that. It's disrespectful. You gotta keep your pants on."

Scar couldn't stop. Some bammas yelled rap lyrics; Scar dropped his drawers.

We couldn't stay mad at Scar, though. He was such a cheerful dude. Didn't have a mean or angry bone in his body. He was our project, I guess. Scar was exactly the kind of kid Steve, Tooky, and I wanted to help.

But guys like Scar helped me, too. Everybody on tier helped me. Being up there, away from the fights and the stabbings, eased my mind. It took the stress level down, which was exactly what I needed, because I had been working on my college degree for five years and I was in the final semester. I had one class I had to pass for my degree, my old enemy: math. I was never good at math.

But now I had the perfect environment. I studied in the morning before breakfast, then in the dayroom with Steve and Brian and the rest of our study crew. I pounded the weights with Juan and Scar in the afternoon. Thanks to my photo business "salary" and the support of the Edwardses, I had credits at the commissary. I ate five meals a day, including dinner every night in the dayroom with Steve. We cooked feasts: sausage, chicken wraps, homemade soup. I never ate sweets, and I watched my carbs, so we made protein and vegetables, enough to share. Other guys pitched in when they could, but Steve and I were supplying food for half the tier.

After dinner, I hit my math books like I hit the weights. I drank coffee and stayed up late, punishing myself with push-ups for wrong answers. Mr. Shipe, who ran the school, gave us extra access to the library, classrooms, and computers. The prison had a computer program for math tutoring that kept score of right answers, so I started Math Wars, a competition for points. Mr. Shipe gave me a key to the computer room so we could use the program after hours.

"You guys are wearing that computer out," he said one morning. "There was one person, I don't know who, but they missed the same problem sixty-seven times in a row."

He shook his head, like he couldn't believe it. *Sixty-seven times!*

"Hey, Mr. Shipe," I said after class, after everyone else was gone. "That was me. I missed that problem sixty-seven times."

"I know that, Chris," he said. "You're the only person I know who would keep trying that long. I just didn't want to call you out. But I can tutor you, if you want."

So Mr. Shipe started staying after class to tutor me. Steve tutored me. Even Bingo put in long hours. And the more we worked, the more I wanted it. That's a great secret for life: The harder you work, the more you care. And the more you care, the more you get. I had trouble sleeping for a month before my math final. I didn't want to waste a second.

I knew I passed the moment I finished the test. I just knew. I was so pumped, I went to the yard and destroyed my workout crew. We pumped for a solid hour, and I wasn't even tired.

"I killed it," I told Steve. "I don't need to hear my grade. I know."

It became official on May 25, 2006. More than twelve years after being kicked out of the eighth grade, ten years after my crime, nine years after receiving life in prison, and eight years after adopting my Master Plan, I *earned* my associates degree from Anne Arundel Community College.

Nobody came to the ceremony. Nobody but Steve, who was also graduating college that day, saw me walk across the stage, shake a white man's hand, and receive my diploma. Did you expect it to be any different? I didn't. I knew exactly what that day would be like. It was just my best friend and me, crushing goals. It was the happiest day of my life.

Chris Wilson, college graduate!
(STEPHEN EDWARDS)

SIX MONTHS LATER, I was walking in the yard, speaking Spanish with a friend from El Salvador. It was summer 2006, more than a year since I had told Showstack I wanted twenty. I was mentoring a group of young Latinos, and we spent a lot of time talking about each other's worlds. They taught me about food, holidays, traditions, and the difficulties of trying to make a better life in America. Latinos are loyal to their families, out to second and third cousins. Family is their support network. It also gets them in trouble, because they respond to violence against a family member. Many Latinos I knew at Patuxent were in because they stood up for their family.

We were talking about freedom, and how my only hope of ever stepping outside my prison cell was a sentence modification hearing.

By then, I had been denied five times, three times by Judge Wood, twice by Judge Serrette.

"*Tienes que rezar*," my friend said. You have to pray.

I started to object, but he stopped me. "*Tienes que rezar.*"

I had a prayer list. I kept it in a beautiful inscribed Bible Mr. Edwards had given me as a gift. I didn't have much faith in God, but I prayed for every person on my list every night, just in case. "Dear God," I always started, "please take care of my mother and keep her safe."

That night, at the end of my list, I prayed for myself. I asked for a sign that what I was doing mattered, because I needed hope. I challenged Him: *Give me a reason to believe in You. I haven't had one for so long.*

I prayed that prayer for six weeks, until my lawyer stopped by to tell me, "Good news, Chris," and I was expecting the usual excuses that weren't good news at all, until he said, "Judge Serrette has granted you a hearing."

I couldn't believe it. *I did it. I worked my Master Plan. I got my chance. Now all I have to do is crush my hearing.*

Of course, that's exactly the moment Mom reentered my life.

Darico

I DIDN'T HEAR from Mom directly. I received a letter from child protective services saying a hearing was scheduled to determine the custody of Darico. As his father, I was invited to attend.

I had committed my crime on Darico's first birthday. I barely saw him when I was in Upper Marlboro. I didn't get to say good-bye before they took me to solitary a year later. Mom lost my father's house not long after that, so she and Darico moved constantly, and I never knew where to reach them. Even as he grew up, Darico never wrote to me. Mom wrote about once every two years, but she never mentioned him. My last meaningful contact with my son was when my sister brought him to Patuxent in 1998. He was two and a half and could barely walk. Now he was eleven years old.

I knew how it was without a father. I was reminded of what a difference that made the year before, when Scar got quiet. He was a talker, always joking and having fun, but that day, he wouldn't say a word. He pounded the weights like he hated them.

"What's up, Scar?" I said.

"That's my father over there," he said, nodding behind him.

I looked across the yard. I saw the new guy, and I laughed. "Dang, Scar, he looks exactly like you. You gotta go over and talk to him."

"I'm not going to talk to him," Scar said. "I'm gonna kill him."

Scar's dad had abandoned him real young. He was still hurting on that.

"No, Scar," I said. "You're going to talk to him, and you're going to tell him how you feel."

I could see the fear on Scar's dad's face when our crew approached him. We were five muscled-up men. I stopped ten feet from him, because you don't press in prison. "Go on, Scar," I said. "We got your back."

Scar did it. He didn't want to, but he walked over and said something to his father. His father said something back. Scar had an inch on him, but otherwise they looked like two versions of the same man. I couldn't hear what they said, but after a few minutes they went and sat on a bench, and the rest of us drifted back to the weights.

Every day after that, Scar sought out his father in the yard. Sometimes they sat together, but mostly they walked the perimeter, talking. Scar was with us on tier. I don't think he ever saw his father except in the yard, but their relationship changed him. He stopped dropping his pants for the female COs. He got a job in the administration office and started dating a civilian who worked there. That wasn't allowed, so when the warden found out, the woman was fired.

Scar put her on his visitors' list.

I was like, "You're crazy, Scar. She can't come here. You know how much trouble you two will get in for that?"

The next weekend, she showed up. "That's my woman," Scar said with the biggest smile. "You don't understand, Chris. We love each other."

I wanted for Darico whatever Scar's dad gave him. I knew it wasn't too late, not if we both wanted it. But I was afraid of what my son would think of me. I had abandoned him. Would he want to fight me? Or worse, would he want nothing to do with me at all?

I walked into that courtroom on eggshells. But when Darico saw me, he started crying. He ran to me and gave me a hug. I felt a lump in my chest so big it hurt.

"Where'd you get those muscles, Dad?" he said.

"What, these? These ain't real. They're just letting me wear them to impress you."

The bailiff was watching. "Can you take these off?" I asked. I was wearing shackles and handcuffs, so I couldn't hug my son.

They unchained me, and Darico and I went into a side room alone to talk. I don't remember a word. Some conversations are so important, you remember everything. Some are even more important, and you can't remember a thing. They feel like a dream. That's how it was when I finally spoke to my boy.

Then the hearing began, and I heard the details of his life. The police had found a body in Mom's house. It was her third husband. He had died of a drug overdose. The police found evidence of drug abuse in the home. That was their term, so businesslike: "Evidence of drug abuse in the home." I don't know what the place looked like, but I can imagine. The last ten years had been tough on me, but they had been worse on Darico. He didn't deserve that. He was a child, and the only thing he'd ever done wrong was to be born my son.

I looked at Mom. She was at the next table as the defendant, but she seemed miles away. I almost didn't recognize her. She was sunken, and she had aged so much her face was different. Her hair was messy and her eyes were glassy. She was wearing a ratty sweatshirt. I remember thinking, *Dang, Mom, you didn't even dress up for this?* I knew she was a drug addict, but she looked more like an alcoholic. Like her life had been ruined slowly, over a long period of years.

But she was in there. The woman who built a good life for us, before the abuse. The mom who sat at the kitchen table and explained entrepreneurship to me; the friend who taught me how to treat a girl right; the special person who wrapped up her own birthday present and let me give it to her, because neither one of us had anyone else that mattered in our lives.

Mom wanted custody of Darico. So did the state. "You're the father, Mr. Wilson," the judge said. "This is your decision."

I didn't want Darico in foster care. It was a terrible way to grow up. But Mom looked bad, and I kept thinking about that dead body in the house. And Mom's addictions. And her bipolar disorder. I knew there was abuse. According to testimony, Darico had once been hospitalized with broken ribs, after my brother Derrick punched him in the chest.

"I just want my son to be safe," I said.

Mom was crushed. I could see it, even in her haunted face. It must have been the way I had looked when she wished I was never born. She didn't understand how her son could choose foster care over her. I didn't feel like I had a choice.

The state arranged to bring Darico to Patuxent for regular visits every two weeks. Mr. Mee reserved a private room for us. It was low-key, but perfect. It was the best thing in my life. Darico and I talked, hung out, played chess. How cool is that? My son was a chess player, like me.

I have one picture of us from that time. It's me, Darico, and David, Steve's older brother. We're on the grounds of Patuxent, at the picnic I cofounded for inmates who had received no infractions in the past six months. The sun is shining. We're squinting at the camera, just a bit, and we're smiling. I've kept that picture near me, through every triumph and defeat, since the day it was taken.

That was October 2006. A few weeks later, on November 3, I finally got my twenty minutes in court.

One Shot

I DON'T LIKE courtrooms. Even today, if I'm giving a speech, I hate doing it in a courtroom. I don't understand the rules there, but I know they are against us: the poor, the dark, and the accused—rightly or wrongly—because that's the room's purpose. These are the places America created to finish us off.

I felt that fear as soon as I stepped through the door for my sentence modification hearing. For weeks, everyone at Patuxent had been encouraging me. "You strong, Chris? You know what you gonna say?" It was like they were more nervous than me. The guys in there, the ones who watched me all those years, needed this. They needed hope.

"I'm cool," I told them. I wasn't worried. I had the truth on my side.

But as soon as I stepped through that courtroom door, I had doubts. The executioner was above me in her box: Judge Cathy Serrette. She smiled when I walked in, but it was impossible to figure out what it meant. Then I saw my lawyer, Keith Showstack, laughing with the state's attorney. Like this was a joke they were playing on the poor black sucker who didn't understand this world.

I had trusted Keith. Over six years and twenty-five visits, we had built a friendship. He had come to me a few weeks before the hearing and said, "Harry Trainor's back in the office. He can step in as your counsel."

Harry Trainor, my original lawyer, was a partner at the firm. He was one of the most respected lawyers in Maryland. Keith Showstack was just a twenty-nine-year-old junior associate with a South Boston accent and slicked-back hair.

"I'll stick with *you*," I said.

Keith looked surprised. "Harry's a big deal, Chris. He's a great attorney."

"Yeah, but you know me."

Now, in the courtroom, I was like, *What's going on here? That's my enemy you're talking to. She's trying to keep me inside for life.*

Keith nodded to me like, *We got this*, then he turned and addressed the judge. "Your Honor, we're prepared, if the court is ready."

He started with my age—seventeen when the crime occurred, now almost twenty-eight. He mentioned Darico, and how we'd recently been reconciled, and how I wanted to be a father to him. He listed my accomplishments. He quoted a letter from my Anne Arundel sociology professor, saying I was "a rarity among all students who have taken this exam!"

"And that's with an exclamation point, Your Honor," Keith said. "That's the enthusiasm of these professors who are actually allowing him to enroll in college curriculum."

He told the court how I was an adviser to other inmates, and how the administration often asked me to help resolve complaints or behavior issues, and how I had recently stepped down from the IAC youth board to focus on my education.

"Every four to six months, I see him at Patuxent Institution," Keith said. "And I've never seen an inmate with all these corrections officers . . . they come up to me and, um . . ." He hesitated.

"Let me stop for a second," he said, and when I looked over, I couldn't believe it. My lawyer was crying.

"These corrections officers, they come up to me, and they say, 'Mr. Showstack, do something for him.'" He paused again, wiping his eyes and composing himself. "I think I could have packed the courtroom with every correctional officer at the Patuxent Institution," he said, "because they care about Chris that much."

He continued for several minutes, describing my foreign language program and photo business, and smaller projects, like my real estate group. But that pause . . . those tears . . . that was the moment. That's why I stuck with Keith Showstack. He had been visiting me for years. He didn't have to keep coming, especially without good news, but he did. The detail with the COs was something only a dedicated lawyer would know, and an emotion only a friend would feel. *Chris doesn't belong here.* That's what the COs told him. What's more powerful than that?

I remember glancing over my shoulder as Keith described my three-year mural project. When I walked in, all the strangers in the public area had been slumped, waiting for their loved ones to arrive. Now they were sitting up, listening, thinking, *This black man is for real. My God, his lawyer cares.*

Keith called Mr. Mee to testify. Therapists rarely appeared on an inmate's behalf, so his presence caused the experienced spectators to shush their children and to lean forward, eager to hear what the man had to say. *My God, he's got jailers speaking for him.* Mr. Mee answered my lawyer's questions carefully and calmly, and only at the end did the state object.

"Do you think that, based on these ten years, Christopher Wilson could be a productive member of society?"

"I do."

"Objection."

"Overruled."

Then it was my turn.

It's rare in life, very rare, to stand before a human being with your life in her hands. To plead with the executioner to turn away the weapon and spare your life. Judge Serrette could set me free, or she could doom me to death in a cage. This was my last shot.

It was so quiet, I could feel my heart beating. I tasted my own tongue. The judge was staring intently, studying me. The only person moving was the stenographer, ready to record the most important words I would ever speak. Words I'd thought about since my solitary confinement at eighteen years old in Upper Marlboro. Words I'd practiced and outlined and rehearsed in my cell, but that totally escaped me now.

I got nothing, Your Honor. Nothing but the truth.

And realizing that—that the truth was on my side. It set me free.

"First of all, I would like to apologize for what I, um, done, you know. I understand the damage I caused. I took someone's life. And you know, I'm not the same person I was back then. You know, I've matured a lot and I learned from my mistakes."

It wasn't a pretty start. I was falling over myself. But I knew what I wanted to say. I wanted to tell the judge that I knew every person who stood before her said they were sorry, that they'd changed, but I was for real.

"Even if I never do go home," I said, "I want to be the guy that, even if I'm seventy years old, I'm still doing positive things. Because it's in me. It's not fate. And I ask the state's attorney, and you, Your Honor, to look at the consistency over these past ten years. Every day I say I am going to do something. I set goals. I'm disciplined . . . I got a schedule, my 2006 goals are almost complete."

Anybody could work for a few days or weeks or months when you dangle a reward. But look at my dedication. I worked every day, for a decade, for this chance. But also because I wanted to be a good person.

"I needed to pass a math class in college, and math was my worst subject . . . I'd sit up all night and study, really nervous. And I finally went in and passed the test. And when I walked across the stage for graduation, no family members came to see me. I walked across by myself. But that was the best day of my life, Your Honor. I was the first one out of my family to get a college degree. And I'm locked up. And they're out here."

I thought I talked about my Master Plan. I remember Judge Serrette smiling down at me, like she was impressed by that. But according to the transcript, I never said those words. I said, "I'm trying to give to people so they can conduct themselves out in society. I want to help other people show remorse and give something back, because I took something, Your Honor. And I beg the courts just to give me a chance. Let me set it right. Let me make up for my sins. I won't let you down."

The state's attorney didn't argue my rehabilitation. She agreed I was a changed man. Instead, she described my crime, the victim "shot six times by that man," pointing directly at me. In the middle of the chest, she said. In the lower right side of the chest. In the right buttocks, left hip, the right elbow, "all as he was running away."

"You hear about how this defendant is doing great things," the state's attorney said. "The victim will never be able to better himself.

He will never be able to say, 'I'm proud of myself, I got a college degree.' He will never know children. He will never know grandchildren. He was shot down at thirty-one years of age . . . *That defendant*, without any thought to what his life was like, took it away."

I remember thinking, as the judge asked me to stand, that this was probably the only time this older white woman ever spoke to someone like me. Then I realized it was the opposite: she probably did this ten times a day, five days a week. Could she see who I was? Or did she simply see another guilty man?

I felt dizzy, but I stood straight. I didn't bend. I looked her in the eye as she passed judgment on my life. She talked about how punishment honors the life taken, and the importance of deterrence, both for the individual and the community. She said justice was a gamble, an attempt to be fair both to the person standing before her and the society that would bear the burden if I hurt someone else. My lawyer had asked for twenty years. The courtroom gasped, as one, when she modified my sentence to twenty-four.

Twenty-four years.

My maximum time in prison was twenty-four years.

I came back to Patuxent like a king. Like the nobody who pulled the sword from the stone. I wasn't a king, I was inmate 265–975, but that's how it felt. COs high-fived me. Guards yelled congratulations. My fellow inmates whooped and screamed and rattled their cages. *Chris did the impossible. Chris beat the system. He knew what he was doing this whole time.*

We partied that night. Chicken and tuna wraps. Coffee. Music. The COs let us stay out of our cells past curfew, and the whole tier celebrated. I was pumped. I was getting out! I had earned my second chance. It felt like ten thousand pounds had been lifted off my back. I knew I'd been carrying weight, but I never knew it was that heavy.

It was around midnight, the party raging, when I realized Tooky wasn't there. I found him in his cell. He was lying in his bunk, staring at the ceiling.

"I'm getting out, Tooky," I said. "I got my sentence reduced."

He glanced at me. "Oh, that what's up, slim."

He turned to the wall. I waited, but he didn't turn back.

"Is he mad at me?" I asked Ray-Ray when I got back to the dayroom.

Ray-Ray shook his head. "It's hard on some guys," he said.

I knew what he meant. I'd seen a hundred guys go out ahead of me, wondering if I'd ever get my shot. Now I was getting mine, but Tooky wasn't getting his. He still had life. He was stuck inside. I thought he was comfortable here. I thought he was okay with this life. But he wasn't. Of course he wasn't. He hated it like the rest of us. I felt stupid for not realizing that, and selfish for not thinking how hard it was to be left behind by a younger brother like me.

"Should I tell the guys to chill?" I said. "I don't want to be disrespectful."

"No, slim," Ray-Ray said. "Hell no. That's on him. That got nothing to do with you." He smiled. "You did the impossible, Wilson. You going home. You got to celebrate that."

The Dream

I DREAMT another dream. Not the snake or the old-man-in-a-cell dream, although I still had that one, too. I have never stopped having it, or thinking that outcome is a possibility. I will never commit another crime, I guarantee that. But that's no guarantee I'll stay free.

In the new dream, I was sitting by the ocean. I was wearing white pants, rolled up, my feet dangling in the water. It was a calm day, hardly a cloud in the blue sky. The sun was reflecting off the rippling water, a light breeze on my skin. I looked at the horizon, but there was nothing to see, only a thin line where the water met the sky, and that's exactly the way I liked it. Empty space. Stillness. Peace.

Then someone yelled, "Hey, Chris," and I realized I was on a boat, hanging my bare feet over the side. So I turned, and everyone I had ever known was standing behind me, even Mom and Dad and Big Daddy and my cousin Eric, and James Brown was playing, and everyone was smiling. *Over here, Chris*, they were shouting. *We got you, Chris*. It was a party, there was a frozen drink in hand, and they were calling me back, but not like I'd been gone, more like I'd walked away to steal a second for myself and now they were bringing me home.

Then I opened my eyes, and I saw my cell, and it hit me: the dream was real. I was going home. I was leaving this cell with the chance to do everything I had thought about for the last ten years. Start a business. Buy a Corvette. Help my community. Find a woman to love.

I thought about the last thing Judge Serrette had said to me. After her sentence was passed, and I was on my way out, she leaned over her bench and said, "I expect you to follow your Master Plan, Mr. Wilson."

"Yes, ma'am," I said, because there was no doubt.

That's what I was going to do.

"My Life Goals" ....by Mr. Chris Wilson

My Long Term Goals:

- Get out of prison, remain out in society and be an active member of my community.
- Reach financial independence and buy a home.
- Remain a life-long learner and focus on continual self-improvement.
- Start my own business one day that makes a difference in people's lives.
- Be able to travel around the world.
- Write a book about my life story that would help young guys handle life's challenges.

My Short and Mid-Term Goals:

- **My Home Plan:**
  - o Buy an apartment in a nice neighborhood.

- *College Educational Goals :*
  - o Earn my General Education Diploma, 1998.......................................(Done)
  - o Graduate from the Carpentry Vocational Shop, 2000..........................(Done)
  - o Graduate from the A+ Computer Repair Shop, 2007.............................(Done)
  - o Learn to speak Spanish...(Done)
  - o Get my A.A. Degree from Anne Arundel Community College................(Done)
  - o Get accepted into the University of Baltimore's Merrick School of
    Business(2008)...(Done)
  - o Get letters of recommendations from my former college professors.........(Done)
  - o Earn a **Interdisciplinary Studies Bachelor Degree**, which will allow me to mix
    Community Studies and Civic Engagement with Social Entrepreneurship into one degree
    (2yrs)
    - Get accepted into university of Baltimore's Leadership Program
    - Work in the Entrepreneur's Opportunity Center
    - Earn a Post Baccalaureate Certificate in Marketing (5months)

  - o Earn an **International M.B.A Degree**

- *List of Occupational Objectives:*
  - o Complete a basic resume for an entry-level retail position.....................(Done)
  - o Create a resume for a Youth Mentor position ....(Done)
  - o Get hands-on experience working in the career center and coordinating study
    groups...(Done)
  - o Research potential future job opportunities in the career center..............(Done)
  - o Improve my job interview and job searching skills.............................(Done)
  - o Work in the Federal Work Study Program ....
  - o Gain employment in the nonprofit business sector................................

⬥ *List of Therapeutic Goals:*
  - ○ Identify and correct my faults and bad habits that led me to prison...........(Done)
  - ○ Maintain a positive relationship with my therapist and continue to seek advice in my therapy sessions ....(Done)
  - ○ Continue to increase my knowledge through reading self-help books and motivational autobiographies (started in 1999)...................................(Done)
  - ○ Help other guys embrace self-improvement through the Patuxent Mentors Program (Earned five certificates for five years of mentoring)..............................(Done)

⬥ *List of Specific Program Objectives:*
  - ○ Complete Alternative to Violence Module, 1997....................................(Done)
  - ○ Complete Alternative to Violence Advanced Module, 1997.................(Done)
  - ○ Complete Alcoholics Anonymous Module,1998...................................(Done)
  - ○ Complete Drug Education Module, 1998..(Done)
  - ○ Complete Narcotics Anonymous Module, 1999...................................(Done)
  - ○ Complete Youth Mentor Module, 1999-2002, 2005..............................(Done)
  - ○ Complete Assertiveness Training Module, 2000..................................(Done)
  - ○ Complete "Steps to Success" Module, 2001.......................................(Done)
  - ○ Complete Victims Impact Module, 2005..(Done)
  - ○ Complete PDRM-12 Drug Module, 2006..(Done)
  - ○ Complete Anger Management Module, 2007..(Done)
  - ○ Complete Life Skills Module, 2007...(Done)
  - ○ Complete Interpersonal Relationships Module,2008.............................(Done)
  - ○ Complete the Further Studies Process, 2008......................................(Done)
  - ○ Make Status...
  - ○ Go to the R.E.F program/Halfway House...
  - ○ Complete the R.E.F Program..

⬥ *Other Program Accomplishments:*
  - ○ Remained infraction-free for entire incarceration (14 years).
  - ○ Over 11 years in *Advanced Youth Therapy Group.*
  - ○ Earned a Certificate for completion of a *Family Relations Module* 1996
  - ○ Has been on fourth level, the highest level in the institution for over five years.
  - ○ A member of the *Youth Planning Committee* for two years. Helped establish '*Family Day*" events that continue annually.
  - ○ Vice President of the Inmate *Youth Advisory Council* for three years.
  - ○ Completed the *I-Rehab Computer Module* 2005
  - ○ A member of the *Patuxent Mural Project* for over three years. Helped paint artistic designs around the institution. 2000 to 2003
  - ○ Received a Certificate of Appreciation from the *U.S. Department of Agriculture* 1999
  - ○ Co-founded the *Inmate Picture Project*, which raised well over $20,000 for the Inmate Welfare Account since its launch in 2003.
  - ○ Created *The Language Study Group*, learning Spanish, Italian and now studying Mandarin , **2004 to 2010**
  - ○ Created *The Real Estate Study Group*, **2005 to 2007**
  - ○ Manages the *Patuxent Institution Career Center*, specializing in resume writing
  - ○ (2)-Certificates of Appreciation for volunteer work in the school
  - ○ Created The Book Club **2009 to 2010**

2

PART 4

The Middle Passage, Part 2

Help yourself, so that you can help someone else.

—JAMES BROWN

Lucky

THE LAST THING I want is for you to read this far and think the system works.

Chris was provided opportunities.

He took them.

He got out, despite a brutal sentence, despite "Life means life."

So the system works.

The system doesn't work. I've spent a lot of time talking with prosecutors, judges, inmates, and returning citizens, which is what I call released inmates, because that's what we are. We're not ex-convicts, and we're not parolees, because those negative words make it okay for people to treat us worse than others. We are returning citizens who have served our time, paid the required price, and earned the same right to life, liberty, and the pursuit of happiness as everyone else.

What's become clear, over the years, is that I was lucky. I was lucky to be sentenced to Patuxent instead of ECI, Grayskull, or one of the DOC prisons. The prison population in Maryland is around 22,000; Patuxent's capacity is 987—and the youth program is about 200. Less than 1 percent of inmates received the chance I was given.

I was lucky to have been convicted in 1997, because anyone convicted in Maryland after July 1, 2004, has only *five years from sentencing* to receive a modification. This sets an impossible standard. I
didn't meet Keith Showstack until I'd served four years. I wasn't
granted a hearing until ten. Under the new law, my opportunity
would have expired. I would have died in prison. The next Chris
Wilson—the next one hundred Chris Wilsons—are in Maryland
prisons right now, with no chance of release.

And for what? Why take away the reward for becoming a better
human being? Why take away hope? Hope powers change. Would
you work as hard at your job if your boss said, "Look, you'll never be
promoted. You'll never make more money. You're going to sit in this
cubicle, no matter how well or poorly you perform, for the rest of your
life. From here on out, nothing you do matters."

Why prove to us, the incarcerated, that the system doesn't care if
we change? That we are not wanted back? That society's only goal is
punishment, and every action is designed to take away our already
few chances to succeed?

I was lucky to be granted a hearing. I was lucky to be assigned to
Judge Serrette, who took a personal and professional risk for me.

I had no money. No extenuating circumstances. No irregularities
in my case. If I had a public defender, like most young people in my
situation, no lawyer would have followed up and spent the time to
know me. Many public defenders don't even file the necessary paperwork within ninety days of conviction, as required by law, to make a
sentence modification possible. My mom lost her house paying for
Harry Trainor. Her sacrifice saved my life, because it put me in
Patuxent, and it allowed a young, ambitious lawyer to find me.

I could have gone with Harry Trainor for my hearing, the more
accomplished lawyer. Thank God I didn't, because he never would

have had Keith Showstack's sincere belief in me. It was the trust Keith Showstack and I had built over six years, along with being assigned the right judge, along with being convicted at the right time, to the right prison, that allowed my hard work to matter.

That's a narrow door. Too narrow for most good people to make it through.

Now everybody asks, "How can we create more Chris Wilsons?"

I say, "It's simple. We have to *want* more Chris Wilsons."

We have to have a system that cares about rehabilitation. That's where our system is broken, in my mind, even more than sentencing. I know this is controversial, but I'm okay with long sentences for young guys with a rap sheet like mine. I mean thirty, forty years, not life. No juvenile should ever receive life. But lost kids need a shock. They need to get crushed.

But they also need a way out, because we don't need any more Steve Edwardses—fundamentally good, incorrectly sentenced, and trapped in the system. We don't need any more Tookys, written off and forgotten. Give bammas thirty—but with a real chance to reduce that time for good behavior. Tell them, "We're taking the best years of your life, but we'll give them back if you earn them. *As soon as you are rehabilitated*, we'll let you out."

Does that seem too generous? Well, in my experience, it takes three years to adjust to prison. And five years of work, minimum, to truly reform. So everyone will serve at least eight years, and I'd guess even the best men and women will serve ten.

Still too generous? Well, I'll get Socratic on that with you, because I know my system will be cheaper, reduce the violence on our streets, and end recidivism as we know it.

But only if we're truly committed. If we truly stop focusing on punishment before all else. If we truly see every man and woman put into prison not as a waste and an expense (or a profit maker), but as an opportunity.

We need a system that identifies good people in prison and rewards them for their efforts. We are watched inside twenty-four hours a day, seven days a week. You seriously think those watchers can't figure out who's made a sincere change and who's doing the work?

We need to get rid of that five-year rule, and all the arbitrary deadlines that keep good people locked up on technicalities, and let everyone who has earned their freedom to achieve their freedom.

People in prison have the potential to achieve great things. I'm not talking about working minimum-wage jobs, although those are important. A hard worker is a positive example and a pillar in a community. I'm talking about entrepreneurs, executives, and artists. I'm saying we can turn prison into a success factory. We have the information, the infrastructure, and the human potential. All we need is the desire.

You think that's the way the system works now? You think my story is proof?

Nah. It's not like that.

They didn't want to reward me. They didn't want me to succeed. They didn't even want to let me out. I'm not talking about the prosecutors, and I'm not talking about the politicians. I'm talking about the people who knew me best: the administrators at Patuxent.

The System

I BELIEVE Judge Serrette gave me twenty-four years for a reason: it made me eligible for parole at twelve years. The Patuxent youth program rules required an evaluation and hearing two years before that eligibility. Prisoners found worthy were given work assignments outside the prison or sent to the halfway house to ease their transition back to society. So I think that's what she wanted: to start moving me toward release.

There was no reason for Patuxent not to accept her judgment. I was in a rehabilitation program. Its purpose was to reform and release inmates, and that is exactly what the program did. At seventeen, a judge deemed me so broken I could never be allowed to walk the face of the earth a free man. I was so terrible, the state was willing to pay an estimated $31,000 a year—about $2 million if I lived an average American male life span—to warehouse me. Ten years later, I was completely changed. I was a model person—not just a model prisoner, but exactly what society wanted out of every citizen—who set a positive example and actively helped those around him. Another judge, with the same authority as the first, deemed me reformed. She ordered me eligible for release. I had done it. *I proved the Patuxent youth program worked.* They should have celebrated. If not, what was the point?

Instead, the administration threw their efforts against me. Governor Glendening was long gone and his "Life means life" decree was no longer official policy, but that poison had sunk deep into the bones of the system. In the 1970s and '80s, between twenty-five and ninety life prisoners a year were paroled by the state. As of September 2017, only four life prisoners have been paroled in Maryland in the twenty years since "Life means life" was uttered in September 1995. Twenty-two years, four paroles—and three were for hospice care.

I wasn't a life prisoner anymore. That didn't matter to the powers at Patuxent. I had been a lifer, so to them, I was always a lifer. This wasn't about justice. Bingo had twenty years. They paroled him, and nobody complained. He beat a fifteen-year-old girl to death with a toilet!

I'm not upset about Bingo. He earned his. What I'm saying is: It wasn't my crime that bothered the administrators. It was my former sentence. They thought if a "Patuxent lifer" got out and committed a crime, it would reflect badly on them. So they held an emergency meeting. They decided to keep me in as long as they could. They even changed their own rules so they were no longer required to give me a hearing for placement in the halfway house, since there was no way, with my record, they could legitimately deny me. In fact, Mr. Mee wouldn't even give me the evaluation that was needed for the hearing.

"It's a waste of time," he said.

"I don't care. I want my evaluation."

"It won't do any good, Chris. The board has already decided."

"Did you speak up for me?" Mr. Mee was the head of therapy. He had power.

"There was nothing I could say, Chris. The director is involved."

I didn't know who the director was—I still don't—but I knew what Mr. Mee's answer meant. "So that's a no, then. You didn't speak up for me."

We had spent a decade building trust. We *liked each other*, even though we came from opposite worlds. All this time, I thought he had my back. Now I wasn't sure. It was Mr. Mee who wanted me to be a mentor. He pushed for our special tier. The evaluation wasn't a big deal for him. It was only paperwork. But to me, it was huge. It was like finding a door, after searching ten years for it—a door everyone insisted didn't exist—and having my trusted companion grab my arm and say, "Don't touch it, Chris. Don't even try. It's locked."

It's like: *Maybe, but you got to let me turn the knob and find out for myself!*

It wasn't even losing work release that bothered me. It was the broken trust. Mr. Mee had encouraged me all those years, but . . . did he actually want me to get out? Or was it all a lie? Did he really just want me to be a docile prisoner?

Everyone knew me in Patuxent. They knew I earned my sentence reduction. They knew I had followed the program since writing my Master Plan in December 1997, a few days before my nineteenth birthday. Heck, I made my own program that was harder than theirs. I'd gotten dozens of inmates to buy into rehabilitation. I wasn't going to commit a crime on the outside. I'd proven that.

So why did they turn on me?

The answer is the system. Once you're in the system, you're no longer a human being to them. It doesn't matter what you do or how many days in a row (more than three thousand in my case) they see you work and follow the rules. You gave up your humanity when they stripped you naked at the door. You were a number now, and the only important rule was this: numbers stay inside.

The last thing they wanted, at Patuxent, was another Chris Wilson. I'm serious about that. They didn't even want *me*.

The other inmates were upset. They were like, "Why you doing this to Chris? Everybody knows he worked harder than anyone."

It wasn't just their treatment of me. Everything was changing. Patuxent had hired a new associate warden and people thought it was her. She had come up through the Department of Corrections, and she didn't like the program. *Too soft. Too many rewards.* She truly was the enemy of everything good in the system, but I don't blame her. She wouldn't have changed the culture at Patuxent so easily if a lot of people in power hadn't agreed.

Steve and I call that period "the memos," because every few days there was another memo telling us what we could no longer do.

Open-tier privileges? Gone. Everyone had to be locked in.

The right to wear our own clothes? Gone. T-shirts or prison issue only. No Positive Delusion of success.

Extra time in school studying? Nope. Security risk.

Punishment became collective. If anyone on a tier did something wrong, the whole tier was punished. The policy was supposed to make us snitch, but it had the opposite effect. Guys said, "Well, that bamma has an illegal phone, I might as well get one, too, since I'm gonna get the same punishment whether I have it or not."

Changing their own rules to thwart me was the last straw. Guys were like, "Wait, now. You been selling us on this idea, be good and get out. Follow the program. Turn your life around. Well, nobody turned their life around more than Chris. And now you're turning on him?"

Guys were saying, "If you do that to Chris, after all he's done, then what you willing to do to me? How can I trust you now?"

It got so bad, the administration pulled me aside. They said I was causing inmate unrest, and if I didn't do something about it, they were going to punish me. I was ten years inside, and I'd never had a single write-up. Of everything I accomplished, to me, that's the most impressive. Even Steve had multiple infractions.

I said, "No offense, but it's not me. It's you."

I was upset. I admit that. I forgot, in the excitement of my sentence reduction, why I didn't want thirty years: Because once you have life, they'll never parole you. They'll keep you in as long as they can. But I wasn't causing problems. I was still working every day, following my Master Plan.

I talked to Keith Showstack. "Patuxent changed the rules to keep me inside," I said. "They're saying it's my fault. I need your help." I wanted him to file motions, lodge protests, tell Judge Serrette.

He said, "I don't know, Chris." He wasn't with Harry Trainor's firm anymore. He was going out on his own. The next time I heard from him, he wanted a thousand dollars up front for his services, but I didn't have the money. I didn't hear from him after that.

Then the state tried to take Darico from me. They had discovered while processing him into the foster system that he wasn't my biological son.

"How long have you known?" I asked Mr. Mee.

"The whole time," he admitted.

The state had tested me when I entered Patuxent and discovered I wasn't a biological match. My mom knew, but she raised Darico anyway. I credit her on that. Mom tried to do right. She had a good heart. What about Mr. Mee, though? He said he kept the secret for my own good. He said he thought it would help Darico and me to have each other.

I told him that was my decision, not his.

"I didn't want you to abandon him," Mr. Mee said, and I think that changed our relationship, his looking down on me like that.

"That kid cried when he saw me," I said. "He rushed to hug me, and he cried, and he called me his dad. I don't care what the tests say, Darico is my son. I'm not going to abandon my son."

I wrote a long letter to the state of Maryland. I told them I didn't care about biology. Darico was my boy. I cared for him when he was a baby. My mother raised him. He had to be with me, because I was the only father he had ever known, and I loved him, and that would never change.

The state found Darico's "real" father in federal prison. He didn't want anything to do with a son he never knew, so they granted my request. Darico's caseworker started bringing him to see me every other week, as promised, and Mr. Mee made sure we had time and space to ourselves. That was special. It was only two hours a month, but it made a difference. There's no better motivation than the love of a child.

It was Steve Edwards, though, who once again turned my attitude around.

The Man in the Cave

THEY TOOK OUR tier. They were busting up the whole incentive program, so of course they had to scatter us and take away the privileges we'd earned. Even old heads like Tooky and Ray-Ray were shuffled around with no respect. Like almost everyone, I ended up with a cellmate for the first time. At least they let me room with Steve, but even that had a downside. I was neat. I scrubbed my toilet every other day. I kept all my worldly possessions in three plastic bins under my bunk. (I had expanded from one—*I was rich!*) I tied my shoes in shower caps to keep off the dust. Cleanliness was part of my discipline.

Steve was messy. He left books and clothing and old newspapers everywhere. It drove me crazy, seeing his *Showboat* magazines, *Wall Street Journal*s, and ramen wrappers scattered all over my home. A man needs his space. Suddenly, Steve was all up in mine.

I couldn't be angry with him, though, because Steve was suffering. He had that forty-five-year sentence hanging over him, and a man can't do forty-five, especially in an environment like "the memos," and come out with his mind.

His family had probably spent $100,000 on lawyers, and other lawyers were helping for free. They were working on a medical appeal. Steve was convinced something physical had gone wrong when he took that brutal beating at fourteen years old. His lawyers had been skeptical. PTSD? Brain trauma? Never heard of it. It took years of effort—that's prison, where things measured in weeks on the outside are measured in years—but now, with the Iraq War, brain trauma was finally being taken seriously.

Columbia University Medical Center had come on board. They were looking into Steve's records, testing him, and doing a full medical analysis of his brain to see if anything physical had led to his paranoia and violent outburst. It was a long shot. All those tests might not prove anything. Even if they did, the state might not care. At best, the process was going to take years.

And Patuxent was crushing him. As part of the new emphasis on "security," they took away the one thing Steve truly cared about: his computer lab. It's one thing to work toward a goal; that feels like progress, even when it's slow. It's another to have your passion taken from you for no reason at all.

Steve fell into a depression. He'd been tutoring for twelve years, but they took that, too. They put him on kitchen duty, breakfast shift, where the odors gave him migraines. Steve had suffered terrible headaches ever since his beating, but these were the worst. There were days he couldn't get out of bed.

He started having nightmares. I'm sure he had them before, everybody in prison does, but now he thrashed in terror. He was on the top bunk. One night, he fell in his sleep and almost knocked himself unconscious on the concrete floor.

I didn't want to leave him. I wanted to be out. I would have walked out in a second if they'd let me. And yet that thought kept coming back: *How can I leave Steve behind?*

I thought about Plato's cave allegory, and all the ways I'd been the man who got out. As a child, I focused on his escape—the possibility of another world. In solitary, I dwelt on the horror, because in the end, the free man was returned to the cave. He had to live with the knowledge of what he had lost.

Then I got out. But I didn't get out. I only got the promise of being out one day. I was still in the cave, just like our man at the end of the story. Every life is lived in a cave, that was Plato's point. We never know the truth, only the shadows.

But there was something I missed the first four times I read the story: The man wasn't recaptured. He wasn't forced to return. He went there of his own free will, to *teach the truth* to those left behind. To tell them the shadows weren't real and there was a better life. All those other characters I thought I was over the years: They were shadows, too. Or maybe they were just steps along my journey. I needed to be the man who shared his knowledge, of his own free will, with the people still in their bonds.

Look around, Steve had said all those years before. *Think of all the good you could be doing for people in here.*

My sentence reduction created an opportunity. *You got life*, inmates had said, laughing, for years. They didn't think I would convince a judge to let me out. They didn't think anyone got out that way. Now they saw, and they believed.

"Tell me about those books, slim," they said. "Tell me how to create a Master Plan."

I had tried to talk to my friend Brian Carter about making a Master Plan for years, but he never embraced it. Now he came up to me, in the humble. "My lawyer asked if I knew a guy named Chris Wilson," he said. "Apparently your story is going around. He told me, 'You want to get paroled, you need to do it like this guy Chris.'"

I thought, *Use it. Don't worry about the extra years. Create a legacy that lasts.*

I expanded my real estate study group to teach the basics of entrepreneurship, like financing, corporate structure, and pricing.

I created a book list so people could read what I'd been reading all those years.

That didn't seem like enough, so I started a self-improvement book club. I still have the flyer. I'm sitting on a stack of books, Photoshopped against a tropical beach at sunset.

I had a lot of commissary credits through my photo business and friends. Steve and I ate well: chicken, tuna, fresh vegetables, and spices. We had enough to share, so I started giving tuna, crackers, stamps, and other supplies to inmates short on commissary.

"What's this for?" they asked, suspicious. You rarely get something for nothing in prison.

"I know you're hungry, that's all. I know you been studying toward your GED. I just wanted to say keep up the good work."

I sent hundreds of letters seeking support for my foreign language program. The University of Maryland sent workbooks and class materials. Linda Moghadam, the head of the sociology department, helped me add classes and solicit materials for the prison school, the prison library, and my other programs. My foreign language program started with eleven inmates. The University of Maryland helped it expand to other prisons. Today, there are more than 250 inmates enrolled.

Ms. Moghadam even helped Bingo get into the university. She looked past his crime, like we all hoped the world would, and saw his potential.

My main project, though, was the career center. For years, I had been frustrated by the lazy, unprepared inmates leaving ahead of me. *I have a plan,* I thought. *I been working. Those guys haven't. They should be letting me outside instead.*

Now I realized that wasn't an injustice, it was a need. Instead of complaining about my situation, I should have been spending my time helping those inmates.

Parole is brutal. Our system is not set up for men and women released from prison to succeed. It's actually set up for them to fail. I'm not sure that's intentional—I think it's the result of a lot of small decisions that piled up over the years—but one thing is certain: society turned its back on its returning citizens long ago. It doesn't want us back. It wants permanent retribution, and it wants to separate us from the ordinary, the normal, and the good. It refuses to consider us citizens, even though it's against the law and the Constitution to continue punishing us once we've served our time. In many places, just like our African American ancestors, we're denied our most basic right as citizens of the United States: the right to vote.

I didn't know that inside. I didn't know how many hurdles the system throws in your way until I hit the streets myself. But I knew starting a life, after years in prison, had to be hard. You're out of touch with the modern world. You have no job experience. You're broke. You're homeless. You're a dung beetle, pushing your giant ball of crap.

I'd been in long enough to see too many young men get out only to end up back inside. Omar, the bamma from first tier, served his five years. He talked all that time about never coming back. But within a few years of being out, he was robbing banks. A job went wrong, and the cops cornered the getaway car. There were four young black men inside. The other three gave themselves up. Omar sat in the backseat, staring straight ahead, while the cops screamed, "Put your hands where we can see them! Put up your hands!"

Omar put the gun in his mouth and pulled the trigger.

"Omar said he wouldn't come back," guys yelled with respect when the story went down the tiers. "He said they couldn't have him, and he meant it, son. Ain't nobody putting the cuffs on Omar!"

They were right. Omar had said it again and again. If I had listened, I would have known he needed help. Omar was getting out, but he didn't have a plan for success. So he was doomed. Omar didn't win like those stupid bammas were yelling. We all lost.

Patuxent already had a career center, but it was nothing but a couple of pamphlets and basic advice. I turned it into a workshop on creating a Master Plan. My friends and I sat with inmates scheduled for release in the next few years and went over their skills and interests. We discussed the kinds of jobs they wanted, and what those jobs required. Did they have the necessary skills? If not, how could they get them inside?

We showed them how to create résumés—which is important, because it tells potential employers who you are. And since you control what's on it, a résumé is a chance to turn your weaknesses, like being in prison, into strengths. For instance, by listing your training.

Most inmates didn't understand. They came in young, with no work experience. They said, "I got an uncle owns a junkyard. He'll hook me up."

I said, "Really? He's been out there working every day, busting it to make his business successful, while you been in here playing cards. And now you think he's going to trust you to run his business? Why would he do that?"

"Because we family."

"He doesn't owe you, slim."

"Say what?"

"We can't get out of here and be a burden on our families, cuz. We can't be expecting our loved ones to take care of us. They been giving this whole time. They come to visit you, right? They send you money for commissary? They been supporting you while you're doing nothing. Now you expect them to just *give* you a job? Nah, it can't be like that."

That made them think. Nobody wants to be a burden on their people.

"So, you like cars?"

"Yeah."

"Well, here's a bunch of jobs you can do with cars."

Here are the requirements. Here's the training you can get inside. Here's how to look good on a résumé. I told them straight up: You can't start working at this once you're out. Don't fool yourself. You have the time and opportunity now. You need to work *now*.

"Now let me ask you another question: *What's your endgame?*"

"How's that?"

"What you want to do with your life? How do you want to be remembered?"

"I dunno."

"Okay, let's say you're eighty years old. You've lived a good life, but now your time is short. Got it? Now look around. What do you see?"

Most didn't have an answer. In their minds, they were forever young and in the streets. But after thinking about it, they knew what they wanted: grandchildren in good schools, a nice house in a quiet neighborhood, a certain car. Most guys were like me with my Corvette: they had a dream car. That's the scale of success young men from the streets can grasp.

I said, "Okay, slim, we see the dream. Now let's figure out, step-by-step, how you can get there. You know what I call it, right? You heard about this? I call it a Master Plan."

Saying Good-bye

EVENTUALLY, THEY LET me out. They had to. Inmates receive credits for service, education, and therapy that lower our sentences, in the same way infractions can lengthen them. For ten years, the prison hadn't even counted my credits. Why bother? There was no way to shorten a life sentence.

When I got my sentence reduced, they were like, "We didn't count them, so you can't get them. Sorry."

I had to threaten a lawsuit before they finally went back over my records. When they did, my maximum imprisonment dropped from twenty-four years to sixteen. So in the late fall of 2010, four full years after my reduction of sentence, Patuxent reluctantly scheduled my transfer to the halfway house for me to serve my last two years before mandatory release.

"I'm going to college," I said when my new therapist, Mr. Fleming, asked my plans. Mr. Mee had retired, in part as a protest against the dismantling of the youth program. "Maybe Towson University. Maybe Johns Hopkins." They were both in Baltimore, where the halfway house was located.

Mr. Fleming's mouth dropped open in astonishment. He was no Mr. Mee, but he was okay, once you acknowledged to his satisfaction he was the smartest guy in the room. "Do you know what kind of people go to Johns Hopkins?" he asked.

I had a college degree. I ran a successful business. I spoke three languages fluently, and I was working on Mandarin Chinese. "I don't know," I said. "Someone like me?"

"No," he said. "Someone like me."

Years later, when my businesses were thriving and receiving public recognition, I received a letter from Mr. Fleming. He noticed I never credited Mr. Mee in any of the articles about my success. "You wouldn't be where you are today without Mr. Mee," he wrote.

Maybe. Mr. Mee did a lot for me, that's true. He met a boy, and he helped me become a man. But he didn't do it *for* me, you know

Finally back with my son (STEPHEN EDWARDS)

what I mean? He was a good person. We made up in those final years. Before he retired, he made sure the caseworker would keep bringing Darico to see me twice a month.

He knew how much that relationship meant for both of us. In the end, though, Mr. Mee was doing his job.

The people who truly cared about me, who taught me and encouraged me and loved me like a brother, were my friends inside. I wouldn't be who I am today without them, especially Steve and Tooky. We are the heroes of our own story. It was being there for one another—not for a job, not for money, not for credit—that changed our lives. I had always wanted a family. Well, I found one.

So it was hard to say good-bye to Tooky. We tried to be cool, just a dap and a hug, but we had tears in our eyes. I didn't know if I'd see him again. I had overheard an intern ask Mr. Mee why Tooky wasn't getting his sentence reduced, too. After all, Tooky deserved a second chance as much as I did.

Mr. Mee shook his head. "Tooky may never get out. He killed a real person."

That's a sick phrase, but I knew what he meant. Tooky killed someone who was going to college or had a job; someone society thought had a future. Tooky was fifteen at the time. I heard it happened at a McDonald's, or maybe a KFC. Tooky never talked about it, but fast food was always mentioned in rumors about his crime.

I don't know if what Mr. Mee said was true. Judge Serrette says who you killed doesn't factor into a judge's deliberations, but that's impossible to believe. The system is weighted. Some lives, in our society, are worth more than others.

What's sad is that Tooky believed it. He didn't like it. I saw his pain the night I got my sentence reduced, when he was too depressed to come out of his cell. He wanted to be free, but he believed he was done. Patuxent was his life. Maybe accepting that was the only way to keep him from losing his mind.

"Don't worry about me, Chris," Tooky said. "I'm living through you now. Go out and do your thing, because all of us in here, we're gonna be watching."

It was different with Steve. This was my other half. We had spent thousands of hours in our shared cell, talking about life. I sat with him when he suffered migraines. I focused his mind on the good things: Chicken wraps. Business books and magazines. Coffee. The first Obama campaign in full swing that year, and the crazy possibility a black man could run this world.

Things were looking up for Steve. He sued the prison over his computer lab. They made a big show of resisting, but they gave it back. None of the COs and therapists had wanted to take it from him in the first place. Why would they? They loved Steve.

Even better, the medical researchers had found serious issues with his tests and treatment in the hospital. Steve didn't like to talk about it, because he was paranoid, but his lawyers were saying his case was huge. It could redefine, they said, how the entire legal system dealt with brain trauma, especially in teens.

Still, it was tough to leave him behind. I wanted to tell him that. I wanted to tell him how much his example and friendship meant to me. But Steve wouldn't let me. He drilled me. "You got your Master Plan? You got your résumé? You need anything, call my parents. You got their number."

"Yes, Mom," I said, laughing.

We had trained for this day, we bled together, but now I was going into battle alone. He wanted to make sure I had every weapon and the courage to use them. Or maybe he was just avoiding his emotions. Steve was not an emotional guy. He didn't let down his guard. So finally, I had to hug him, just to shut him up.

"You're coming out right behind," I said.

He pulled back. I could see it in his eyes: he wasn't sure. But I knew. On that, I had faith like a mountain.

"This ain't over," I said. "You're coming out, Steve. And you're coming out soon."

Fifteen minutes later, I was in the transport van, crossing under the razor wire. I was staring at my hands, lifting them over my head, moving them around. I wasn't chained. I was in the van, and my hands weren't chained. It was the weirdest, most wonderful feeling of my life. I thought, *I'll never be chained again.*

But I couldn't forget what Dr. Carter, the grandmotherly African American therapist I had known for years, had just said. They were the last words spoken to me as I walked out of Patuxent, and they will stick with me forever:

"Be good out there, Inmate Wilson," she said. "Always remember, you are the property of the state of Maryland."

Halfway

THE PATUXENT HALFWAY house was an old Jewish orphanage a few blocks southeast of downtown Baltimore. It sat on a busy corner in a densely packed section of town; three floors of small rooms with metal mesh over the windows. It wasn't prison. We were locked in, but we could leave on a prearranged schedule to work or attend class. We couldn't have a social life—no dates, no meals out, no riding around—but at night, I could look out the window and see people walking by, cars driving past, free lives being lived. The only indication this wasn't a regular building were the security cameras and the signs: STATE PROPERTY, TRESPASSERS WILL BE PROSECUTED.

I was ready to get that prize. Erick Wright offered a "get out" present when he heard I was finally being moved to the halfway house, so I asked for a suit. It was a major request, but he didn't hesitate. Geronimo took my measurements—he worked in the prison laundry and made clothes from scraps—and Erick had an off-the-rack suit tailored to fit. I'm sure it was expensive. Over the years, Erick had bought me food and clothes, especially shoes. He sent me CDs and books. It probably cost him more than a thousand dollars all told, but

Erick never sweated how much he spent. He never asked me to pay him back or to do him a favor when I got out. He had a wife and young children; he didn't have to give so much. But he did, and it meant more than money. It meant friendship. It meant faith.

Thanks to Erick, when I stepped out of the halfway house for the first time, I felt successful and confident, because I looked like the Chris Wilson I wanted to be: an entrepreneur.

We were given a special-meal request when we arrived. I asked to go to a nice steakhouse, the Capital Grille. Mr. and Mrs. Edwards offered to pay for it. The halfway house staff said, "That's too nice for you."

Instead, they walked the four new residents eight blocks to Lexington Market. The market was a maze of ratchet plywood food stalls in the middle of an open-air drug bazaar. People were panhandling and drinking out of bags. Old women were nodding out. Men were slouched, with that glassy-eyed stare. It was filthy. Trash and vomit on the ground. Garbage cans overflowing. And there I was in my suit, walking with pride.

I looked so good, prostitutes were calling, "Hey, baby, what you looking for?"

I smiled. "I'm all right, thank you. Have a nice day."

The famous restaurant at the Lexington Market is Faidley's, best crab cakes in Baltimore. But I walked right through to the food stalls. I knew what I wanted: a cheesesteak.

You know what it's like to eat a cheesesteak, in a suit, on the street, after fourteen years of prison food? Listening to that meat sizzle on the griddle. And that melted cheese spilling out the side. Steaming hot peppers and onions burning my mouth. I stood at the food stall and inhaled that sandwich. I thought, *I can do this now. I can do this every day.*

Soon after, I sat down with my caseworker, who was responsible for overseeing my life. I told her about my Master Plan. "I'm going to college. I'm going to start a business and be a social entrepreneur."

She shook her head.

I can't remember her exact words, only that she dismissed my Master Plan. "You're a convict," she said. She used that word as an insult. "You got to lower your standards. You can get a job at a gas station. Maybe. If you're lucky."

That wasn't a good sign, but I thought, *That's okay, Chris. She don't know you. You just have to show her by doing the work.*

Grinding Again

JOHNS HOPKINS COST $30,000 a year. I guess Mr. Fleming was right: it wasn't for people like me. So instead, I walked to the University of Baltimore, less than a mile from the halfway house, in my best (yeah, only) suit. I had an appointment with the dean of student affairs, Kathy Anderson.

"Hello," I said. "I'm Chris Wilson." Firm handshake. Nice smile. Just like I'd learned in my communication and business books.

She motioned me to a seat, and I told her my story. "I was incarcerated for fourteen years, since I was seventeen years old. I've been working all that time." I showed her my résumé. "I'm living in the halfway house, serving the last two years of my sentence, but I have a Master Plan. I want to be a social entrepreneur and start a company that helps people from poor neighborhoods. The next step is a BA in community studies and civic engagement from your institution."

I didn't have to do it like that. I had already been admitted for the spring 2011 semester. Brian Carter, who Master Planned his way to the halfway house soon after me, had also been accepted. The University of

Baltimore catered to part-time students, primarily working people. There weren't many ex-inmates, but the school was used to students taking different paths to an education.

But I wanted Dean Anderson to know me. That's something I learned in my studies. Sit down, spend the time. Create a personal relationship with the people in power.

"What do you need?" Dean Anderson asked.

"I don't want anyone to know about my past," I said. "Do you mind if we keep that a secret? I want to be treated like any other student."

"Absolutely," she said. She smiled and shook my hand. I could tell not many students came and talked to her.

"You'll fail out," my caseworker had said, but I proved her wrong. I received top grades on my first few papers and tests. I thought that would impress her, but she proved *me* wrong, too. At that time, I was allowed six hours a day out of the house, Monday through Thursday, but I wasn't allowed to leave campus. So I went to class, organized study sessions, talked to women. It was incredible, walking up to a woman and introducing myself, even if I couldn't date her. Talking, making women laugh, watching them smile—it was a dream. Brian Carter got himself a girlfriend, but I was freelancing. I spent my extra time in the library. I would have studied there all night if they let me. I was used to studying ten, twelve straight hours. I'd been doing it for years.

My caseworker cut my time to four hours, so I could no longer attend after-class study sessions and professor events in the evening. "See how well you do now," she said.

When I still aced my tests, she took away one of my three special eight-hour "home visit" passes. I guess she didn't know I had no family to use them with.

Occasionally, I had lunch with Darico in the student center. He was thirteen, and he had an attitude, like he didn't care anymore about hanging with me. Half the time, he didn't show. I tried to talk options. *What's your passion, son? What's your endgame?* But it was hard to be a father when I was on a schedule, and I couldn't visit him in his neighborhood, I had to rely on him coming to me.

Don't lose focus, Chris, I told myself. *Master Plan.*

Life in the house was rough. Guards were belligerent. The rules were strict. Meals came from the prison cafeteria, and my bag was often smashed. I swear I smelled piss on my food more than once. I knew some of the COs, because the halfway house was a shift for Patuxent guards. When I asked about the treatment, they looked away. "Sorry, Chris. I can't do nothing."

They searched my room multiple times, tore up my stuff and tossed my belongings on the floor. I had a bottle of Joop, my favorite cologne. The guards confiscated it. I said, "Come on, that's expensive. My parents— My friend's parents gave it to me."

"No glass allowed."

"Everybody else has glass." It was true. Guys on my hall had bottles sitting right out on their windowsills, and those same guards walked right past them.

"Sorry, Chris. It's orders."

The worst part: My caseworker was also my therapist. I had to sit with her a couple times a week and discuss my progress. I tried to tell her about my work and my goals, but she had a message for me, and she hammered it over and over: *You have to give up your dreams. You're a convict. You have to accept that you are at the bottom of society, and you always will be.*

That stirred something in me. One word is *anger*, but the better word, I think, is *determination*. I thought, *I'm not a convict. I served*

my time. I'm a returning citizen of the United States of America, and
once I'm out, I have the same rights as everybody else.

The Edwardses wanted to take me to Nordstrom's for a second suit, since I was wearing the one Erick bought me almost every day.

"You can't go to Nordstrom's," my caseworker said.

"Why?"

"That store's too nice for someone like you."

"It's a gift."

"Doesn't matter. I'm not giving you a pass."

She was baiting me. She wanted me to lash out. They'd gotten Brian Carter after only a few weeks. They sent him back to Patuxent because he had a letter from his brother in his room. "You broke the rules," they said. "You can't communicate with people who are incarcerated."

The letter came through the halfway house mail. The guard on duty had inspected it and given it to Brian the previous night. The letter was an excuse. They hated Brian because he wasn't broken. He had ambition, he dressed nice, so they wanted to knock him down. I knew if I gave them a reason—any reason—they'd do the same to me.

But I couldn't go on like this. Not for two years, with no friends for support, no outlet for my frustration, and the people with complete power over my life determined to tear me down. I wasn't sleeping. I was losing focus on my Master Plan. So I reached out through contacts to the only person I could think of, Mr. Mee. I asked if he would come back and be my therapist. He was retired, but he was a good dude. In the end, I realized, he cared about us. He agreed to help.

My caseworker was pissed. The halfway house denied the request, and she came after me in therapy, taunting me for reaching out, for thinking I was too good for her, as she put it.

I did what I had to do. I kept my head down (but not bowed) and threw myself into my studies. I visited Dean Anderson. I talked with professors after class. I locked myself in my room and crushed my schoolwork. It was a battle, but it was one I knew how to win.

After several months, I was granted a pass to stay overnight with Erick. It took a long time to set up, with all the rules and conditions, but after nearly ten years as friends, I finally saw Erick's life: nice house on a quiet street, nice car, his daughter's pink and purple bicycle in the driveway. It was real, you know. Everything a man needed to be happy. It was possible. Erick had it.

He kept an eye on Mom. After my sentence reduction, he reached out to her. She was living on the streets. It took a while for Erick to convince her to come see me, but in 2008, he drove her to Patuxent. It was sad. Mom looked sick. She seemed confused. It had been two years since I'd seen her across the courtroom at Darico's custody hearing, but it felt like she'd aged twenty.

I reached across the table and held her hands. They were rough, but warm. "I'm getting out of here, Mom. You understand that, right?" I looked her in the eye.

She looked back at me, nodding. "You're coming home."

She wrote me five letters after that. She addressed them to "Wonder," her new nickname for me, because of my impossible sentence reduction. Each one started out hopeful, but soon it became how poor she was, how abandoned she felt, how none of her children talked to her. She had plans for me to get money, like from my father's social security.

I never wrote her back. I didn't know what to say to her in that state. But I kept those letters in a special place in my blue plastic bin.

I read them so often, they almost tore through. I studied those letters, because my mom was in there somewhere, between the complaints and the hunger, and I was going to find her, the mom I used to know.

Erick set up a phone call. That's why I went to his house that weekend, to talk to Mom. She was living in Georgia with my youngest brother, Korey. He was starting kindergarten when I went to prison. Now he was nineteen, married, with a baby girl.

"How'd you get out, Chris?" That was the first thing Mom said to me. "Did you escape?" She had forgotten my sentence reduction.

She said she wanted to live with me. I told her that was impossible. "I'm in a halfway house, Mom." She didn't understand. She had a fantasy I was going to take her in and take care of her. We would be mother and son again.

"I love you," she said.

Now, I love my mother. I have always loved my mother. I have a photo of her on my desk right now, the only framed photograph in my house. But I wasn't ready to say that to her. I had love for her, but I had too much hurt to let it out just yet.

"I love you, Chris," she said again.

"Okay," I said. "I'll talk to you soon, Mom."

"Okay, son. Good-bye."

What was I supposed to say? My family had abandoned me. My mother had written me off and stuck to that for thirteen years. Now that I was getting out, we're supposed to flip the switch? We're going to live together, take care of each other, be a family. How's that going to work? I'm *the property of the state of Maryland*, Mom. I don't even have a home.

Erick dropped me at the halfway house on Sunday morning. I wish I remembered more about the weekend. I'm sure we had good times. But that phone call with Mom, my disappointment as well as my hope, was the only thing on my mind.

I was barely back in my room when the CO stepped up. "Wilson. Phone call."

We weren't allowed calls except under strict conditions and at specific times. This wasn't one of those times.

I trudged to the public phone. I could feel the staff watching. "Hello?"

It was Erick. "Ah, Chris, I got bad news. It's your mother. She passed away last night."

I talked to my sister. "Mom had a heart attack in her sleep," Leslie said, and it felt . . . unfair. So unfair. It was cruel for God to take her, just when we were so close to being together again.

Korey called a few hours later. "It wasn't a heart attack," he said. "Mom overdosed on pills." My baby brother was shook; I could hear him crying.

"It's okay," I told him. "She's okay now."

"It's not okay, Chris," he said. "She left a note. Mom committed suicide."

Crying All My Tears

"IT'S YOUR FAULT," my caseworker told me.

Really, that's what she said. My caseworker crushed me over Mom's death. She said I was an embarrassment. I was a burden. She said, *Imagine how hard it must have been to live with the shame of a son like you.* And even though I could see she was trying to break me, it hurt. I'm glad she didn't know about the phone call. How I turned my mother away when she said she loved me. How she ended her life that night.

I have trouble living with that, even today.

But I wouldn't break. So my caseworker denied me a day pass to attend my mother's funeral. Right up to the day, she told me I couldn't go. Finally, at the last minute, she granted me a short-term pass. The funeral was in DC. The pass wasn't long enough for me to stay for the burial or the family gathering afterward, but I would be there for my mother's final viewing.

I slipped into the back of the church as the service was starting. The place was full of people I was related to, who I grew up around, who loved my mother—strangers to me now.

My four siblings were up front with the coffin. My sister did most of the talking. At one point, she said, "Her son Chris couldn't be here today."

"I'm here," I shouted, and before I knew it, I was walking down the aisle to sit up front. People were looking at me like they had seen a ghost.

"I thought they gave him life," I heard someone whisper.

The pastor invited the immediate family to come up and view the body for the last time, but I didn't move. I had heard stories of how bad she looked. I wanted to remember the beautiful woman who had sat with me, helped me write love notes to girls, and sang along to James Brown.

"What's wrong, Chris?" my sister asked.

"I don't want to see her like this," I said. "I can't take it, Leslie."

My heart was pounding, but my sister, like always, told me what I needed to hear. "Yes you can, Chris. You'll find the strength."

She grabbed my hand. She led me up to join my family at the coffin. But my mother wasn't inside. It had taken my family five days to raise the money to transport her body back from Georgia. That emaciated woman wasn't my mom.

Why'd they have an open casket? Why'd I have to see her like that?

The pain that surged through my body is almost indescribable. Tears poured out of my eyes and onto my suit. Memories of Mom flashed in my mind. How she used to kiss on me when I was young. How she would ask me how she looked in a new outfit, when she still had pride in herself.

My sister read from the suicide note. She called it a journal, because we were covering the truth. The reading was meant to assure us her pain was over, that Charlene "Mona Lisa" Harvey was in a better place. It didn't work.

Dearest Christopher . . . I am so happy you are home. . . . You can do it Chris, you know you can . . . Please continue to grow. I don't know what you imagine of me. I know it's not good . . . But I am still your mother regardless of the pain. I did my best Chris . . . I'm just lonely. I am in pain. Don't regret your life Chris, especially because of me. I don't want to go away from you or Korey or Derrick, Leslie or Kenny. It's just . . . a lot of things happened to me that you don't know about . . . and I cannot make up lost time.

Mom was hurting so much, and for so long. She had lost the love of her children, or so she thought. She had lost her self-respect. Her husband died of an overdose, and she blamed herself. She was alone. That's what the note kept coming back to. She had nothing and nobody left. It was terrible, this life she'd fallen into while I was away. It brought tears to my eyes, thinking about that pain.

Everyone was crying, even Leslie, trying to read. Everyone but Grandma. She was in the front row, sitting stiffly and staring straight ahead. She'd cried all her tears.

I confronted my sister outside. "Why didn't you help her, Leslie? You could have put her into a drug treatment program! You could have got her into therapy!" My hurt was so strong, it had turned to anger. "That's our mother, Leslie. You let her die!"

"You don't understand, Chris," Leslie said. "I helped her so many times. We all did. We took her in. We paid for so much. If you had been here, you would understand. I did everything I could, but Mom couldn't be helped. This isn't the first time she overdosed or tried to kill herself, Chris. We took her to the emergency room, thinking she was dead, so many times."

If you had been here, you would understand.

No. If I had been here, Mom wouldn't have died. I'd have taken care of her.

"You abandoned her, Leslie." *Just like you abandoned me.*

"No, Chris," she said sadly. "Mom abandoned us."

My caseworker said I had to talk about my feelings. I had to open up for my own good. I wasn't going to open up to her. I knew she would use my feelings against me.

"I want to talk to Mr. Mee," I said. When he heard about my mother's death, Mr. Mee had volunteered to come to the halfway house to talk to me.

"You'll talk only to me," she said. "It's a mandatory part of your treatment."

I didn't talk to her. I couldn't, even though I was falling apart. I was having terrible dreams. I would be sitting in class and realize tears were streaming down my face. All I could do was put my head down. I always thought we'd make up with each other. I thought we'd have years. I needed to be Mom's son again, not the kid she wished had never been born. I was different now. I was a good son. But Mom never knew that because she died on the day of our second conversation in thirteen years.

It was the darkest time of my life. I was half free and fully alone. Steve Edwards was gone. Brian Carter was gone. Tooky was gone. All my friends were in Patuxent, and I wasn't allowed to contact them. The only thing keeping me sane was Narcotics Anonymous. Attendance was required, but because of rules about where I was allowed to go, I was forced to take three city buses to a meeting way out in the suburbs.

Those men and women saved my life. They weren't like me, but they knew addiction. When I told them about my mother, they understood. When she died, they took me in. It was all love. I belonged.

I don't think I've ever talked like that in a therapy session, but once I started, it came out. For weeks, NA was my safe place.

Finally, I went to Dean Anderson and explained the situation because I was falling behind. "I can't focus on my work," I told her. "I try, but I'm too messed up."

"You need to talk to your professors," she said. "You need to tell them everything."

I was nervous, but I did it. I told my professors the truth. I was a prisoner. I lived in a halfway house. My mother died. I was depressed and alone.

They were, every one of them, surprised. They never suspected my background—which, given how our society thinks, was a compliment. I thought they might look at me differently, even hate or distrust me. If they knew my charge—murder—they might have. But every single professor was supportive. They told me not to worry. They knew I could do the work because I had excelled for two months, and they would help me.

I'm glad I did it. I'm glad I was open with Dean Anderson at the start so I had someone to confide in when things went wrong. I'm glad I was honest with my professors. It made a difference, because a few days after speaking with them, I was cuffed, stuffed in a transport van, and transferred back to Patuxent on the recommendation of my caseworker. It happened so suddenly, I never had a chance to tell the college. As far as they knew, I simply disappeared.

Revenge

THEY DIDN'T SEND me back to the Patuxent youth program. They sent me "behind the red door" to the mental health ward. This was the tier where I had seen men strapped to their bunks and an inmate eating his own arm.

"What you doing, picture man?" the naked inmate said. "You got my pictures?"

"No. Sorry. Not this time."

It was a terrible place. Just the flies, man. And the roaches. I could hear them crawling, even when I closed my eyes. I could hear my fellow inmates, lost in their delusions. They screamed all day, every day. I could smell them, because they crapped all over their cells. They burned their mattresses. I don't know how they got the matches. They pissed through the slots in their doors. It was the place for lost souls. Besides meal delivery, the only person who ever came on my tier was the man who cleaned the hallway every three days. He wore a full-body hazmat suit, in case he was bombarded with feces and piss.

I was isolated, cut off from the rest of the prison, where my friends were still walking their rounds and doing their work. I had nothing, because the halfway house had boxed all my possessions and mailed them to Erick's house (which I used as my home address) when they sent me back. There was another inmate sent back from the halfway house next door to me, Big Danny. The halfway house had thirty beds, but when I was there, there were only eleven inmates. By later that year, the number dropped to two.

"They got Osama bin Laden," Big Danny yelled. He had a small TV in his cell. "They killed that motherfucker, yo!"

"Did anybody see a body?" I said. "I'm not believing it until I see a body."

They sent Danny away soon after, but I knew enough people at Patuxent to get word to Steve I was back inside. He bought the essentials: coffee, a hot pot to warm the water, and paper. Sympathetic COs smuggled them to me.

I was in the middle of a course on civil rights when they sent me back. Steve was able to get his hands on two of the assigned books: *Parting the Waters* by Taylor Branch and Martin Luther King Jr.'s *Letter from Birmingham Jail.*

It was a lucky break that, at the worst moment of my incarceration, I could take comfort in the wisdom of that great man, when he referenced a higher justice and asked his fellow clergymen not to condemn him for his civil disobedience, but to help. When he refrained from being angry and calmly said, as Steve had said to me so many times over the years, "Let's do the work."

I pulled the sheet off my bunk, sat on the floor, and wrapped it around my body like a cocoon. That's how I read, because it was the only way to keep off the flies. I wrote a term paper in that cocoon, in pencil, scrawling on the front and back and all the way to the edges because I had a limited supply of paper. I could feel the roaches crawling. I could see their shadows when they scurried across me, because the overhead light shone through the sheet. I kept my head down for days—I even slept in that cocoon—and did the work. I wasn't going to pass that class, obviously. I couldn't even turn in my paper. But that didn't matter. What mattered was the work. I didn't realize until later how much that experience was like my childhood in Lincoln Heights, when I wrapped myself in blankets and read books on the floor because I was too scared of stray bullets to sleep in the bed.

Steve tried to get COs and counselors to visit me. He begged Dr. Carter, the woman who declared me the property of the state of Maryland, to talk with me. She came, but it took weeks. She kept telling Steve she couldn't do it, it was against the rules, she couldn't break the rules.

My first visitor was my caseworker. I don't know how long I'd been on the mental health tier, because those conditions distort your sense of time. I'm guessing two weeks. She came to gloat, that was my impression. She seemed pleased with how things had turned out.

I said, "I'm going to get out of here one day."

She stepped back. "Are you threatening me?" Oh, yeah, she wanted me to threaten her.

"No," I said. "Listen up now. I'm getting out of here one day, and I'm gonna be successful. I'm gonna be more successful than you. And that's gonna be my revenge."

Home

THEY TRANSFERRED ME to the Eastern Correctional Institution (ECI), a maximum-security facility two hours away on the Maryland shore, to serve out the last thirteen months of my sentence. ECI was a rough prison. It was in the boondocks, and it was black and Latino gangs versus hard-hitting white COs. There was no school, therapy, or vocational training. Rape, violence, and murder were the constants of life at ECI, and the gangs ran the place. You couldn't even get in the weight pit to work out because the gangs blocked off all the time for themselves. For the first time in my long history of incarceration, I didn't know a soul.

I kept my head down. I didn't make any friends, and I barely spoke. I didn't even bother to shave, so I finally grew that big-ass beard. What did it matter? The prison was so far from the city nobody visited me, not even my son.

My first day in the yard, I put on my headphones, laced up my rubber prison-issue sneakers, and ran. I ran as fast as I could for the entire hour. The yard was small, about the size of a baseball field, and it was crowded. Inmates glared at me, wondering who the hell I was. Rocks stabbed my feet through the thin bottoms of my shoes. I didn't stop. I must have circled the yard twenty-five times. By the end, my body was hurting. My shoes were bloody from the torn blisters all over my feet. Didn't matter. A man can endure anything when he sees freedom ahead. Especially when he lived ten years without that promise at all.

In the end, I was paroled. I had a hearing. The board looked at my record and said they didn't understand why I was still inside. By then, I had only two months left on my sentence, so the prison slow-rolled the paperwork and kept me in until my mandatory release date.

May 11, 2012. That was the day they rolled up the door at the DOC processing center and released me into downtown Baltimore. I had a white T-shirt, state-issued blue jeans with no pockets, a notebook, and $50 in cash that the state gave every released inmate to start a new life. I was a free man after sixteen years, but I had no family, no home, no job, and no immediate prospects. No one was there to pick me up. Erick Wright was supposed to be waiting, but I wasn't allowed to contact anyone during my three days of processing, and he somehow missed the when and where.

So I walked to the only place I knew, the University of Baltimore. Halfway there, it started to rain. I walked fifteen minutes without an umbrella, arriving unannounced and wet at Dean Anderson's office. I wasn't sure she'd recognize me. It had been almost two years. I hadn't told her I was leaving. I hadn't been able to contact her from inside. But I could tell immediately she knew who I was.

"I'm out," I told her, "and I still have my Master Plan."

She came around the desk and hugged me. "Welcome home."

PART 5

From Plan to Action

It is the task of the enlightened not only to ascend to
learning and to see the good but to be willing to descend
again to those prisoners and to share their troubles
and their honors, whether they are worth having
or not. And this they must do, even with
the prospect of death.

—PLATO, "THE ALLEGORY OF THE CAVE"

Get Out of Prison

PRISON STRIPS YOU down to the essentials; the release system steals everything else. When you come out of prison in the United States, you have nothing of your own. No money beyond the $50 they hand you in an envelope. No possessions except four outfits (the maximum) and a few personal items. No job. You're not allowed to contact anyone inside, so you're completely cut off from your friends and mentors. There are no therapy sessions. No training programs. No services. Maybe a few little things, like a dusty, outdated job center, but no bed, no food, no shelter, and no support.

The system provides you with three things:

1) A criminal record;

2) A parole officer; and

3) A bill for your freedom. In Maryland that includes $100 a month for parole and probation fees (called restitution) and/or (depending on the county) $40 a pop for two mandatory drug tests a week. Two a week! That can run $400 a month. I was lucky. My judge waived my parole and

testing fees. I assumed I was home free, until my PO told
me I still owed the state $4,400 for *supervision*, payable
at $50 a month.

Charities help, but not nearly enough. Fee waivers like mine are
inadequate and far too rare. For the most part, society throws returning citizens back on the families and communities they came from.
This is disastrous, since those families and communities are often
poor. They can't afford thousands of dollars in fees and drug tests.
Like the exorbitant price of prison phone calls, the system is a vac-
uum, designed to suck money out of the pockets of the people struggling the most.

And that's *if* returning citizens have people to stand with them.
Of the four strangers released with me on May 11, 2012, only one
had a ride. The rest of us walked away alone. Our $50 wouldn't rent
a room for two days, much less an apartment—even if landlords
rented to people with no credit, no rental history, no collateral, and a
criminal conviction, which (spoiler alert) they won't.

It's illegal to discriminate against a person in housing . . . unless
they have a criminal record. Then it's encouraged. Most public-
assistance housing complexes, where the rules are set by the government, no longer allow convicted felons on the premises. That means
the poorest returning citizen, saddled with parole expenses and no
job, can't move back with his own mother without risking her eviction. In some buildings, he can't stay even one night. Often, he can't
move in with his wife or girlfriend, either.

Other countries understand the math: $1 spent making sure a
returning citizen finds a good situation is worth $10 later when we
don't have to warehouse him in prison.

In America, we don't even care about the money. We don't like returning citizens, period. We don't believe in redemption. We don't want so-called ex-cons to vote. We don't want them to have good jobs. We don't want them to succeed, because if they succeed that means *they aren't being punished enough.*

So we set up systems to make success hard, then blame them for their failure. We push them back to prison in hundreds of small but significant ways, then claim data shows returning citizens are "career criminals" and use that claim to make the system even worse.

I know men and women in Baltimore who sell drugs to pay their parole expenses. These are good people who want straight lives, but they can't get out from under their debt to the state of Maryland. So they sell a little to keep ahead of their obligations. Then they get caught, and they go back to prison on long sentences as repeat offenders. How does that help anyone?

I'm not trying to be naive. In my experience, 30 percent of the men and women in prison aren't ready to change. They're dangerous. But 70 percent of released prisoners return to prison within five years. That's 40 percent pushed back into incarceration by a system so broken that it hurts every American, and not just because punishment instead of rehabilitation creates more (and more violent) criminals. The cost of housing our massive prison population, after all, was estimated by the Vera Institute of Justice in 2010 to be $39 billion—*every year.*

So how did I make it? How did I go from homeless and broke at thirty-three to a respected and successful businessman by thirty-six?

The first step was finding a good living arrangement. One family member actually offered to take me in: my grandmother. She was almost ninety, but she was still in her house on Division Avenue, with the same rocker on the front porch covered in plastic and Big Daddy's chair in front of the television, his fraternity cap hanging from the corner of it just like he'd left it almost twenty years earlier.

She said, "Stay here, Chris. The neighborhood's better now."

I could see that on my first visit. The junkies were off the corner; a charter school was being built over the field where my elementary school track team used to run; and the city was closing the Lincoln Heights House, although the buildings still loomed half empty across the alley where Eric had died.

But I turned down her offer. I couldn't live there. It violated the number one rule of staying out of prison: *Don't go back to the people and places that got you in trouble.*

How serious was I about that rule? A month after getting out, I walked into a TGI Friday's and heard, "Yo, Wilson." It was two returning citizens from Patuxent. So I went over, bumped hands. "What up, slim? Good to see you home. Sorry I can't stay." And I walked out. I didn't even get food. Those guys were fine, we didn't have beef, but

With Erick Wright

they were bammas. And if bammas were hanging at Friday's, it wasn't the place for me. That's how serious I was about avoiding bad influences and situations.

I couldn't stay with the Edwardses, either. In fact, I never even asked. Their house was too far from Baltimore, where I wanted to be, and there was no access to public transportation.

So Erick Wright took me in. He barely knew me before Patuxent. He was my sister's six-month boyfriend from seventeen years earlier! And yet he put himself out for a man in need. He let me sleep on a sofa in the basement, and I'll be honest, it wasn't fancy, but it was the nicest place I'd laid my head since the cop started beating my mother into a shell of her former self.

With that settled, I started grinding. I was up early every morning, working out: push-ups, sit-ups, jogging, dips. I cleaned the house and mowed the yard. Erick and his wife didn't ask for that, but I wanted to give them something. Then I convinced a few of Erick's neighbors to let me mow their lawns. They were a little embarrassed to hand me $30 cash, like that wasn't much for a grown man's labor, but I was like, *I been working for $1.35 an hour for sixteen years. This is as much as I made in a month!*

I wasn't one of those returning citizens who comes out and is amazed by everyday things. Oh my God, *pizza!* Oh my God, *flat-screen TVs!* I knew about smartphones because guys smuggled them into Patuxent. Steve worked on modern computer equipment in his lab. I used Rosetta Stone software to learn languages. But I admit, I was amazed by one thing—the Internet. I mean, with the Internet, I could find out anything *in seconds!* In Patuxent, I had to give my questions to a librarian, she'd do the research and, three or four days later, give me a printed sheet of information.

So I stayed up most nights researching on Erick's computer. How do I get an EBT card? Type the question into Google and, *bam.* Here's the information to bring and the address of the nearest office. Within days, I was getting $200 a month in food stamps. I spent

$100 on myself—about $3 a meal, but I knew how to stretch a dollar—and gave the other half to Erick.

How do I take a bus from the northern DC suburbs to my parole officer in Baltimore? *Bam*. Here's the route map and schedules.

I found out on the Internet that people in Erick's area were charging $150 to create your résumé. I'd been doing that for six years for free. So I made business cards offering résumés for $100 and gave them to everyone I met. I made a thousand dollars on that business, just working at night and on weekends.

I had to go to Baltimore twice a week for drug testing and to meet with my parole officer. Most returning citizens hate their PO, because the PO is a symbol of the system. I definitely hated that it took three buses and two hours to get there, but I embraced that relationship as an opportunity to prove myself. I dressed in my suit. I was always on time. I was polite, even when she said I owed her $4,400. I told her about my Master Plan. The first few meetings, she was hard, like my caseworker at the halfway house, but she warmed up pretty quick. When you're putting in the effort, most people appreciate it.

She cut my mandatory drug testing since I was clean. She got me a few job interviews. After I explained our relationship, she granted me permission to talk with Steve, even though contact with prisoners wasn't allowed. I got a message to him through his parents, and Steve started calling me every Sunday at 1:00 p.m. during his break in the dayroom. No matter where I was or what I was doing, I answered that call. I knew how important a call like that was inside. And hearing from Steve—hearing his voice, asking his advice—kept me strong.

Steve's parents were there for me, too. They took me to dinner once a week, and they bought me basic things like clothes and cologne (I love my Joop). They took me to a baseball game and gave me calling cards for my prepaid phone. I called Mr. Edwards twice a week for advice and inspiration. He told Bible parables, like the story of Job, who lost his family, his money, his land, and his freedom, but kept his faith in God. Job was rewarded in the end. "It will happen for you, Chris," Mr. Edwards told me. "God's not through with you yet."

I tried to move out of Erick's house. I spent a night with my cousin. I lived with Steve's brother in DC for a week. I called my aunt, who had a five-bedroom house in the DC suburbs, and asked if I could stay with her for a while. She laughed in my face. "I can't have someone like you around here," she said, then hung up.

Finally, Erick sat me down. "What's up, Chris? Why you looking for another place?"

Fact was, I was embarrassed. I was in my thirties, sleeping on his sofa rent-free, and it was humiliating. I remember the night Erick's family ordered Chinese takeout. I looked at the menu, and the chicken was $12. It had been $2 back in the day on Division Avenue.

"I'm not hungry," I said.

Erick's wife looked at me. "You're our guest, Chris. Get anything you want."

"No, I can't."

"Well," she said, "then I'm ordering for you. You like shrimp?"

They were so nice. They never asked for anything. They had the greatest kids. Their son, who was in the second grade, even started wearing a tie to school because he said he wanted to be like me. He thought of Chris Wilson as a guy in a suit! How cool is that?

But the nicer they were, the more I felt like a burden. And that was one thing I promised myself in prison: to never again be a burden on anyone.

"You're not a burden," Erick told me. "Camille and I want to do this, Chris. I mean that. You're a good dude. We want you to stay here as long as you need."

It was hard to accept their charity. I'm proud. But it's a good thing I did. I thought it would be three weeks, maybe four, before I got on my feet. I had a résumé. I had skills. I had a plan.

Nah, it wasn't like that. I lived with Erick and Camille for *four months*. And they never complained.

Remain Out in Society

A LOT OF returning citizens lose themselves, because in prison everything is theoretical. You sit in a cell, imagining everything you could do, and it seems easy—if they'd just give you the chance. *Of course I'm gonna bust ass! Of course I'm gonna make it!* Now, suddenly, you're waking up on a sofa in a basement, and you have the day in front of you, and you can go anywhere—except out of the area, because you're on parole. But still, the world is wide open compared to where you've been. And it's overwhelming.

I had a plan: Attend the University of Baltimore for the fall semester. Get a meaningful job I could reach by public transportation from the university. And as soon as I had the money, move to Baltimore. New city. No entanglements. Perfect second chance.

But how was I going to do that? It would cost thousands of dollars, and even after six weeks I was struggling to afford a hamburger, much less a steak. Women laughed at me when they found out I didn't have a car.

"What you gonna do, pick me up on your bicycle?"

It wasn't even my bike. It was Erick's bike. For so long, freedom had seemed incredible, like nonstop awesomeness. And it was. Holding a phone. Eating shrimp. Riding in a car. Can you imagine how that felt after sixteen years? After believing for a decade you'd never do any of those things again?

Sometimes, I'd sit out in the backyard alone, completely overwhelmed by the trees and the quiet and the feeling of breathing free air.

But it was depressing, too, because I had all these dreams and plans, and I was failing so bad.

Mr. Edwards straightened me out. He said, "Make a budget, Chris. I know your goals seem too far away, so break it down into steps. How much do you need for the bus? How much to buy your own bike? How much for an apartment?"

Fifty a month for a bus pass. Two hundred for a used bike. Two thousand a month to cover my expenses and rent my own place. Yes, that was a lot, but looking at it like that, it felt realistic. I made enough for the pass by mowing lawns. I could see myself saving for the bike. I could find a good enough job to afford an apartment.

College was the problem. The University of Baltimore was a lot cheaper than Johns Hopkins, but it was still thousands for a semester and supplies. How could I possibly get that kind of money together in less than three months?

Mr. Edwards said, "In my first semester in the masters program at the University of Maryland, I realized that I needed additional income to provide for my wife and three kids. So I reached out to the university. They provided me with the support I needed, which helped to cover my expenses.

"So don't be too proud, Chris. Don't be stubborn. It never hurts to ask."

I listened to that, and I took it to heart. I put on my suit every day, and I took the bus to the University of Baltimore. I applied for everything available in the financial aid office. I talked to administrators in the public policy and business departments. I scheduled meetings with my old professors and deans. I wanted them to remember me and understand how serious I was about education. They recommended books; they told me about upcoming classes; and most important, they tipped me off to scholarships. They even recommended local entrepreneurs and businesses I could contact for informational interviews. I love informational interviews, because when you sit down face-to-face, you make a connection, even if they don't have anything for you at that time.

I worked, in other words, at my Master Plan. I had to, because every Sunday at 1:00 p.m. I needed something to tell Steve. We always talked for at least thirty minutes, but only the first few were about him and Patuxent. There wasn't much to say about the prison grind. His case was moving slowly, and Steve didn't want to jeopardize that progress with loose talk on the phone.

So instead, we talked about my week. I told him everything, from the furniture in the nice offices I visited to the disappointment on a girl's face when she found out I was broke. Steve loved those stories, but even more, he loved giving me advice. He was living through me, so he liked talking about what he would have done, and then telling me what I should do next. I didn't mind. I had my own ideas, but Steve was smart, and I valued his opinion. I told him those opinions were stupid, of course, that's what brothers do. But I listened. Everybody needs a person to keep them responsible and on track. For me, that person had always been Steve.

And every time I hung up the phone, I thought, *How lucky am I? How lucky am I to be out here, when Steve is inside? Don't waste your chance.*

About the only thing I was missing in my life—well, except for a job, a place to live, money, possessions, and a girl who would give me the time of day—was Darico. He hadn't been hard to find, even though we hadn't spoken since I was behind the red door at Patuxent. He was just hard to *reach*, because by the time I got out, my son was in county lockup awaiting trial on stealing a car, drug possession, and resisting arrest.

I remember him walking into the visiting room in his orange jumpsuit and cuffs. He was thirteen when I last saw him, with the fat cheeks of a boy. Now he was thin and hard. Taller than me, peach fuzz on his lip. We'd known each other for six years, but we'd only been allowed about forty-eight total hours together. Now I couldn't even hug him because he was still on the other side of the glass.

I said, "How you doing, son?"

He said, "I need money, Pops. I need a couple thousand for a lawyer." He was staring at me, like he was testing me, trying to see which way I would move.

"I'm sorry, Darico," I said. "I just got out. I'm broke."

He looked away. "Then what good are you?"

It hurt, but I recognized. I knew the hardness in his eyes. Darico was like me at that age. He felt abandoned and unloved, just like I felt when I told my father to fuck off, the last thing I ever said to the man before he died.

"I never wanted to leave you, Darico. They sent me back."

"Yeah, whatever, Pops."

Those four extra years inside—I did the crime, so that's on me. And I helped a lot of people in those years, especially Steve. But I can't help thinking that Darico was eleven when Judge Serrette reduced my sentence. He loved me then. He craved a father. I could have been there for him as he went from a boy to a man.

Now he was almost seventeen. He had grown up in foster homes, abused and neglected, until he finally ran away and found a family on the street. He was in the cave, like I used to be. He no longer believed in hope and change and all those words. He didn't even believe in me.

I gotta let him go for now, I thought. *I gotta get myself straight so I'm ready when he wants my help.*

They gave Darico five years. I figured he'd be out in three. That gave me a thousand days to go from broke and homeless to the man my son needed me to be—the man I'd promised everyone, including myself, I'd become, if they gave me the chance.

Become Financially
Independent

FIFTY-TWO DAYS. That's how long it took me to find a job.

That is a short amount of time, considering my record, but it wasn't luck. It was years of hard work. That work started, appropriately enough, in the civil rights class I took while in the halfway house. After they threw me in the mental health wing of Patuxent, I could have quit. I was going to fail, because you can't pass history from a locked ward. But I finished my term paper, under my sheet, while the roaches crawled and the sick men screamed. After I was released, I went to see my professor, Dr. Betsy Nix. It had been more than a year, but she remembered me. Steve had mailed her my term paper, and I doubt she'd ever gotten a term paper from prison before. I told her I was out for good, and I told her about my Master Plan.

Soon after, Dr. Nix got a call from Karen Stokes, the director of a local nonprofit that worked in poor Baltimore neighborhoods. At the end of the conversation, Ms. Stokes asked if Dr. Nix had a promising student to recommend for a job. This happened every six months or so, and Dr. Nix always said no.

She started saying the same old thing, then stopped herself

midsentence. "You know what? I do know someone. I think he'd be perfect for this work. His name is Chris Wilson."

I did my homework. I didn't just walk into the job interview and ask, "So what's up with you guys?" I studied the organization, the Greater Homewood Community Corporation, now known as Strong City. The GHCC had been around for almost fifty years, very old for a nonprofit in Baltimore. They had offices in thirteen poor neighborhoods where they worked in schools and with community leaders to increase the quality of life.

The open position was in Barclay, a neighborhood just west of downtown Baltimore, and I wanted it bad. I needed the paycheck. I cared about communities like this, since I grew up in one. The job was entrepreneurial because I would be accessing problems and finding solutions. And Barclay was only a few blocks from the University of Baltimore, so I could walk from my classes to my office.

By the time I arrived at the interview in my best (and still only) suit, I knew my pitch: I understand these citizens, and I love them. They will trust me because I'm one of them. I didn't want to talk about prison, but I wasn't hiding my experience, either. After all, I had spent my time at Patuxent doing exactly the kind of work I'd be doing in Barclay: talking with people, learning what they needed, and figuring out how to get it for them. I knew Greater Homewood hired mostly people with college degrees in social work, but it was also important, I would argue, to have employees who had lived the challenges of poverty firsthand.

My interviewer had grown up in Italy. We talked about the job, but we also talked about her childhood, in Italian, of course. She was a fan of my favorite Italian television show, *The Octopus*. I never thought being fluent in Italian would help me get a job, but the world is complicated, and knowledge opens doors.

My caseworker at the halfway house had told me I'd be lucky to work at McDonald's or at a gas station. My parole officer, who was much more supportive, worried at every meeting that my goals were too high. My own grandmother doubted I'd amount to anything. But here I was, less than two months out of prison, a workforce outreach coordinator, working twenty-four hours a week for $21,600 a year.

And the need was great, because Baltimore is the Detroit of the East Coast. In 1970, the population was 906,000. By 2010, it had dropped to 621,000. There were thousands of abandoned row houses in the inner city, and burned-out shells stood half collapsed for years because nobody cared enough to knock them down. Less than a mile from the ritzy Inner Harbor, you could walk for blocks without seeing a single building that looked inhabited. Then, suddenly, you'd come up on four little kids sitting on a stoop, and you'd realize that families were living in these shuttered buildings, in an urban wasteland without grocery stores, parks, or even trees. And almost all those families were black.

Barclay had been one of those areas, but by the time I arrived, it was changing. Development had started along North Avenue, the neighborhood's southern edge. There were white "urban pioneers" on a few of the blocks. But the strength of Barclay was the people who had been there all along. There were gangs. There was high violence and unemployment. But there were resources, too: thriving churches, women's groups, hardworking men and women, mentors, advocates and, as always, those pillars of the community, the grandmas.

I tried to meet them all. Instead of calling people into the office for appointments, like GHCC had always done, I walked to their homes so I could see their challenges. I knocked on doors. I went into the churches. I talked with the dealers on the corners and the unemployed on the stoops and the homeless people begging on North Avenue.

I was interested in business, so I stopped into the mom-and-pop shops to ask questions. What do you do? How do you do it? What do you need to reach your next goal?

I talked with the gang runners who ran the soldiers on the corners. I didn't lecture, and I definitely didn't turn them in. Like in prison, I used the Socratic method, which means listening and asking questions to get them thinking differently. What's your endgame? Where's this gonna lead? You're nineteen now, that's cool, but you want to be out here when you're thirty? Yeah? Well, what about fifty?

Mostly, they cursed me out. "Man, you ain't from this neighborhood. You ain't even from Baltimore."

"That's true, but we're businessmen, right?"

"So?"

"Well, what does a businessman need?"

"I don't know. *You* to stay out of his business."

"A safe neighborhood. The safer this neighborhood, the better for everyone. So let's work together on that."

"Ah, fuck you, you DC motherfucker," but said with a smile somewhere between *Who this fool think he is?* and *This suit-wearing brother's all right.*

Once classes started in September, I began looking for an apartment. Between college and the job, I had to be in Baltimore early every morning, and that two-hours-both-ways bus commute was killing me. I hadn't made my $2,000-a-month budget number—I was at $1,783—but I had a steady job, and I could afford something small.

I couldn't find an apartment. Once they saw my record, nobody would rent to me. Five, ten, twelve apartments turned me down, at

$50 a pop in application fees, eating up every cent of my extra cash. Even in Barclay, nobody would rent to me.

Then it got worse: the human resources director called me to the main GHCC office. It was in an old house on the other side of Johns Hopkins. I took the bus. I had never been in a neighborhood that nice. GHCC was pretty high up in the white world.

Ms. Stokes was having second thoughts. She knew I'd been to prison when she hired me, but she never asked the details. She'd assumed I'd been in for a year or two, maybe five at the most. When the HR director told her it was sixteen years, she got worried. So I told them the truth: I took a life at seventeen. I received a sentence of life in prison. But I turned my life around. I worked my way out. I earned this chance.

Ms. Stokes and I had a good relationship. She knew how hard I worked because I made sure we had a personal relationship. She wasn't my direct boss, but I talked to her all the time. That didn't make me feel safe. I knew a place like GHCC was political. If I messed up, Ms. Stokes would be blamed for hiring a "felon." No, for hiring a murderer. She could get fired if I screwed up bad enough.

I thought she was going to fire me. The three people I worked with in Barclay were young white women from good colleges, and those were safer hires than a man like me. I thought I'd be back on Erick's couch, broke and discouraged. Getting a foot in the door is hard, especially for a returning citizen. How long would it take me to get another job? Would I ever get another opportunity like this?

But I was wrong. Karen Stokes took a chance on me.

"I have some ideas," I told her when I finally caught my breath with relief. "Can we have lunch some time?"

I came with a written proposal for a job placement program. We talked about it, reworked the idea, and Ms. Stokes took it to a few

GHCC benefactors and received donations to fund it. Instead of being fired, I was promoted to thirty-two hours a week and placed in charge of my own program. In barely a month, I almost doubled my salary to $36,000 a year. I even received health care.

Two weeks later, I found an apartment. The chaplain at Patuxent heard about my situation through Steve. His daughter owned a few buildings, and he convinced her to rent to me in Reservoir Hill.

"I don't know about this," Erick said when he drove me to the block. Reservoir Hill was a transitional neighborhood, and my building was in a stretch of dilapidated row houses. There wasn't a business in sight—although I found out the first night that there was a busy marijuana trap house right next door.

"Stay with us, Chris," Erick said as I unloaded the three blue plastic bins that still contained almost everything I owned. "This is dangerous."

He meant dangerous for a guy on parole. Dangerous for a man who had to be watchful—of knuckleheads, drug dealers, and cops—because he would never get the benefit of the doubt.

I wasn't crazy about the spot, either, but I had to start somewhere, and the apartment was half a mile from my job and school. So I bought a bicycle, since I couldn't afford a car, and a hundred packs of ramen, since I couldn't afford to eat out, and settled into my own place, by myself, for the first time in my life.

Start a Business

To ME, jobs are the key to changing a neighborhood. I believe in education and training, especially for young people, but the first thing people in desperate poverty need is cash. Once they can afford basics like food and clothing, *then* they can start to get the rest of their lives in order.

People scoff. They say: No handouts! Pull yourself up by your bootstraps!

Here's what they don't understand: The very poor don't even have boots. I mean that literally. When one man got an interview at a construction site, I told him, "Show up in appropriate shoes." His eyes dropped, and I realized he couldn't afford shoes. So I took him to a store and bought him a pair of Carhartt boots.

The older people in Barclay had grown up in a segregated school system, and some couldn't read. Others couldn't see well enough to read, but couldn't afford to do anything about it. So I bought them glasses. I bought women office-appropriate dresses. I babysat their kids so that they could go to interviews. I bought tires to replace flats. I paid for bus passes. Karen Stokes shook her head every time I brought her the expense reports—boots? Glasses? A tire?—but she always supported me. For GHCC, these purchases were small, usually $50 to $100, but they were insurmountable obstacles for unemployed people with no means of support.

There were more intractable problems, too, like the fact that most of the men had criminal records, which said more about Baltimore than the community. Baltimore was a lock-'em-up-and-sort-it-out-later city, especially in "high crime areas," where the police were aggressive and plainclothes officers, nicknamed "knockers," accosted citizens every day. I was jumped by four knockers in Barclay for carrying a backpack. Do you know how scary that is, to have four armed men suddenly and violently assault you? There is no way, when they jump out shouting, to know they're cops. Even when they slam you against the wall and pull out badges, your mind is telling you, *It's a robbery, these guys ain't real.*

They let me go when they realized I was a student, but how is that acceptable? Why can't a black man in that neighborhood carry a backpack? The knockers didn't stop crime. The only thing they accomplished was burdening hundreds of young men and women with minor charges, like drug possession, loitering, and the infamous "resisting arrest," which an officer could slap on anyone at any time, usually just to make other charges stick. Sending us to court, to them, was "just a warning," but court appearances get people fired. Even a minor conviction—probation, a few months time—could cripple their job prospects for life.

That kind of existence—in and out of prison, followed by long periods without work—leads to terrible habits. Many clients at GHCC were in their thirties or even forties, and they didn't understand how to function in a job environment. Working hard takes practice. Knowing what to work on without being given detailed directions is a learned skill.

I can't count how many times people failed to show up for interviews because they didn't understand the importance of meeting obligations every time. GHCC used to mark that down as a failure and say, "Next time." There was always a next time, and a next person in line. I knew we had another tool: I called their grandmothers.

Sure enough, ten minutes later: "Yo, slick, why you get me in trouble with my grandma?"

"You missed your interview."

"The water got turned off." (Or the electricity. Or the kids were hungry.) "I had to go round up some cash and wait in line to pay the bill. I'll do that interview tomorrow."

"There's no interview tomorrow. You understand? You only get one shot."

"Nah, you kidding? Nobody told me that."

"Look, homey, come on in here. Let's talk about how this works again."

I met one young woman, real smart. She was in an abusive relationship with an older married man, but we got her out and into her own apartment. I pitched her hard to a firm looking for office help because I knew she didn't have money for rent. The company agreed to take her on, pending an interview.

"They drug test," I told her. I knew she smoked weed because I'd smelled it on her a time or two. "If you're not clean, let me know and I'll work around it."

"No, no, I'm fine," she said.

She didn't show up for the interview. For days, I couldn't find her. About two weeks later, I happened to see her waiting for a bus on North Avenue. She was dressed in a nice skirt and blouse, and I had a bad feeling about what that meant.

"You're not . . ."

She nodded. "I'm on my way to the interview." She had quit smoking and waited for the weed to leave her system. Now she was ready to go.

When I didn't respond, I saw her face drop. "There's no interview, is there?"

"No," I said, "there's not. They gave that job to somebody else."

It's easy to fall into hopelessness when stuff like that happens. To become overwhelmed by the problems of poverty and inexperience. To stand on the side and say, *They're doing it to themselves*. But when you're there, among the people, you know that's not the story. There's a lot of hardworking folks in a neighborhood like Barclay. A lot of small businesses being run out of kitchens, garages, and back rooms. Black folks are entrepreneurial. We've been shut out of the regular working world so long—by prison records and a hundred other means, too—that we've made our own.

So I started a weekly program to bring these small entrepreneurs together. I wanted to share what I'd learned in prison and school, and to let them meet and learn from each other. I wanted to ask them the same questions I asked everyone: What's your endgame? What are you doing right now to get there? Do you have a Master Plan?

And I wanted them to show me, in practical terms, how to start a business when you got no experience, no money, and nothing but a dream.

I called it the Barclay School of Business (BSB).

I took it seriously, like I was a professor. I prepped my lessons; I handed out printed class plans and reading lists; I brought food. I was working and going to college, so we started at 8:00 p.m. The classes were scheduled for two hours, but often they lasted three or four. As long as people had questions, I stayed.

I remember, once, staying until midnight, trying to explain why you don't mix your business income with your personal money. People couldn't understand that.

"Why not? I made the money, right?"

"That's your business money."

"But I need to eat."

"Pay yourself a salary. I'm not saying you starve. But you have to plan."

I've found this everywhere, at every level of income. People look one step ahead. When they get out of prison, they want to celebrate, like they've made it. No, you're just starting. When they make money, they want to spend it. No, you need working capital so you can grow. I hit that for weeks: basic accounting, budgeting, growing a business. It's a hard concept for people living hand to mouth. They struggle to plan for tomorrow because they're too focused on getting through today.

I met my first business partner, Warren Savage, at BSB. He was a former gang associate who had spent seventeen years in the state penitentiary. He came out a Christian and a master upholsterer. Warren was in his fifties, running a street ministry for gang members as well as a garage where he fixed furniture. I checked out his work. He was talented. He had used his prison time wisely. He wanted to expand his business, make it steady enough to support his ministry. That was his endgame. I thought we could help each other, so I invested my life savings—a few thousand dollars—and we created a partnership.

There's a saying in business school: Find your first follower. That's step one for any business, finding one client who believes in you.

In my life, that first believer was Steve, then his parents. In my social entrepreneurship, it was Karen Stokes at GHCC.

For T&W, our upholstery business, Warren already had a possibility. He knew someone opening an upscale lounge, and they needed upholstery on chairs, banquettes, and even the front of the bar. It was a massive job. In a sense, Warren was bringing me in to secure and manage the contract.

So I researched fabrics, time commitments, and pricing. I studied contracts, then asked my business professors for clarification and advice. "Legally, I can't advise you on a business, Chris," they said, "but theoretically, that means . . ."

By the time we met with our potential first follower, I was ready. Warren knew upholstery, but I knew the upholstery business. I could talk price, schedules, and contracts. I wrote a proposal, like I always do, and put it in my new briefcase. I shaved and put on my best suit and tie (and my Joop, always). Half an hour before the scheduled time, I took the elevator to the penthouse of a hundred-year-old hotel. The moment I stepped off the elevator, I saw Baltimore spread out below me through the floor-to-ceiling windows. Then I saw Warren, chilling in the corner in his usual tight work apron and do-rag.

Oh, man, I thought. *Come on, Warren. This is business.*

We made a good pair, though. Warren had the easy smile and the technical skills. I provided the discipline and professionalism. It was a good reminder that business is about a personal connection, as well as pricing and proving you can do the job. We pitched, had a few drinks, walked the space to discuss the work. I was sure we had the contract, until Warren started in on racism and violence. This was the year of the Trayvon Martin killing, and it was his favorite topic. It was the favorite topic of everyone in black Baltimore. But that wasn't the time or the place.

"I think we're done," I said, shaking hands and hustling Warren out.

We got a contract for $30,000. It was November 2012. I was six months out of Patuxent, and I had already landed my first business deal.

The only problem was, Warren and I had to start right away to make our schedule, and our payment was tied up in contract negotiations. We didn't have the money for fabric and supplies, and because of our prison records, we didn't have access to a line of credit. At that point, I didn't even qualify for a credit card.

I made a mistake. I got an under-the-table loan. I'd get $3,000 immediately, but I'd have to pay back $4,500 within three months. I thought I didn't have a choice. My business was on the line. I accepted the terms.

Mr. Edwards found out and came to me, steaming. "Be smart, son," he said. "Don't ever take a deal like that."

He was right. You can't get ahead on bad loans, and I felt stupid for trying. Mr. Edwards was a big man, he was a father to me, and it was intimidating to see him angry. But he was on my side, as always. He gave me the money to pay off the loan before the interest accrued.

"Pay me back in six months," he said. "No interest. Just come to me next time."

The last check from our restaurant client arrived right before Christmas, so I paid the Edwardses back over a nice holiday dinner at their house. I know it was their money, but handing over that check felt like thanking them not just for the loan but for everything.

A few days later, I leased my first car, an eight-year-old Acura Coupe. I know, I know, I should have saved that money and invested it in my future. Wasn't that what I'd been preaching? But where I came from, a car was a big deal, because a car was freedom. With a car, it didn't matter where you lived. The cave couldn't hold you. With a car, you could go anywhere, and you could be anything.

For six months, my world had been limited by my bike and the bus. The car was a gift to myself on my thirty-fourth birthday. It was another step in breaking free.

All I needed now was a driver's license.

Remain a Lifelong Learner

I SWITCHED TO the business school for the spring of 2013. I had spent the fall semester in community studies, writing grant proposals, and I thought, *What's the point?* I'd been writing successful proposals since Steve talked me into joining the IAC board at Patuxent in 2003. I may have spent half my life in prison, but my life experience was light-years beyond the program.

My life experience was beyond the basic University of Baltimore business program, too. The other students read about business; I was living it. So I went right to the top. Steve and I talked so much on Sundays, it was like he was auditing my classes. I even shared my notes and our reading list so he could follow along. He asked so many good questions about T&W, it felt like he was helping Warren and me run the place.

I talked with my professors, too. One encouraged me to enter Rise to the Challenge, a competition for business ideas. Instead of writing about a hypothetical business like the other students, I wrote about my work with Warren.

And I won. So I entered a business competition at Johns Hopkins,

and I won that, too. There was a huge reception. Local business leaders kept congratulating me on my victory. They all assumed I went to
Hopkins.

I smiled, remembering my old prison therapist: *Don't you know
only people like me go to Hopkins?*

"I go to the University of Baltimore," I said.

"What's that?" They had never heard of it, even though it was
right down the road.

I felt so good after the reception, I told my friend, "Let's drive."
We had my Acura, but I only had a learner's permit, so he was my
driver for the day. "I don't want to go home," I told him. "I want to
enjoy this."

We were in Bolton Hill, a nice white neighborhood across North
Avenue from Reservoir Hill, when the cops pulled us over. We weren't
speeding. It was late April, the trees were blooming (they had trees
in Bolton Hill, so I knew it was nice), and we were cruising slow,
enjoying the late afternoon.

My friend gave the two cops his license, and I handed over my
learner's permit. I was annoyed, but I didn't worry about it—until the
cops took our licenses.

"These are fake," they said.

They weren't, but that wasn't the point. They sat us on the curb
and threatened to impound my car unless I let them look in the
trunk.

"Whoa," I said. "That's illegal. You can't search my car without
probable cause."

"Well, we're going to search your trunk one way or the other," the
cop said. "We can get a drug-searching dog, if that's how you want it.
But it's the weekend, and the dog's out in the county, so it's going to
take a couple hours."

Okay, this was serious. It was getting dark, and by now there were three police cars on the scene, lights flashing. There were white people out walking their dogs, white kids riding their bikes, everyone staring at the two of us on the curb, probably thinking, *It's a shame young black men can't stay out of trouble.*

Except we weren't young. We were in our midthirties. How old does a black man have to be before it's okay for him to drive in this neighborhood?

"Y'all better call the dog," I said.

I called a friend on the police force I'd met through my work in Barclay. I told him what was happening, and he said he'd come over. He was off duty across town, so we'd been detained for close to an hour when he arrived. It was only the two original cops by then. He huddled up with them and then came over to us.

"They just want to look in your trunk," he said.

"They can't do that."

"I know. But that's not the point. Do you have anything illegal in your trunk?"

"Of course not."

"Then just let them look."

I heard him. Challenging cops, even when they're wrong, is risky. This is how black men get thrown in prison for "resisting arrest." But I was afraid. They could have planted something in my trunk. You don't think that happens? They have six cops on trial in Baltimore right now for doing exactly that. And I knew what would happen to someone with my record if this went wrong. It would be my word against theirs, and something easy to plant like a knife or a bag of drugs could put me away for life.

I opened my trunk. I was sweating, even though I knew I was clean. The cops searched the crevices and under the spare and pulled out the only thing inside: a giant cardboard novelty check for $1,000, my prize for winning the Rise to the Challenge business competition.

The cops reluctantly gave up. They were still impounding my car, though, because neither of us had a driver's license.

"But you took our licenses when you pulled us over!"

The cops wouldn't acknowledge that had happened. They'd spent more than an hour on this stop, and they were getting something for their trouble. But driving without a license was a parole violation. It could put me in prison. And the impound fees . . . And the lost time . . .

My cop friend stepped in. "I'll drive their car home," he said.

"Then we're going to impound *your* car."

My friend just looked at them. "I'm a cop," he said. "You sure you want to do that?"

So he drove us home, and the last thing I remember was seeing the two cops in the rearview, on the side of the road with their lights flashing, angry and empty-handed. I feel bad for the next black man they pulled over, but I guess it's possible they let it go.

Nah, they didn't let it go.

I couldn't let it go, either. Especially as I was waiting four hours at the DMV and paying $50 to get a new learner's permit. Those cops ruined my triumphant afternoon. They almost took my car. What if I hadn't been friends with a cop? What if I hadn't been able to reach him, or if he had been on duty?

I felt powerless, like in prison. I was doing everything right: school, work, business. Staying clean. And it didn't seem to matter. Prison meant being constantly prodded; being a black man in Baltimore was like sandpaper against your skin. Everything in the system rubbed against you the wrong way.

Figure Out How to Afford
to Be a Lifelong Learner

I HAD a classmate a few blocks away in Reservoir Hill. He had a nice black BMW convertible, and every time I rode by on my bike, he was out waxing and polishing it. I asked him one day how he could afford it while in school.

"Oh, they're paying me," he said.

"What?"

"Yeah, I have a full scholarship, and the university gives me money for expenses."

Now, I'd been studying this dude, because that's what I do. I study people to see what I can learn. He didn't work. He didn't have a plan. He was just taking courses, chasing girls, and chilling. When I asked what he wanted to do after he graduated, he said, "I don't know. I'll figure it out."

What a luxury, to have a single day in your life you didn't have to hustle, much less years. I was working seven days a week, ten hours a day, to stay ahead of my expenses. And the university was paying this guy while they were charging me?

I didn't forget that, or Mr. Edwards's advice from that first summer:

always ask. That fall, he had helped me prepare an itemized list with the things I needed but couldn't afford, like a computer. I sent that list in a proposal to nonprofits all over Baltimore, but only one person wrote back: Jane Brown. Her family's foundation was one of the largest in the city.

We met for lunch, and I told her my story. Not some of it—all of it, the good and the bad. At the end of the meal, she said, "My foundation can't help you, Chris, because you're not a charity, and we're not set up to help individuals." I was disappointed, but I was like, *That's okay, I just met a really cool person who's important in this town.*

Then she slid a check across the table. "But that doesn't mean I can't help you myself."

I've since found out Jane Brown helps a lot of people that way, and nobody knows about it. She doesn't do it for respect or accolades; she

Celebrating my birthday with Jane Brown
(JEFFREY KENT)

doesn't do it for the tax break, since we aren't charities. She does it because she cares.

A few months later, I happened to see the dean of the business school, Darlene Smith, getting out of her car.

I had never met Dean Smith, but I had read about her. That's why I recognized her on the side of the road. I knew she was a serious cyclist, and I was riding my bike to class. She was also on the board of Live Baltimore, a nonprofit focused on promoting the city, and I was working to improve our inner city.

So I stopped and introduced myself. I told her how much I liked the business school and admired her nonprofit work. We talked about biking. I told her I had a job in community development while attending school full-time. Then I gave her a little speech I'd been working on in my head, in case I ever got this chance.

"I work in Barclay," I said. "That's only three blocks away, but people in that neighborhood never come here. They've never even heard of the University of Baltimore. I know you want to change that, and I think you can do that by investing in me. This is our city, and I'm going to spend my life helping people. I just need some help right now paying for school."

She stared at me. This might have been the first time a student had recognized her on the street. I'm sure it was the first time a student had ridden up on a bicycle and asked for financial assistance.

She smiled. "Just asking for what you want, huh? I like that. I'm going to waive your tuition for next semester."

"Thank you," I said. "I appreciate that, Dean Smith, and I don't want to sound ungrateful, but, honestly, I don't think I should have to pay for anything at this school ever again."

That stopped her. She stared at me, harder this time. "What's your name?" she said.

"Chris Wilson, ma'am."

"Okay, Chris. Let me think about that."

She must have heard good things about me, because I received an email late that very night saying the University of Baltimore was giving me a full scholarship covering all my tuition, fees, books, and supplies.

Now, that was ballsy, I admit. But that's what it takes, y'all. If you deserve something, ask for it. *With respect*. Don't be angry if you don't get it, but don't be too shy to ask.

I had proven myself. I had a plan. And when the university thought about me, they saw a smart investment. They started having me speak to new students and alumni. They wrote articles about me. About a year after our conversation, Dean Smith asked me to meet with a woman considering making a large donation. I had no expertise in this area, and I didn't know much about the university in general, so I asked the dean what she wanted me to say.

"Just tell her your story."

So a few days later, over lunch, I told this polite, well-dressed, grandmotherly white woman my whole story, from Division Avenue to Barclay. I had her in tears when I talked about my mother, but also when I told her about my financial struggles after prison, and my work with GHCC, and my meeting on the street with Dean Smith.

She gave the university a seven-figure donation. She told them one of the reasons was that the school had the guts to support the inspiring student she had met at lunch. So what goes around comes around, I suppose, the bad and the good.

Focus on Continual
Self-Improvement

IT STARTED WITH a fight on my block. Alarms blared; windows shattered; cars were smashed. The next morning, there were bloody chunks of concrete and broken bricks in front of my building.

"Get out of there," Erick said. "Come back here. The kids miss you."

"Nah," I said. "I don't run."

Two nights later, I was up late talking with a young woman from the building when we heard gunshots. We hit the floor because we'd both been raised in tough neighborhoods, and we knew it was close. Half a minute later, we looked out the window. There was a body behind the house.

My friend called 911, and we ran downstairs. It was a knuckle-head I'd seen a hundred times. He was probably the toughest guy in the area. But someone caught him slipping. They shot him through the neck, and he was alone in the alley in a pool of blood. He was too hurt to move, but his eyes were open, tears were running down his face, and he was moaning, "Momma, Momma, I want my momma."

My friend fell to the ground and scooped him up. She put his head in her lap, put her fingers in the hole in his neck, and held him as he cried.

"He's not gonna make it," I said. "We have to send him off."

So I got down on my knees, and we prayed over him. I didn't know this man, except by his actions, but it hurt to be there, on my knees, when he left this world.

By the time the cops arrived, I was back upstairs. I had a record. I was on parole. This was Baltimore. I couldn't be found by the police at a murder scene.

So I watched from my window as the man's body was covered and the cops shoved my friend roughly into a squad car. They were treating her with disrespect, like I knew they would.

She came back six hours later as I was leaving for work. She was covered in blood and exhausted, and I could see how affected she was. That night changed her life. She quit her job and dedicated herself to helping kids deal with the trauma of the streets. I think it was the tears. I think she saw that hard man's humanity, there at the end, and she could never look away.

It changed me, too. It hit me hard like I didn't expect. I felt so bad, I was depressed for days. I still am, when I think of all the young people dying in the streets. Back in the neighborhood, it had felt like we were in a war and those who fell were the casualties. Their deaths hurt, but they had made sense to me. Getting desensitized was the price of survival.

Now that shell was peeling off, and I could see that it wasn't a knucklehead dying in my friend's arms. That was someone's son. He might have been a father. He could have been my friend, or my brother. Nah, he *was* my brother, and it was wrong that he died like that. No matter what he'd done, it was wrong.

There was a war raging in Barclay at that time. A young gang associate had been causing problems, so an old head from another gang said, "Be cool, man. Don't bring trouble around here." The bamma shot him point-blank in the head. Just like that, for nothing.

The man's friends demanded the gang give him up. They refused. Tensions escalated until disagreements turned into arguments, and arguments into fights, and someone got shot.

Then someone got killed, and the feud was on. The gang leaders went underground. They hunkered down on their blocks and put a kid with an automatic at every entrance. These were the young dudes, the newest soldiers. They were eleven, twelve years old, standing out on the corner with a gun to kill or die.

It was hot. Nobody at GHCC would venture into Barclay. Even the old-timers, the grandmothers and night-shift workers who had lived through decades of violence, hunkered down. I hunkered down, too . . . until that night in the alley. After that, I couldn't stand by.

I had contacts through my work in the neighborhood. I went to the number two in one of the gangs who I knew had the leader's ear.

"Why you protecting this guy?" I said. "You're destroying your business, because you can't move drugs through here right now. You're hurting the people in this neighborhood who you always saying you want to help. Kids are dying. Give this bamma up."

It wasn't happening. The kid was trouble. Nobody liked him. Even in the middle of the carnage, he was shooting off his mouth, standing on corners and screaming his name. He was a suicide bomber, as we called them. He was begging for someone to take him out, but a guy like that, when he's got the protection of proud men, can do a lot of damage. Thirteen people died over that beef, mostly young men.

Fourteen died, really, because the suicide bomber disappeared soon after a truce was finally called. I'm pretty sure he didn't take the Amtrak to Miami.

I said to myself: *Be part of the solution, Chris. Be talking, on the streets, spreading the message of hope.*

But I also said: *Be smart.* I was called to work against the violence, but I didn't have to live in it. I had options. So on the day I dedicated myself to the streets, I told my landlord I was moving out.

I set my sights on Bolton Hill, the neighborhood where the cops pulled me over for driving while black. Bolton Hill had a long history. It had been a wealthy neighborhood in the early 1900s, but like Reservoir Hill and Barclay, it had been redlined during the Depression. In 1937, the government-sponsored Home Owners Loan Corporation, which was created as part of the New Deal, rated all three neighborhoods either "declining" or "undesirable." They weren't talking about the poverty rate. They were measuring the "threat of infiltration by foreign-born, Negro, or lower-grade population."

Because of those government ratings, banks wouldn't make mortgage loans in the area. Housing prices dropped. By the 1950s, most of the white residents had moved out and "foreign-born, Negro, and lower-grade populations" had moved in. It goes without saying that the lack of mortgages wasn't new to blacks, because they had never been able to get mortgages. How could they, when their very existence in an area caused that area to be labeled undesirable?

Reservoir Hill, Barclay, and other redlined neighborhoods never recovered. They are poor, black, and broken to this day. Bolton Hill was different. It was always nicer, with larger row houses and a beautiful church in the center, and its "undesirables" were mostly groups eventually accepted by mainstream America, like Jews and Germans. After it was designated a historic area in 1967, new people moved in and fixed up the homes. By 2013, the row houses cost more than half a million dollars. Grass and trees were everywhere, and that's a big deal in inner-city Baltimore.

Some people still consider the neighborhood transitional. But I knew it was nice, and not just because of the trees. It was majority white, and the blacks who lived there were mostly doctors, lawyers, and other professionals.

I could afford Bolton Hill, but I knew my prison record would be a problem. So I did my homework. I assembled more financial documents than necessary. I got testimonials to my character. I was gaining a little publicity, so I included several articles that had appeared on websites and in fund-raising letters. I even wrote a letter explaining my situation. By the time I went to look at apartments, I had a whole folder to convince someone to take my money.

It didn't work. I was turned down for multiple apartments. Once, I sat with an agent and pitched him for twenty minutes because I really wanted that apartment.

He called the next day. "I appreciate your honesty about your past," he said, "but the owner doesn't feel comfortable with you."

I found a place off Craigslist. It was a third-floor, one-bedroom apartment owned by a young white couple, the Strebs. It was small, but it turned out great, because the Strebs were good people. They took me in. They trusted me. They had two young children, a boy and a girl, and those kids loved me. They always said hi, ran to give me hugs, asked if I wanted to play. They set up a little lemonade stand one day, and when I walked by, the daughter yelled out, "Look, Chris! We're entrepreneurs, just like you!"

You get the picture: blond hair, pigtails, missing a front tooth, never a doubt that I was a good person, a good friend, and someone to admire.

Start My Own Business
That Makes a Difference
in People's Lives

In the summer of 2013, I was accepted into the University of Baltimore's prestigious Entrepreneurship Fellows Program, an intensive two-year course of study with only eight students. That was a major accomplishment. I was proud; I was really making it now. But I wasn't satisfied. I didn't want to just learn about business; I wanted to do it. So I bought a partnership in a small Barclay business that contracted for basic construction and cleaning work. I liked the business model because they hired mostly men and women recently released from prison.

After a few months, I realized they weren't running the business right. The owner was mixing personal and business money, exactly like I told the people in the Barclay School of Business they couldn't do. She took cash for "off the book" jobs and didn't report them as business income, but used the business's equipment and resources. That isn't just unprofessional; it's illegal.

To succeed in business, you *have* to keep your accounting in order.

It has to be checked every week. You can't take off-the-book jobs; you can't forget to write down payments and expenses; you can't use your business money like your personal money. None of this is complicated. For very little money, you can get programs online that will help you keep your books. You just have to do the work.

My new partners weren't willing to change, so I had no choice: I left. I couldn't afford to be in business with people I didn't trust one hundred percent. I lost my life savings, about $10,000, on the deal.

But it was a good business idea, because it matched resources with a need. I had been running the GHCC workforce development program for fourteen months. There were plenty of people I couldn't place, but who I believed could succeed if given a chance. The contractors always told me the same thing: *I don't have time to teach them. Time is money, and I need people I can trust to get the job done right.*

"What if they were part of a crew?" I asked. "What if an outside company oversaw them and guaranteed their work?"

"Sure," a few of the more socially conscious contractors said, "I could give that a try."

GHCC, like most nonprofits, had narrow rules for how money can be spent. We weren't authorized, equipped, or financed to oversee work crews. But Ms. Stokes knew I wanted to be a social entrepreneur, and that my main interest was helping returning citizens transition from prison to private life. This was my opportunity. So we worked out a set of guidelines for how I could run a for-profit business that hired GHCC clients, while working for GHCC, trying to get those same people hired.

Now all I needed was working capital. So I went to Jane Brown, the woman who had helped me in the past. This time, I brought her a proposal with my business concept and a list of expenses. It wasn't just my proposal that sold her (although it was good). We had been meeting for lunch every couple of months; she knew how hard I worked; and she believed in me. That's why she helped with the company, and that's why I love her. Jane Brown has always believed in me.

I spent the fall of 2013 setting up my new business, the Barclay Investment Corporation (BIC). Legal paperwork, corporate registration, banking and accounting systems, licensing and bonding. It's not easy, or cheap, to form a company. It's called "barrier to entry," and it's what keeps most low-income people out of entrepreneurship.

A few years ago, for instance, I secured a contract to clean an office building. The building manager was a great guy named Felton. One night, he told me he owned a barbecue cart. The Artscape festival was that weekend, and he wanted to be there, but he didn't have money to buy supplies, like meat, napkins, drinks, that kind of thing.

"How much you need?"

He shrugged. "A thousand dollars."

I loaned him the money. He paid me back the next week. Then he asked for another thousand for another event. We did that a few times. You know what he did after that?

Felton quit his job and opened a food truck two hours away in Harrisburg, Pennsylvania, where he lived. Now he owns two successful restaurants. For years, the barrier to entry holding Felton back from his Master Plan was one thousand dollars. Now he's living his dream.

Jane Brown's gift was more, but not by that much. All I needed was start-up money, because by the time I launched the Barclay Investment Corporation, I already had my first contract with a large project on North Charles Street. A developer had purchased the entire block between Pennsylvania Station and Barclay. I knew that block. It was only a quarter mile from the university, but it was on the wrong side of Interstate 83, and everything on the wrong side of Interstate 83 was broken. A few blocks away, on both Biddle and Chase, you crossed directly from million-dollar houses to an area referred to as the Ho Chi Minh Trail. It was gorgeous mansions, then highway, then burned-out blocks with nothing but a barred liquor store on the corner of, you guessed it, Barclay Street. The interstate was the modern red line.

North Charles was like a bridge project between the nice part of town and Barclay. I liked that. Even better, it was a big job. My contract was for low-skilled labor, like tearing down walls and removing debris. I hired a Hispanic guy I knew from GHCC with great construc-

Me and a crew (ANDREW HAZLETT)

tion experience but a problematic prison record as my crew chief. He helped me choose four more returning citizens to fill out the crew. That job alone kept those five men employed for more than six months. By the third month, I had hired another crew, and the Barclay Investment Corporation was in the black. You know what that means, right? It means we were making bank.

A Stoop Story

By then, I was speaking regularly on behalf of GHCC. I spoke at community meetings in Barclay, and at churches, gyms, conferences, and private homes. I met with everyone from black congregations deeply involved in their struggling neighborhoods to wealthy women considering donating to our cause. Rodney Foxworth, a well-connected black social entrepreneur I first learned about through his blog, got me a gig at Hack for Change Baltimore, where I spoke to hundreds of the city's technology elite. I challenged them with a call to action: let's focus all the brainpower in this room on one neglected neighborhood and see how much change we can make. Only one attendee took me up on the offer, Jason Hardebeck, who had sold his company to Facebook and was looking to help other Baltimore entrepreneurs through the Greater Baltimore Technology Council. He's still helping Barclay today.

Even though I had a lot on my plate, I took each speaking appearance seriously. To me, each speech was a story, and to tell an effective story, I had to connect with my audience. With inner-city African Americans, I usually mentioned up top that I had been in prison. I never glorified it. I had seen the look in Darico's eyes, at eleven, when he said to me, "I heard you had a Mac-10 back in the day, Pops. You were a real gangster." Somebody had been telling stories, and Darico took it the wrong way. He was looking at me with admiration—not because of my turnaround in prison, but because of that gun. That broke my heart.

So I mentioned being in prison to let them know I understood the struggle. It's like my line if someone white asks if one of my employees has been in prison. "He's black and from Baltimore."

It's a joke, I guess, because after a few moments of silence, they laugh.

But it's no joke. According to a March 2015 analysis published in *The Baltimore Sun*, 52 percent of black Baltimore men in their twenties were in jail or on parole/probation. About 20 percent were locked up. Almost every black person in Baltimore, especially in poor areas, had someone they loved in the system.

I didn't tell white audiences I'd been inside. I figured their reaction would be different. The statistic above made most black people think: *Wow, the Baltimore cops are aggressive and judges are harsh. Our community needs help.* To a white person, I worried, it read more like: *Wow, black people are lawless. Our community needs protection—* from them.

But word got around. The other GHCC employees in Barclay were white women, but they weren't naive. I had to take drug tests. I had to visit my parole officer. It was pretty obvious I'd been in prison. Besides, people in the community knew, and they talked. I wasn't hiding my past. I just wasn't advertising it.

And I definitely wasn't talking about the seriousness of my crime. The only people outside the system who knew my full story were my boss, Karen Stokes, and my benefactor, Jane Brown. I didn't lie, but

I let everyone else assume what they wanted, which was probably that I'd been in for a few years on a minor charge.

Then a woman in my office suggested I try out for Stoop Stories. *The Stup . . . id . . . what?* I had never heard of it. Turns out Stoop Stories was a series of talks in a local theater that were recorded and broadcast on NPR. Ordinary people told true stories about their lives, as if they were sitting on a stoop. I'd been in prison. Now I was helping people who had been in prison. My colleague thought that was interesting enough to share.

My first thought was, *Hell no!* I had a good job. A steady income. Friends from the streets of Barclay to the highest levels of the local nonprofit world. I had just launched the Barclay Investment Corporation, my big entrepreneurial idea and the business I'd been planning, in a way, since Steve Edwards shook his head at me on tier two in Patuxent and said, "Think of all the good you could be doing for people in here." I was working my Master Plan. I'd been working it for almost twenty years! Why risk that to tell the world my story?

Because your story will help, I replied to myself. It might inspire other kids on the street or in prison to work hard and to not give up. It might change the heart and mind of someone who didn't want to give returning citizens a chance. Wasn't that my endgame? Didn't I want to change the narrative about black men like me?

I talked it over with Steve several times. We went back and forth. Was it worth the risk to my reputation? Was it worth the risk to my business? Could it really make a difference for other returning citizens? We always ended with the same questions: *What did I want? And what was I willing to do to get there?*

I did Stoop Stories, in the end, for myself. I was tired of hiding. I was tired of living in two worlds—exemplified by Barclay where I worked and Bolton Hill where I lived—and trying to keep them apart. I wasn't lying, but I was holding back the whole truth in one of those worlds, and that made my past feel like a shameful secret. *Shame*, that's the key word. With its constant monitoring and refusal to grant me basic rights, like the right to vote, society was shaming me for my past. It was making me the other. If I was afraid to tell my full story, I was buying into that shame.

Of course, it took me two months to reach that conclusion, and by then the deadline to apply had passed. I had to rush down to the theater and give them my application. I was a day late, but they let me audition a rough version of my piece. They chose me, along with six others. We were amateurs, so they coached us on story structure and public speaking. No mumbling. No rambling. No f-bombs.

Don't worry, NPR. I haven't dropped an f-bomb in years. Master Plan!

My episode, "The Giving Life," was scheduled for December 19, 2013. And it was cold. It was one of those Baltimore nights that cuts you on every corner. I walked to the theater huddled deep in my new Kenneth Cole jacket, wondering if I was doing the right thing. I had rehearsed every line. I knew what I wanted to say. The producers loved my story. But why? Because they thought it would help people? Or because murder made good radio?

Several speakers were on before me. I don't know what they said. I was in my own world, with the memories of my old life: My cousin Eric. The house in Temple Hills. The darkness and quiet of that terrible night, and the fear when I pulled my gun.

But mostly, I thought about Mom, and how she tucked in my shirt the night of my first date, and gave me a flower to give my girl, and bent down in front of me and smiled as she straightened my collar and said, "Treat her like a gentleman, Chris, just the way we talked about, okay? Treat her like a man should always treat a woman, because you're my little man, right? I'm so proud of you, Chris."

I can do this, I thought. *I can make my mother proud.*

The stage at Stoop Stories was tiny. It was about a foot high, maybe ten feet square, and the audience was close. It was a full house of four hundred people. I couldn't see them because of the stage lights, but I knew they were there. I could feel them. I had talked to big crowds, but this moment felt bigger. It felt like my confession.

I talked about growing up. I talked about the cave. I talked about my brother, shot seven times, and my cousin, shot seventeen times. I talked about my mother and the cop. I talked about my prison escape plan, which I called my Master Plan. I talked about studying and therapy and working out. I talked about my second chance, and making the world a better place, and my mother committing suicide before she had a chance to see me as a man.

"If my mom was out in the audience today," I said, "I would say to her, I only been home eighteen months. I am a student at the University of Baltimore with a full scholarship. I am the owner of two successful businesses. I am the director of a workforce program for Greater Homewood, and my mission is to lead people out of the figurative cave and show them that despite all the things you're going through, despite how hard life is, the world is beautiful.

"I would say, Mom, last week I helped a guy in my community. A guy who was dealt a bad hand, just like me, a guy who struggled to feed his children. You know, tears ran down his face when I shook his hand, and I pulled him close, and I said, 'You gonna be all right, man. I'm gonna help you.' Today, this person is feeding his children. This guy has a career.

"Mom, this is what you raised me to do. I love you."

As soon as I heard the ovation, I could feel the weight lift. No hiding now. After the show, people crowded around to shake my hand and congratulate me, not just on the talk, story, and confession, but on my life. These were white, wealthy, older couples, the audience I worried about the most. But they weren't judging me for my sins. They were applauding my success.

The next morning, one of my Entrepreneurship Fellow professors called me at home. He had heard the broadcast. "You're a businessman, Chris," he said. "You can't tell that story. You can't have that out for clients to hear. You have to tell them to take it off the Internet, and I mean now. Nobody will do business with you."

I felt the weight crushing me, twice as heavy as before. This man wasn't just a professor; he was a successful entrepreneur. He'd founded and run million-dollar businesses. I looked up to him because he was a hundred rungs above me in the ladder of success. So I knew he was right. I screwed up. No one would hire a company run by a criminal—especially not a criminal like me. The truth wouldn't set me free. It would ruin me. Of course. Hadn't that always been the case? Why had I thought otherwise?

I walked to the business school, depressed and embarrassed. The first person I saw was the communications director, Danielle Giles, who I had known since the halfway house. She looked my way, and I saw her pause. A strange look crossed her face. She had heard the broadcast, I could tell. She started walking toward me, and I felt so ashamed of myself I wanted to turn and run, but she kept coming and coming until she was so close she could wrap her arms around me.

"Oh, Chris," she said. "I had no idea."

My entrepreneurship professor was right: Everyone knows my history now. It's on the Internet. It's in this book. It *is* this book! There's no hiding who I am or what I've done.

But he was wrong about their reaction. Maybe some people don't want to work with me. They make excuses, or decide not to take my calls. But that's not most people. Most people believe in the man I am, because now they better understand the man I was. And they want to help. My business tripled after Stoop Stories, and it's been steady ever since.

Positive Delusion

A WEEK AFTER Stoop Stories I finally did it: I put my hands on the dream I'd had since I was nine years old. It was the first possession I ever desired, and my first Positive Delusion. It was the one object I thought about, on all those empty nights, when I dared to dream of a future outside my cell. *I'm gonna get out*, I told myself. *I'm gonna work. I'm gonna get my Corvette.*

This wasn't like the Acura. A Corvette wasn't just something to get me from one place to another. A Corvette was about the journey. It said, "Look at what I've accomplished. Look at the way I'm able to live. Look at the man I've become." In a Corvette, you don't just pull up to your destination; you *arrive*.

The model on the lot was burgundy, and it was slick, son. Top of the line, booming sound system, cool rims. When I rubbed those Corvette curves and put my hands on the leather steering wheel, I felt it. This was what I'd been working for.

Then I thought, *Hold up, Chris. This isn't the dream.*

I had pictured this car, asleep and awake, a hundred thousand times. That car had kept me going when my cell was freezing in the winter, and boiling in the summer, and the system rejected me again and again, and I wanted to lay down and give up and let the state have my life. In all those moments, over all those years, the car was never burgundy. It was black.

So I went online, and I found it. A 2001 black Corvette convertible with smooth curves and that big Corvette ass and the Z06 low-profile rims. I took it for a test drive, and I knew it was mine the minute I felt the motor hum. That car ate the road. That car was more than freedom. It was more than the destination. I didn't have to go anywhere anymore, because every second I was in that car, I had already arrived.

Maybe you've been there. Maybe you've had a moment when you stepped out of your life, looked at yourself, and thought: *I'm here. I did it. I always said I would, even though they said it was impossible. I always believed, but . . . damn, maybe I didn't really believe, because this is like magic, man . . .*

Master Plan! (CLÉO BAKER)

I'm here. It's real. And it feels so damn good.

I made sure I was on the road at 1:00 that Sunday, top down, radio off. "You hear it, Steve?" I said. "You know where I am? That's right. Yeah, that's the motor rumbling. Yeah, I did it. Don't worry. I'm good for it. No, don't worry. Don't worry, brother. Don't worry. You'll be here, too. You'll be here real soon."

A Blessing

IT MUST HAVE BEEN early spring, because the cold was breaking when the University of Baltimore asked at the last minute if I would speak at the law building. Normally I would have said no. I usually insisted on a few days to prepare, but for the university, which was giving me so much, I made an exception.

I assumed I would be speaking to a small group of students, but when I arrived, I saw people of all ages and races, from men in ties to kids in jeans to older women with their hair bound up in head wraps and years of worry on their faces. Even as I walked to the podium, through that room full of diverse people, the only thing in my mind was, *What now, Chris? What do you have to say for yourself?*

I think the light inspired me. This was a large space on the twelfth floor with floor-to-ceiling windows. I could see over the crowd to *my* Baltimore, the redlined Baltimore, where the sunlight was sharp. I could actually see the rays of light falling through the windows. Places like Barclay, when seen in God's light, are beautiful.

So I started telling a story I'd never told before. It was about a visit from Mr. Edwards at Patuxent, during one of his trips from overseas to see Steve and me. We hadn't seen him in a while, so Steve and I were excited. We sat across the prison table from him, expecting his usual laughter, but Mr. Edwards was quiet like I'd never seen him before. He looked at us slowly, from one to the other, and tears filled his eyes as he started to speak from the heart.

He said, "I've had a vision. God came to me in the depth of my despair"—and here he reached across the table and grabbed my hand so hard it hurt—"and He told me you're getting out, Chris. You're getting out."

Then he turned to Steve, and Mr. Edwards grabbed his hand in the same way, and he said, "And you're getting out, too, son. I don't know when. I don't know how. But God showed me the Promise. One day, He will put you here with me."

I don't talk much about faith, but I told the audience that Mr. Edwards's faith was so strong in that moment that I believed him. I believed God had a purpose for me, and that gave me hope. I had been denied five times, but I believed, and the impossible happened. I believe today, I said, that He has a purpose for every one of you.

That wasn't like my usual talk, which was about doing the work. In a way, I was completely off plan. But when people came to shake my hand that evening, they were crying, especially the older black women, with their hard hands and strong hugs. At the end, a young black man pulled me aside and told me, "You blessed this room today, Chris."

That man was Wes Moore, author of *The Other Wes Moore*, a national best seller about the different paths of two black kids growing up poor in Baltimore. It's a book about mentorship and role models. Wes, who had both, made it out; the boy who shared his name got life in prison. Wes told me, "I'm going to hook you up with a national speaking bureau, Chris. You have a message that needs to be heard." And he did. To this day, Wes is a mentor and a friend.

I'm thinking about that right now, though, because of my first mentor and friend, Steve Edwards. It had been eight years since Mr. Edwards's prophetic vision, and all that time, Steve kept the faith. He kept at the work we had started, like the career center, tutoring, and the computer lab. He took over my projects, like the book club and the Spanish school. He always spoke not of himself but of the young men coming up, the new generation learning from our hard work.

The results of the three-year Columbia study had been compiled, and I don't like to say a brother has brain damage, but my brother had brain damage. It was the kind of frontal lobe trauma that causes paranoia, violence, and lack of judgment. Steve's brain healed—I'm not saying he's brain damaged right now (although, I don't know, Steve, what you think?)—but on that fateful night, when the neighborhood knucklehead cornered and confronted him, Steve wasn't in his right mind. It was what his lawyers had promised: a paradigm-shifting case.

Still, the state fought him. They said the new information didn't warrant a hearing and told him to bring it up at parole. Steve's lawyers sued and proved parole for life prisoners in Maryland was a farce.

The state cited regulations. New laws. Missed deadlines. Like I said, the system works, but only in this sense: Once you step through a prison door, it is designed to keep you inside. Doesn't matter if you changed your life and became a model citizen. Doesn't matter if your brain damage was misdiagnosed. Doesn't matter if your case was corrupt or the police lied or new evidence proves your innocence.

Once you step through that door, *even your innocence doesn't matter.* The system will fight to keep you.

So many guys from Patuxent were out. Brian Carter was living in the Baltimore County (known in the city as "County"), the often rough suburban area that ringed the city. He was driving a heavy-duty truck and saving money to start his own trucking firm.

Scar was married to his girl from Patuxent. They had a baby and another on the way. He was mentoring underprivileged kids at a gym and determined to be the father he never had.

Bingo was at the University of Maryland, working on a math degree.

Guys I barely remembered were hitting me up on Facebook or calling my phone. Some wanted to congratulate me. They couldn't believe I was out. "You had life, Chris. Now you own a business? That's crazy. You always a worker, though. You always said this would happen."

But you never believed it, did you?

Others were looking for jobs. I hired a few, like Jimmy, who got stabbed in the neck with that Christmas tree knife. I didn't hire him because of guilt or anything like that. It took him ten years, but Jimmy got his GED. He worked longer on his GED than anyone Steve ever tutored. I respected that effort, so I put him on a cleaning crew.

I gave the bammas their medicine, just like my sister with me back in the day. "You remember us talking back in Patuxent?"

"Yeah, we was tight."

"Remember how I told you to get your GED, read books, put together a Master Plan?"

"Yeah, sure. You were always on that."

"Well, you didn't do any of that, did you? All you did was ball and talk trash while other guys worked. So why would I hire you now?"

"Yeah, well, Chris, you know how it is."

"Yes, I do. So I'm sorry, I can't help."

Some guys didn't take that well. They had a baby, they had bills, they were hungry. But they knew I was right. They hadn't done the work, and I'd been straight with them: if they didn't do the work inside, they couldn't expect to get the work outside.

Meanwhile, the Patuxent administration was leaning on Steve, the best guy of them all. They took his computer lab for the second time. They put him in the kitchen, where he once again suffered migraines. When they found out he'd been granted a hearing, they took him out of the kitchen and put him on garbage duty, the worst job in the prison. Before sunrise every morning, Steve was lifting and emptying one-hundred-fifty-pound garbage containers into trucks. I guess the administration thought they could break him with hard labor. Maybe they were punishing him for trying to get out, I don't know. They made him a hero instead, because Steve didn't complain. He didn't miss shifts. Inmates had always been suspicious of him, thinking he was soft or a kiss-up to the administration. After all, he *was* the model prisoner. But in those last months, when the administration tried to crush him, Steve earned the other inmates' respect.

I wanted to testify at his hearing. Steve wouldn't talk about his case because he was paranoid, but I begged his parents. This was my best friend, the guy who inspired me and taught me how to use my life for the greater good. I wouldn't be who I was today without Steve Edwards, and that's what I wanted to say. Steve Edwards didn't belong inside. I had a thousand stories to prove it.

Steve insisted I stay quiet. He thought it was too risky. Steve didn't believe good behavior could get him out, and he was right.

"Even we're not testifying," Steve's mom told me.

My heart was breaking. *I'm a public speaker*, I wanted to yell. *I can do this.*

But I was only a spectator, sitting beside Mr. and Mrs. Edwards, when Steve finally got his day in court on June 20, 2014. Unlike at my sentence reduction hearing, the courtroom was packed with his supporters. Even so, it was silent. Everybody was tense. This was Steve's shot. He wouldn't get another.

Then Steve walked in. It was the first time I'd seen my best friend in four years, and he looked exactly the same. He had the same tight haircut. The same confident posture. The same calm eyes. When I saw him like that, I heard Mr. Edwards's words: *God showed me the Promise. He is with you.*

The hearing was more than two hours long. Steve's original judge came, to say Steve was never supposed to be in prison this long. Mr. Fleming, the prison therapist who replaced Mr. Mee, testified on Steve's behalf. There was a lot of medical testimony I never understood. The one moment I remember clearly is when the state's attorney told the panel of judges that Steve had bad parents. They let their son slip through the cracks; they abandoned him to the streets; they couldn't be trusted, she said, to take responsibility for him now.

I was so mad I wanted to jump out of my seat. Steve had the best parents in the world! Mr. Edwards would take a bullet for his son. But I looked, and his face was stoic. He didn't even blink. He kept his eyes straight ahead, like her words couldn't hurt him, because this wasn't about him, this was about Steve.

Eventually, the three judges retired to their chambers. They took with them a recent article about my successes that discussed Steve's influence on my life, but otherwise I made no contribution. I sat, like everyone else who loved Steve, and waited quietly as three judges decided what to do with the rest of his life.

When they returned, it was over in an instant. They said, essentially, "We don't know why you're still in prison, Mr. Edwards. You're free to go."

It was a punch in the chest. It felt so good, it hurt. I looked at Mr. Edwards, and he was still staring straight ahead, with that stoic look on his face. Then he closed his eyes, bowed his head in prayer, and hugged his wife. Both of them were crying. I was crying. I was as happy as the day Judge Serrette set me free.

Three days later, I drove to the prison in my Corvette to see my best friend walk out the doors of Patuxent a free man. It was June 23, 2014, the day before Steve's thirty-seventh birthday, and it was perfect: clear, sunny, warm but not too warm. I'm not sure what we said to each other, or if we even spoke. What was there to say? The moment was too big for words, but it's there in the image: the two of us, in my Corvette, in the parking lot of the building that had been our grave. I remember Steve putting on sunglasses for the first time in twenty-two years. He looked at me and smiled. *Yeah, we alive.* We hugged for a long minute, then Steve got out of the Corvette, into the car with his parents and headed home. I put on "My Speakers" by Ace Hood and blasted back to Baltimore with the music thumping and the top down. That was one of the best drives of my life.

Steve told me later that the hearing was a last resort for the state. He was on the verge of getting a new trial based on Columbia's medical findings. The state was worried the evidence of PTSD and brain trauma would set a precedent that would allow hundreds, maybe thousands, of inmates and accused criminals in similar situations to go free or have their sentences reduced. By releasing him through a hearing, they sealed his medical records so that no other prisoners could benefit from those years of work.

In low moments, Steve doubted himself for taking the deal. Had he been selfish? Should he have held out to help others?

I told him he was crazy. He had to take the hearing. With that much on the line, the state would have done everything—*everything*—to keep him inside. Steve may have had the evidence on his side, but a trial was the state's hand to win, and they always held aces.

"A miracle happened, Steve," I said. "Your father's vision came true. We had life in prison, and now we're free. We're free, Steve. All those years we talked about it, all those plans we made. We're free. Now, let's stop worrying and change the world."

Be an Active Member
of My Community

STEVE SPENT the first few days with his parents, then moved twelve minutes from me in Severn, Maryland, just outside Baltimore. By then, I was renting a large corner apartment on Charles Street, in the first big project that had hired my company. It was a nice block: an old automotive shop and parking garages on one side, connected apartment buildings with industrial brick walls, large windows, and exposed metal beams on the other. From my window I could see the railroad depot, Pennsylvania Station, and a few of the taller buildings at the University of Baltimore.

I knew it wasn't going to be like in prison, when Steve and I sat together and talked all day, because my business was booming. In addition to my college classes, I had several small projects and a large contract at an office building being converted into condominiums. I had twenty-three employees. I was on-site ten hours a day, managing problems and organizing crews. I was up half the night trying to figure out permits and regulations, because this was the first time I had to deal with that. But that's what it took to put numbers on the board.

As my entrepreneurship professor said: "Anybody can start a company. The hard part is making money."

Steve was grinding, too. He worked on his code every day. But I could tell right away it was different for him. His parents bought him a new car, the Audi A5 he'd been dreaming about since I was with him in Patuxent.

I was like, *Yeah, he deserves that.* We were celebrating in those early months, mostly with late-night talks and *gambas al ajillo* (shrimp with garlic) at Tapas Teatro, a Mediterranean restaurant on my block. I love shrimp. Love it! It was like, "Can you believe this, Steve? We sitting at a restaurant, eating shrimp."

Then Steve went to computer conferences in San Francisco. He said he needed to make industry contacts. Well, I had contacts right here in Baltimore. Jason Hardebeck ran the technology planning and promotion group for the city, and he and I spoke all the time. He was a big supporter of my work.

Steve's parole officer was strict, though. She called the other party beforehand to clear meetings, and it was embarrassing for him. It didn't matter that Jason Hardebeck already knew his record; Steve didn't want to start professional relationships that way. He didn't want to do business in Baltimore because of that.

I told him, "I understand, Steve. That sucks. It's a stupid system. But you're spending a lot of money."

He said, "You've got a Corvette."

"Yeah, but I worked for that car. I rode a bike for a year."

I was on rocky ground. It was natural for Steve's parents to support him. He was their son. I didn't want to be arguing with him like this. And I definitely didn't want to seem resentful.

"Look," I said, "I been out here two years. I'm just saying, it's not easy, that's all."

For me, the challenge wasn't getting work. There was plenty of work. It was managing employees and making a profit. There was a reason other companies didn't hire my guys, and it wasn't work ethic. They did what you told them. But then they stood around, arguing with one another or on the phone. "Oh, we finished that job," they said. "We cool."

"No, you're not finished until five. There's plenty more work here. Look at that pile of rubble over there."

Payroll was the worst. My guys knew how much they were making an hour, and how many hours they worked, and when that amount wasn't on their check they got angry. "Yo, Chris, where's my money?"

"That's what you get. I have to take out taxes and social security so—"

"Nah, man, I just want my money."

"Look, I'm not stealing from you. That's the system."

It got heated. Every pay period, I was yelled at and threatened. I had a gun pulled on me by one of my employees.

It wasn't just lack of understanding. These guys had girls in their ears, and family members on them about needing cash. Their moms and girlfriends would call during work hours, saying go pay a bill for me or buy some Pampers.

I was like, "Look, this is how you get the Pampers. You work. You have a responsibility to be here. Those people need to take care of their own problems."

On my early projects I barely made a profit, my employees were costing me so much money. It was Mr. Edwards who explained, "You have to build a twenty percent cushion into your estimates, Chris. That's not cheating clients. That's to cover when things go wrong, because things always go wrong."

Steve watched all that. He saw how hard I worked, and he heard my complaints. We talked about it at first, like old times, but I could tell he was more interested in his own company now, and I didn't want to burden him. I mean, this was on me. This was why I hired these guys. BIC was about building men, not just walls.

Steve said, "I understand your struggle, Chris, but I'm not like you. It's going to be different for me."

I knew what he was saying. Steve was in technology; he was laying the groundwork for a multimillion-dollar breakthrough. I was grinding to make a little money and provide a few good jobs every day. But it's hard, as any type of entrepreneur, to put those points on the board.

So when Steve decided to raise funding for his company, I said I'd help. That's my boy. I wanted to support him. But Steve hesitated. He said, "Well, Chris, the smallest investment unit is like ten thousand dollars."

I had $10,000, but I could tell Steve didn't know that. That's when it hit me. It was like, *Dang, my best friend's looking down on me.*

Those were tough times in Baltimore. The opioid epidemic was starting to hit, but nobody understood it then. Murders hadn't spiked, but crime was up, and the street was hot. Cops were aggressively sweeping the neighborhoods. They took your ID, took your photograph for their records, then wouldn't give your ID back. I'm not sure, even now, if that was policy. Seven cops have gone to prison for running wild through black neighborhoods during that period, including getting addresses so they could rob people's houses while they were in lockup. But the whole department was spanked by the federal government for racial profiling, and there was a major street initiative in 2013 to 2014, so it's hard to know where the line was.

All I know is, frustration was high. Guys were missing work because they got popped in sweeps. They were hassled and sent back to prison on minor parole violations. That's when I started getting pulled over. I think it was ten times in 2014 alone. It wasn't for my driving. Every black man in Baltimore knows you stay in your lane, watch your speed, and signal every turn when a cop is around. It was my Corvette. Cops were profiling it, and that's dangerous for a man with my record. In a street stop, you're at their mercy. It's their word against yours, and your word don't count. It's like Patuxent. Ninety percent of cops were good people, but there were enough assholes to make it a grind, especially when aggression was being encouraged from the top.

And it didn't slow the crime. Two of my employees were shot and wounded in separate incidents, but nobody thought to mention it to me, since that was common in their world. Twice, I came home to find a heroin addict passed out in the vestibule of my building with the needle still in his arm. Both men worked in the kitchen of the Chinese restaurant down the block. The whole kitchen crew was addicted—they were dumping needles everywhere—but the owner refused to do anything about it.

Then Tapas Teatro was robbed at gunpoint. I happened to be sitting at the bar, and I jumped up, chased the man down the block, and tackled him. He was a kid, about fourteen. For some reason, it made me feel bad that I'd caught him.

"What were you thinking, Chris?" Steve said when he heard what happened. He was pissed.

"I don't know," I said. The truth is, I didn't think. I just reacted. And once the adrenaline wore off, I was shook.

"You have to make better decisions," Steve said.

Steve was careful. He was private. He didn't like to drink, he didn't like to go out. He met a girl in the building, and before long, he basically moved in with her. That was Steve.

I liked meeting people. I loved talking with women. We both

worked hard, but Steve had support. He had the luxury of the long view. I had to see immediate results, at the work site and in my checkbook. We were brothers for life, but we were different, and being outside brought that into perspective.

That life wore me down, no doubt. I came home every night exhausted. I laid awake past midnight, thinking about how to fix what had gone wrong that day, not just on-site but in Baltimore, in the neighborhoods, in the lives of my men. Once you climb in the hole, you realize how deep it is. And it's pretty scary. It feels like, at any moment, the walls could fall in.

But it was exhilarating, too. I had a purpose and a plan. I had a job to do. I was up every day at dawn, working out, and it was like, *Hook up the jumper cables and recharge the batteries, Chris is ready to grind!* Ready to get more returning citizens working. Ready to argue with the pushers, the dealers, and the guys on the stoops. Ready to convince people we can save this city, one building and one returning citizen at a time.

And if I worried about my progress—which I did, all the time, because that's the nature of being an entrepreneur—I got a nice little boost one morning when I pulled up to a work site in my Corvette. I happened to look in my rearview, and I noticed a woman down the block. I looked three times to make sure, because I couldn't believe it, but it was her. My old caseworker from the halfway house was walking right toward me.

I waited for her to get close, then stepped out and leaned casually on my car. She didn't notice me at first, but then I saw her flinch. She looked at the car, then at me, then back at the car. I was wearing a dark suit, a crisp white shirt, and a solid-color tie, the same outfit I wore every day. And I was smiling. I couldn't help it, I was grinning ear to ear.

"Hey, Chris," she said. "Do you work here?"

At a construction site? In a suit? Please. You know better than that.

"No," I said. "I own this company. All these guys work for me."

"Oh," she said, and walked on. I couldn't see her face, but I knew she was thinking about the same thing I was: the day she came to the mental health ward at Patuxent to rub my face in her power, and I said, *One day, I'm going to get out of here, and I'm going to be more successful than you, and that's going to be my revenge.*

"Who was that?"

I turned around. I must have zoned out in that dream, because one of my guys was standing right at my shoulder, watching my old caseworker walk away.

"Who, her?" I said, turning back to the work. "That was nobody."

Make (Another) Difference
in People's Lives

THAT WAS a tough spring. Murders rose from 211 in 2014 to 342 in 2015, the highest per capita rate in Baltimore's history. Opioid overdoses spiked into the thousands, and police were busting heads. It was so rough that Steve, after raising funds for his business, moved to the DC suburbs. We talked every day—he'll always be my brother—but he wasn't part of this fight. We were different people with different paths, and I couldn't help feeling disappointed about the distance between us.

I was into the struggle: voting rights for returning citizens, a cheaper parole system, bail reform. I became the spokesperson for a group called the Campaign for the Fair Sentencing of Youth (CFSY). I spent a week in Annapolis, the Maryland capital, in support of a bill to give every teen sentenced to life in prison a mandatory parole hearing after fifteen years. I told my story to dozens of legislators in private meetings. Each one shook my hand and said, "You're an inspiration, Chris. I wish there were more people like you"—then voted against the bill.

I called Grandma twice a month, at least. I used a fake voice, like, "Hello. I'm calling from the city. Is Kathleen Harvey in?"

"That you, Chris?"

"No, this is Bob from accounting."

"Don't be playing, Chris. You can't put nothing past me."

Grandma was sharp. She always knew. And yet, she never once mentioned that the family was planning a big party for her ninetieth birthday. I didn't find out until a few days before the event, when my sister, Leslie, called to invite me.

I guess I shouldn't have been surprised. Returning citizens from Patuxent Facebooked or Instagrammed to congratulate me whenever an article or interview came out. Criminal justice advocates used me as an example. Even prosecutors and judges asked me to give speeches and offer advice. I was walking to the bank one day when two former Patuxent guards recognized me. They were high-fiving and hugging me, they were so happy I was out. I finally had to tell them I was busy, because they wouldn't stop talking about our time together, as if they hadn't been on the other side of the war.

Nobody in my family ever said a thing.

I saw my brother Derrick once, about six months before Grandma's party. I was in my suit, walking to a meeting. Derrick was in rumpled clothes. I heard through friends that he'd lost his job as a plumber and was living on a friend's couch. When I saw him, I thought, *Success is my best revenge*, but I didn't rub it in. I said, "Hey, Derrick, what's up?"

He didn't say a word. He just looked me up and down, like he'd seen a ghost.

The next time I called Grandma, she said, "Derrick's mad at you, Chris. He said he don't want to talk to you no more."

What? Derrick's mad at me? After everything he's done!

I thought, *Don't take the bait, Chris. He's trying to hurt you.* But it did hurt, knowing Grandma blamed me. That she couldn't look at the two of us, as we were now, and tell what was really going on.

"I'm not going to the party," I told Leslie. "Nobody wants me there."

She hesitated, because it was true. I was still a criminal and an embarrassment in their eyes. "I want you there," she said.

The Edwardses were my family. The Wrights were my family. The guys on tier four were more family than anyone who shared my blood, but these people did share my blood. I didn't want to care about them—it hurt too much—but I wanted them to accept me back.

"I'll come for you," I said.

The party was a catered buffet at a community center. There must have been eighty guests. They were my cousins, aunts and uncles, neighbors from back in the day. I knew their names but not their faces. They had become strangers to me. Even Leslie, who pushed me through track, and wrote a letter to Judge Serrette on my behalf, and ran Mom's funeral while I sat in the back row crying, was a stranger to me.

Derrick? He didn't show. But I heard he came by as soon as I left. He must have had a spy on me.

"You look nice, Chris," Grandma said, checking me out from her seat in the center of the room. She must have said it five times. She'd never seen me in my suit, with my Napoleon cuff links, my perfect tie knot, and my watch.

"I hear you're driving an expensive car," she said.

"It's a Corvette, Grandma. You remember how I always talked about a Corvette, and how Mom would buy me those Corvette Matchbox cars?"

I could tell she didn't remember. "I want to see it," she said.

"No, that's okay. You don't need to do that."

"Help me up, son," she barked. "I'm gonna see that car."

She marched out, bent but proud, and the whole crowd parted before her. She went right to my Corvette and placed one hand on the hood. "Umm," she said, "that's nice."

It was almost a blessing, but not quite. Grandma never understood me, no matter how many times we talked about my work. She told a writer who came to interview her, "Yeah, Chris out living his fantasy." She stopped to chew on that, sitting in her living room with the blinds drawn, like she had for seventy years. "But he'll learn."

My grandma loved me. She took me back. But even she didn't believe in me.

That hurt, but it wasn't what bothered me most that spring as the deaths piled up and the police descended on the neighborhoods. Nothing—not even Steve's leaving—bothered me half as much as the thought of going back to Patuxent, back behind those razor-wire fences and that hell-mouth of a door. That thought gave me nightmares. It made me sick to my stomach for weeks. There's a reason that Omar killed himself rather than go back. For all the good that happened for me in there, Patuxent was torture.

But I was going, and I couldn't back out, because this visit wasn't for me. It was for my brothers inside.

So I got up one late-spring morning, put on my best suit, and drove my Corvette to the far edge of the prison parking lot, where it would be visible from the cell block. The cell windows still opened then (they've since been remodeled), and I could see arms sticking out. I could hear shouting. I knew word would get around. *That Wilson? You for real? That motherfucker driving a Corvette, just like he always said.*

A two-man crew was recording me for a documentary that a young brother was trying to put together. I was talking to the camera in the parking lot when I saw Mr. Flood, who had been a CO back in my day, running toward me. He started laughing when he got close. "Wilson," he said, "you know you can't film on prison property."

I laughed back. "You right, Mr. Flood. You right."

Dr. Carter, who had invited me to speak, met me at the door. "I clip all the articles about you, Chris," she said as she walked me down the long entry hall and past the guard bubble. "I laminate them and hang them in the dayrooms. You're a real success story for this institution."

I like Dr. Carter. She's a good person. But when she said I was a success story *for this institution* I could hear the echo of her last words as I left for the halfway house: *Remember, Inmate Wilson, you are the property of the state of Maryland.*

Then we passed into the cell block, and the memories hit me hard. The sticky heat. The shouting and banging up and down the tiers. That awful smell of rot and antiseptic. I got sick thinking of those sixteen years. Then I went cold, remembering the old man from my dreams, dying in his cell with a bowl of watery farina in his hands.

Dr. Carter walked me to a therapy room. There were articles about me on the walls. *Were they always here?* I wondered. *Did the inmates read them? Did they know my story was about them, too?*

Tooky was the first to arrive. He still looked twenty-five, not a gray hair on his head. He smiled, and we hugged, man-to-man. "Good to see you, Tooky."

But it was terrible to see him, too, because Tooky wasn't twenty-five. He was more like forty-five. I thought about the words Steve had said to me fifteen years before: *Think of all the good you could do in here, Chris.* I thought: *Think of all the good Tooky could do out there.*

He was a voice of reason. A peace maker. With five words, he could take the heat off any situation. We needed Tooky in Barclay, in Baltimore, in our communities.

He'd been turned down for parole. The board had said his record was impressive, come back in another ten years. I hated thinking of Tooky doing another ten—while costing the taxpayers another $300,000. He'd be in his fifties at his next parole hearing, and even then his odds were long. Why are we wasting a man like Tooky? What are we afraid of?

Tooky said, "Don't worry 'bout us, Chris. I mean that. Keep doing what you doing. We living through you."

After that, the room filled up. Dr. Carter had invited twenty inmates, ten of the best and ten of the worst. I was planning to talk about my Master Plan, but these guys knew about that already, even the bammas. They were talking to me about everything I had done. In the half hour it took me to get through security, they had heard about my Corvette, just like I had hoped.

"I didn't think you were real," one young man admitted. He had face tattoos and gold teeth, but he was studying, reading, working on his Master Plan, and getting his college degree. "Dudes said they knew you, but I wasn't sure you was really one of us."

"Sixteen years," I said. "Tooky knows."

We started talking, not about a Master Plan, but about the weight pit, the food, the guards, the mural of dung beetles Steve and I had painted on the wall. I laid everything out for them. I explained the books I had read, the courses I'd taken, and how all my work, even Italian, helped me succeed. That was important for them to understand. But it was getting to know me—a lifer who made it—that made them believe.

I was supposed to talk for forty-five minutes. After an hour and a half, Dr. Carter told me it was time for count. I had to leave or be locked in until it was over. Count took an hour.

I didn't want to be locked into Patuxent. I *really* didn't want that. But I looked at those twenty prisoners, watching me in anticipation, and I said, "Lock it up. I'm not leaving."

I always wondered about my work. Did it matter? Was I helping enough people? I had twenty-nine employees, but thousands needed jobs. I was winning battles, sure, but this was a war.

Back with my people at Patuxent (The State of Maryland)

The message gets out, though. That's what I learned that day. The message spreads, even when you don't see the change. It reaches even into Patuxent, where a guy with gold teeth and face tattoos hears rumors of a dude like him who made a success of his life, and he decides he wants that, too.

I said, "Do the work, y'all. Read. Study. Act respectful. Earn every degree and certificate you can. Make a Master Plan. Understand your endgame. Decide what success means to you, then figure out how to achieve it. The world ain't fair. Prison ain't right. But you're getting out, and I'm expecting great things."

My grandma didn't trust me. She just couldn't believe, I think, that a kid who came from where I came from, who screwed up as bad as I had screwed up, could succeed. That's sad . . . but just think of what she lived through. Segregation. Busing. Housing discrimination. Civil rights and its violent opposition. They killed Martin. They killed Medgar. They destroyed her comfortable black neighborhood with two housing projects. They decimated black communities with Nixon's war on drugs. Then the crack epidemic, police battering rams, and mass incarceration. The death of a son. The death of a daughter. She lived to see a black president, only to see him repeatedly called a traitor, a criminal, and un-American. Even then, an opposition was already rising to undo everything he'd done, and in that opposition there was only one black person of influence, a man my grandma knew well and had followed for years.

I can't adequately explain how important Ben Carson was to poor blacks in Baltimore and DC when I was growing up. We were dying for a role model, and here was a black surgeon from Johns Hopkins, world famous but living in Baltimore, like one of us. Our schools didn't just have Ben Carson come to speak. We had whole weeks dedicated to him. Those were bleak days—crack, guns, a military occupation by the police—and in some sense, he was all we had. The poor blacks of DC and Baltimore raised Ben Carson up. We supported him with our hard-earned pennies, even though he had more money than half the blacks in Barclay put together. And he turned on us.

Do you understand that? *He turned on us*. He told the world *we* were lazy, violent, and good for nothing. That his success was proof the system was fair, and that our struggles were nothing but our own fault. In other words, as soon as we helped him climb high enough, he wasn't one of us anymore. He was one of them.

So I can't blame my grandmother for a lack of faith in me, because it wasn't about me. I can't blame her for not believing the world would let a man like me win, not without me selling my soul.

But sitting in the Patuxent parking lot in my Corvette, after two hours with my inmates, I felt inspired. It was another little moment—like seeing my halfway house caseworker and realizing how far I'd come—that made me believe. I thought: *It doesn't matter what they've done to us. It doesn't matter what they do. We can change ourselves. We can break the cycle. All we need is a chance.*

Less than a month later, Freddie Gray died.

The Uprising

HERE'S THE STORY: On April 12, 2015, the Baltimore police arrested Freddie Gray for carrying an illegal switchblade. That's not a real charge. They don't arrest people in Howard County or at Columbia for that. But they cuffed Freddie Gray, put him in a metal transport van, and gave him a rough ride. That means they hit potholes at speed, took sharp corners, and slammed the brakes to smash him around the back of the unpadded van. When they arrived at the station, his neck was broken and he was struggling to breathe.

People were angry. People were like, *Again?* Everybody in black Baltimore knew about rough rides. They were infamous.

Six days later, on April 18, with Freddie Gray still in a coma and nothing but excuses from the police, thousands marched on city hall. I marched with the Strebs, my old landlords in Bolton Hill. They were pushing their youngest daughter in a stroller.

On April 19, Freddie Gray died. The police commissioner apologized, saying, "All Lives Matter." Y'all need to stop saying that. As a response to "Black Lives Matter," it's a slap in the face. It's not meant to humanize us and make us equal. It means: *Shut up, black people.*

Society's fine. You aren't treated differently. There's no need for us to change.

But we have Trayvon Martin, whose stalker was called a hero. We have Michael Brown, executed in broad daylight on a crowded street. Eric Garner, choked to death for selling cigarettes. Tamir Rice, twelve years old, killed by cops for carrying a toy gun in a city where carrying a gun is legal. And Freddie Gray, killed for carrying a switchblade.

WHO EVER DIED OF A ROUGH RIDE? a billboard over North Avenue says. And then the answer: THE WHOLE DAMN SYSTEM.

It's a declaration of resolve. *We won't stand for this.*

It's also a plea: *Stop killing us. Help us. Please.*

For a week, the demonstrations were peaceful, and we marched: the Strebs, me, and thousands of others. The worst violence I saw was drunks in Fell's Point throwing bottles and calling us n*ggers. But the tension kept rising. Black Baltimore had been mistreated by the police for decades. Neighborhoods had been marked for aggressive patrols. Citizens had been profiled. Two generations of black men had been decimated by out-of-control incarceration. Thousands had been given rough rides, just like Freddie Gray. The whole black population of Baltimore had been given a rough ride.

We wanted answers. We wanted respect. We wanted help, not persecution. After Freddie Gray's funeral on April 27, a few people threw rocks. Fearing a riot, the cops swarmed Mondawmin, a rough neighborhood just west of Barclay. I was in Druid Hill Park, at a picnic with friends from Patuxent. We called it level five, because level four was the top at Patuxent, and we'd gone beyond. There were about fifty of us, chilling, having lunch in the park, when we saw convoys of police cars booming past with lights flashing.

"It's starting up," someone said, and we all knew what he meant. The tension had gone past the tipping point.

Three hours later, I was home on North Charles when a friend called. "They stopped running the buses, Chris. My little sister was at school. I can't find her."

He was out of the city, so I said I'd go. By this time, North Avenue was barricaded, so I walked. It was about a mile. There were maybe a hundred people in the street, rocking cars, screaming, holding up crowbars. Nobody was trying to stop them.

I found my friend's sister, thank God. She was huddled up at her elementary school with a bunch of teachers and other kids who couldn't get home. I walked her back to North Charles. By then, the city was on fire. They say 155 cars and fifteen buildings burned, but it felt like more. The power was off, but the evening was lit up with flames jumping ten feet high.

I saw the windows of a 7-Eleven smashed in. A store on the next block was on fire. Along the street, store owners were standing in their front doors. These were small minority-owned businesses, and the owners weren't giving in without a fight. Some were clutching brooms or bats. Most were holding guns. People were standing on their porches with shotguns, telling people with a look to move on. They watched us pass, a grown man walking slowly down the middle of a major city street holding the hand of a ten-year-old girl.

Stay calm, I kept telling her, because it was scary. I thought the city might fall. *This is my neighborhood. Nobody gonna hurt us here.*

It was post-apocalyptic. Alarms were blaring. People were running and shouting, but the only cars moving were the ones on fire. There were no police. The cops had pulled out of the black areas, possibly on the mayor's orders, and when that happened, black Baltimore collapsed. I never would have believed it, but large parts of a major American city fell into anarchy in less than a day. And it stayed like that, in my part of town, for a week.

News coverage tried to say the violence was coordinated, that criminals were in charge and police officers were targeted for assassination. I was interviewed on national television during one of the marches still going on downtown, and I said, "No, no, no," because it was nothing like that. This was spontaneous. This was the honest frustration of the people. This was foolish and illegal and harmful, but it wasn't a riot. This was an uprising.

WHOEVER DIED FROM A ROUGH RIDE? the billboard asks.

THE WHOLE DAMN SYSTEM.

I went out every day. I walked Bolton Hill and Barclay, checking on my friends and employees. At night, we set up sentries to protect our block. We placed people with walkie-talkies at both intersections. The rest of us stayed ready. The second night, with the police still huddled in their stations, a large group showed up with buckets of rocks. They were planning to throw them through our windows and at the nice cars in the parking deck across the street.

We met them in force. It was tense. Baltimore was chaos; it was every person for him- or herself. A friend lost everything when her hair business was destroyed. A store I shopped in almost every day, where the same older Korean couple were always behind the counter, was smashed and looted. But we turned them aside on North Charles. I'm sure they went to another block. I'm sure those rocks went through windows somewhere, and I'm sorry about that. But there's only so much you can do when the people in power pull out. I couldn't stop the worst aspects of what was happening. This was the powerless grabbing control any way they could. I could only protect my own.

I'm proud of what happened in Baltimore. I don't approve of the violence and destruction, but I'm glad people took a stand. You can only kick a chained dog so long, and I say that knowing it might bother you, because people care more about a dog being kicked than someone from Barclay. It's like . . . you can imagine the pain of that poor dog, right?, more than you can see how much it hurts to get pulled over and frisked every time you catch a cop's eye the wrong way. More than you can see the casual violence of plainclothes police officers jumping and punching black men for carrying backpacks. More than you can feel the pain of having half your community's young men thrown into prison for things other races in other cities get a warning for, and then the way those young men are burdened and stunted a thousand ways by that conviction for the rest of their lives.

You can imagine the pain of that helpless dog more, even, than you can imagine four cops on bicycles riding down Freddie Gray for running when they stared at him. He wasn't doing anything illegal. He has a right to protect himself. Why'd he run, people say, if he had nothing to hide? You'd run, too, if you'd spent your life being treated that way.

So they rode him down. And threw him to the ground. And searched him with rough intent. And jerked his arms backward to cuff him. And threw him in a metal van and drove in a manner intended to hurt him, and accidently broke his neck.

The cops said, "We knew Freddie Gray." That was the excuse. He was a known drug dealer. That's why they said it was okay to treat him that way. *We knew Freddie Gray*, they said, *and he was worse than a dog.*

Burning the Boats

THE UPRISING CHANGED the air in Baltimore. There was energy in the streets, an anger turning toward action. The churches in Barclay and the community organizers in Sandtown were demanding respect. Mothers on devastated blocks were demanding a better life for their children. Poor citizens were speaking up about their reality, making their voices heard. None of this was new. The frustrations had been obvious, and they had been building for years. But now people were listening who hadn't been before, and I mean wealthy, influential people, not just in the city, but everywhere. There were weeks of national news stories. Everybody came to Baltimore that summer: Al Sharpton, Newt Gingrich, Charles Barkley.

With the cameras rolling, the city government was suddenly interested in our plight. The mayor fired the police commissioner and, although it took a year, disbanded the knockers, the plainclothes police division that had been terrorizing poor blacks for a generation. She promised basic services, like infrastructure repair and heaters for our dilapidated schools. She reached out to people in the community. I was asked to join several working groups, including the board of Safe Streets, a group that included the new police commissioner and top city officials. Everyone wanted my opinion. They said, "What's the pulse on the streets, Chris? Why are people upset?"

I was like, *Really? You serious? You been here for years, and you can't figure that out on your own?*

All right, fine, let's break it down: guns, poverty, policing, racial stratification, over-incarceration, and lack of opportunity.

"Let's do a gun buyback!" I was on five task forces that summer. On every one, some well-intentioned white liberal suggested a gun buyback.

I'm for gun buybacks. I have a friend who trades computers for guns as a way to get young people interested in education. But we need a lot more than that from the powers that be. We need to address the underlying issues. For me, that's jobs. Poor people can't move up without jobs. For you, it might be education. Or housing. Or gang remediation. Or racial profiling and police violence. I'm not saying I have the answer. I'm not saying you have the answer. There is no single answer. It took us two hundred years to get into this situation, through slavery, lynchings, official segregation, redlining, unofficial segregation, and the "war on drugs," and we're not going to solve that overnight. It's going to take more than a photo op. It's going to take a generation of hard, smart, dedicated work. It's going to take millions of dollars and ideas nobody has even thought of yet. But let me ask you this:

What's our endgame?

What does success look like? Let's define it. What, specifically, do we want to achieve?

What do we want our legacy to be? What kind of world do we want to leave behind us?

Now . . . What's our Master Plan to get there?

"It's not going to last," the old heads said. "We have their attention for a minute, but that's mostly because the cameras are on."

My inner circle at that time was Ben Jealous, the former head of the NAACP; Wes Moore, the author and activist; and Fagan Harris, the CEO of Baltimore Corps, an organization focused on social issues in the city. We were all young, black, and ambitious, and we were dedicated to Baltimore, because everyone but me had grown up there. Ben and Wes, who were a little older, kept telling us: "Be leaders. Do your part. But don't just talk. Make your move. Get what you need for your work now, because this is the best chance you're going to get."

I knew what I wanted. It wasn't a handout, and it wasn't a contract. It was a $100,000 line of credit. For years, I couldn't get a credit card. Even now, I had such a low credit limit I had to run my business essentially on cash. I tried to keep $30,000 in the company accounts, but large jobs—like a multiphase contract or buying and rehabbing a row house—took a lot more up-front money. I couldn't work for Johns Hopkins and other large city institutions because of their long "float." With those places, I had to finish the work, then bill them, but they wouldn't pay the invoice for sixty days. Well, I had to pay my guys every week, or they wouldn't be able to buy the Pampers and feed their families. I didn't have the money to "float" the difference in the pay schedules.

Now, with millions of dollars being publicly pledged to help the inner city, I wrote a proposal. I had twenty-nine employees, but several were part-time. With a $100,000 line of credit, I said, I could build my company to fifty full-time employees, all returning citizens, and develop my own projects in Baltimore's poorest neighborhoods.

I had everything necessary to succeed: experience in the construction market, a solid employee base, and relationships with the men and women who needed jobs. I was already working to improve the neighborhoods: stabilizing an old industrial chimney on North Avenue, clearing piles of rubble from a vacant lot where transvestite prostitutes were taking johns and disturbing the peace.

There was a problem with garbage pickup. City services were never good, but after the uprising, they fell apart. People complained. *This city is always like this. They never treat us right.* I went to buildings in the less desirable part of downtown, where the problems were piling up, and signed them up for a late-night trash removal and cleaning service.

A friend from the University of Baltimore's Entrepreneurship program was like, "Are you serious, Chris? Trash pickup? That's dirty work."

Steve said the same sort of thing. "Work with your mind, Chris. Not your hands."

Well, no offense, but neither of you has made a penny. Meanwhile, my garbage company put two men from Barclay to work. I bought a truck to haul the garbage, and I use it to put other men to work during the day. Sure, trash removal won't change the world, but it clears $70,000 a year, and it makes Baltimore a better place.

Do you want to help Baltimore's worst neighborhoods? I wrote in a proposal. *Then trust in me. I'm already doing it. All I need is the credit to expand.*

I took my proposal to every bank in the city, since they were shouting their commitment to disadvantaged communities. They turned me down. I took it to dozens of charities and philanthropic organizations, both local and national. One offered me $2,000 if I went through six months of business training. I was like, "Really? Is that what you guys do? I think I'm a little past that."

Another promised to back me for the credit line, but abruptly pulled out. Then I heard that the head of the foundation was dragging my reputation all over town. He was telling everyone that my business was unsophisticated, underfinanced, what have you. Yeah, well what did you expect? No, I'm not rich. I'm not well capitalized. I came from nothing—from a place where $100 is a big deal and $1,000 is an insurmountable barrier to a better life. But I'm working. I'm profitable. I have a nice car and a place to live. I'm providing jobs. Yes, I only have $30,000 in the bank, at most, *but why do you think I need the line of credit?* Why do you think I take contract work instead of running my own projects? What do you think it's like when you start at the bottom? The real bottom—not whatever people born into success think the bottom is.

Finally, a bank officer I'd known for years sat me down in his office. He said, "I keep approving this loan. My boss approves it. But it gets kicked out by the system every time. The truth is, Chris, nobody's going to give you a line of credit. Not with your prison record."

I felt like saying, *But my friend served twenty years of a life sentence. He's only been out a year. He's never made a penny. And he got money for his business.*

But I knew it wasn't the same. Steve got his money through his family and their friends. That's what the guy at the foundation who dragged me and all the other privileged people didn't understand. There's a barrier for entry for poor folks around getting that first $500 or $1,000, but there's another one around getting that first credit line. Our backgrounds, whether prison or lack of collateral or just coming up from nothing on the wrong block, keep us from getting financed. It's a red line. Our opportunities are stunted because of it, and always will be.

The old heads were right about the attention, of course. By the fall, the cameras were gone and the public's interest had moved on.

The city government spent the summer listening to input from the neighborhoods, then went right back to doing what they'd been doing before. Nobody saw any money. I'm not talking about the foundations or the faces on television. I'm sure all those pledges went somewhere. I'm talking about the people on the streets. The ones who show up in the neighborhoods. The ones running one-room community centers and food pantries and day cares on the blocks. The ones putting themselves on the line not once a year, for a tour and a photo op, but every day. I talk to those people all the time. I'm one of those people. Nobody I know got funding after the uprising, and nobody I know can point to a project that's affected real change.

WHOEVER DIED OF A ROUGH RIDE? the billboard asks.

Not the system, I'm afraid. The system don't change.

That half broke my heart. But it set the other half on fire.

So I quit my job at Greater Homewood. I'd been holding on to it like a safety blanket, but it was long past time to let it go.

I took the spring 2016 semester off. I told the university I was coming back because I believed in education, but I had other things I needed to do right now.

Then I gave up the lease on my Corvette.

That hurt. I loved that car. I loved the way people looked at me when I was in it, and I loved the way it made me feel. People from the inner city are visual learners. When my employees saw me pull up in that Corvette, they believed. They said, *If Chris can get that, after all he's been through, then so can I.*

But that car was dangerous. I mean that. I had my Corvette for two years, and I was pulled over twenty-six times.

These weren't traffic stops. They were *Looks like we got a criminal here* stops, and they were tense. First thing I did, every time, was put my wallet and registration on the dashboard and my hands on the top of the steering wheel. The cops came to my window, many times, with guns drawn, but I was prepared. No reaching. No sudden moves. Honestly, I was shocked, once they checked my ID and saw my record, that I was never arrested. I found out recently I was lucky; there was an error in my files. The name on my driver's license didn't match the name on my prison record because I had been spelling my middle name wrong my whole life. So every time the cops pulled me over, they found a clean record.

That might have saved me. If I had known how to spell my own name, I might be in prison right now. I'm not even joking about that.

So I got rid of my Corvette, and it was . . . a declaration of intention, I guess. It was like the conquistadors burning their boats when they landed in the New World. There's no turning back now. I'm all in on Baltimore. I'm going forward with this city, no matter what happens, because I burned the boat, and there's no other direction left for me to go.

Be a Father

Darico and I get to work
(ACRES)

DARICO WAS RELEASED from prison in late 2015, right around the time I threw myself into the work. For the first time since his first birthday, my son and I were free together. And I was ready. I had successful companies, so I could give him work. I had moved to a three-story townhouse in Bolton Hill so I could give him a place to live. I had been mentoring young men for seventeen years, so I could give him advice. And I had a passion burning me up to make this situation—to make every situation—right. This was my chance to know the boy I'd gone to court for in 2006, the one who smiled every time he visited me in Patuxent. I still have the photograph from our first prison picnic: Darico, Steve's brother David, and me.

I didn't pick him up from prison. His mother did. She never left the life in the old neighborhood—she had several kids with other men—and since we never meant much to each other anyway, we didn't talk. I figured Darico would live with me, since his mom didn't have room, but he wanted to live with his girlfriend, who had stuck by him throughout prison. I was disappointed, but I didn't press. Darico knew her better than he knew me.

I hired him, though. I made him a foreman and put him in charge of a five-man crew. I called them my C team because they did the most basic jobs—hauling, cleaning, that type of thing. They were all teenagers with prison records, but they were solid. I knew they wouldn't resent my son being in charge.

I had scolded guys inside for lounging around, avoiding opportunities, and saying they were going to enter the family business when they got out. *They been working,* I said. *They been building that business. Why would they hire someone like you?* Now I could see the appeal. There's nothing as important as family, and I should know. I'd been missing mine for twenty years.

I had spies on Darico since I couldn't be with him every day. I put his crew on larger work sites where I was tight with the people running the project. They praised him every time. He was polite, they said. He was respectful. He listened to his crew, but he made them work. He had a good work ethic and instincts. He was a leader. I was a little surprised. Darico was only twenty; he'd gone to prison at sixteen; and he'd never worked a full-time job. I was impressed, and I told him that.

We had dinner together at least once a week. We talked about his work, his Master Plan, appreciating the good things on the outside, like shrimp—I still *love* shrimp, I eat it practically every night—and the freedom to talk to anybody, at anytime.

What's your endgame, Darico?

He didn't know. He was happy with what I'd given him, and he wasn't thinking beyond right now. I didn't push him, because that's not how it works. He needed to come to a Master Plan on his own. And he had time. Darico was young, and he had the three things every returning citizen needs: a paycheck, a mentor, and a chance to prove himself.

Within a month, he ran into trouble. He was pulled over in a "random" traffic stop and found to be driving without a license. The cops threw on a couple extra charges, including resisting arrest, for good measure. It was the kind of stupid mistake a young man in Darico's situation can't make. It was reckless to drive without a license, even to his parole meeting.

And that's where Darico had been headed: to his parole meeting. His girlfriend lived out in County, and there was no convenient bus. He made a mistake trying to save time, and since he was on parole and couldn't afford to pay his fines, he was on his way back to prison. Lots of young men go back to prison that way.

I got him a lawyer, who kept him out on bond while he awaited his hearing. I told Darico, "It's not gonna be like this, son. I can't pay your way, and it doesn't make sense for you to be out in County. Your job is in the city. Your parole officer is in the city. The drug testing center is in the city. If you want to work for me, you need to live with me."

So Darico moved to one of my spare bedrooms in Bolton Hill, and that's when things started clicking. We worked all day, then stayed up late, getting to know each other. I remember him sitting on my sectional, looking down at his hands, the night he opened up about what he'd been through: physical abuse from my mother, which broke my heart, because I love my mother. Physical and verbal abuse from Derrick, bad enough for Darico to hate him to this day. By seven, he was living without supervision. No food. No clothes. No rides to school. He often left home and lived with friends or on the street. It took days for anyone to come looking for him.

The foster system was worse. The parents he was assigned to didn't care about the kids. They were in it for the money. One couple wouldn't buy him shoes. One "father" beat him every time the man was drunk. That's how Darico ended up running with a gang. It was less violent than the world he came from.

That killed me, to see my son with his head down, but I appreciated his honesty. I didn't yell like my father had when I tried to explain myself. I didn't cut him off. I didn't tell him, "Grow up and be a man. This is on you," like everyone had said to me. I let him talk, and I listened. I had learned that much at least.

Construction is slower in the winter, but I had a snow-removal contract with Zipcar. They had more than 100 cars and 250 designated parking spots around Baltimore, so it was perfect work for my company. When snow closed work sites, my crews would be shoveling for Zipcar.

So when a large storm was expected in late January, I was pumped. I met with my crews the night before for a pep talk: *This is gonna be big, it's gonna be hard work, and it's gonna be cold like you never felt cold before. But you are going to earn a lot of overtime. You're gonna feed your families for a month on this.* Wear boots, I told them. Bring gloves, heavy jackets, several pairs of extra socks. Bring a hot beverage in a thermos. Bring snacks and big bottles of Gatorade, because the stores won't be open if this blizzard is anything like they say.

The blizzard was worse. The snowfall reached thirty-five inches, with drifts four or five feet high. It was the largest recorded snowfall in Baltimore history. The news called it Snowzilla.

That wasn't a problem; that was an opportunity. As soon as the morning light showed, Darico and I were out the door to meet the crew at my garage/storeroom/office near North Avenue. It was only a few blocks from Barclay, but only half the guys showed. Half of those weren't prepared. No gloves. No heavy jackets. No boots.

That's when it hit me: *These guys don't own winter gloves.*

After a couple hours, we were down to eight men, but we kept at it. We worked nonstop for thirty-three hours. The last ten, I was seeing visions, I'd been running on adrenaline so long. But we shoveled. We lugged snowblowers. We smashed ice. I was driving my SUV while Darico drove my work truck. Six hours in on the first day, the SUV got stuck in a snowdrift. We couldn't dig it out, so we ditched it in the middle of the road and drove the truck to the next spot.

"Hard work is good for the soul!" I screamed to nobody in particular. "I'm looking for warriors! People call *us* lazy?! Then how do they explain this?"

By the second night, Darico was running the operation. A few more guys had showed up, so he was dispatching four three-man crews, checking the work, making sure nobody's toes fell off from frostbite. I was loving it. This was the dream. After forty hours of working side by side, I saw the future: my son as my trusted partner, helping my business grow.

I felt so confident, I went back to Bolton Hill and went to sleep.

The next morning, I was up at 4:00, shoveling out cars and clearing walkways on my block. My relationships in Bolton Hill were rocky. I told one neighbor I was an entrepreneur and he assumed I was a drug dealer. He laughed about it later, sort of ashamed, but no, sorry, that's not all right. Another neighbor watched me out her window. She called the cops on my crew when they were moving some furniture out of my row house. Yeah, you see black men with a moving truck, you assume it's a crime.

So I didn't make a big deal out of blowing my neighbors' walkways and digging out their cars. To this day, I don't think they know it was me, because I didn't see a single person the whole three hours I worked. It wasn't about recognition. I can't worry about what other people think. I take pride in being a good neighbor, that's all.

The next day, I flew to Florida. After the uprising, an organization called Breakout had asked me to speak to young entrepreneurs in Baltimore. They liked my talk so much, they made me a keynote speaker at their conference in Miami. So while my son guided my company through the worst snowstorm in Baltimore's history, I spent three days in the sun. That's a boss's life, right there, and it was good. Life was very, very good. It was a picture right out of my big notebook of Positive Delusions. I sat on the beach, drink in hand, Prada sunglasses on, and for the first time in years, I remembered that old dream from Patuxent: the one of me on a boat, in the middle of a calm ocean, with the sun shining off the waves. I had my feet in the water, and it was warm like a bath, and I was smiling, looking out at the horizon. Someone yelled, "Hey, Chris," and I turned around, and everyone I had ever been close with was on the boat—even Mom and Dad and my cousin Eric—and everyone was smiling, welcoming me to the party, like no one had died and I'd never been gone.

A few weeks later, Darico showed up at my house in the middle of the night. He was upset. He was staying with his girlfriend for the weekend, and they had argued. She was pregnant, but that's not what they had argued about. Darico was determined to be a good father.

"She slapped me," Darico said. "She attacked me, Pops." He looked down, in the same way he had when he'd told me the horror of his childhood. "And I punched her in the face."

She called the cops. Darico ran. He started crying as he told me this. "I blew it, Pops," he said. "I had a good life. I had a job. I was

making money. I was happy. And I blew it. I'm gonna lose everything."

I remember a calm coming over me. I was disappointed, but as
Darico broke down, I felt all the lessons of my life working inside me,
holding me solid.

"You messed up, Darico," I said. "You can never lay a hand on a
woman. You gotta take responsibility for your actions. With your record, you're gonna serve time, maybe a year, maybe two. But you're
gonna learn from this, Darico. You're gonna come out a better man.
And I'm going to be here for you. I'll have a crew ready to go. This
doesn't change our Master Plan."

He came around on it. We talked until three or four in the morning, and Darico came around to embracing the opportunity still in
front of him. He was ready to turn himself in. He just wanted to get
a few hours' sleep first.

What can I say? I fell for it. I went to sleep on the sectional in the
basement, sure everything would work out, and when I woke up
three hours later, Darico was gone.

He texted me the next day. He was in DC with his half brother,
down in the old neighborhood I'd put behind me so long ago. I told him
to come home, turn himself in, take responsibility. He didn't reply.

There was nothing more I could do. I was on parole, and Darico
was on the run from the law. Any contact between us could land us
both in prison. It was up to Darico to make his own decisions and to
do the right thing, just like it had always been.

The White House

THAT SPRING, I received the President's Volunteer Service Award. I was invited to the White House by President Obama for a Rose Garden ceremony, one of sixty-four minority men being honored for their contributions to a better society. The ceremony was scheduled for May 20, 2016, nine days after the fourth anniversary of my walking out of the DOC holding facility in downtown Baltimore a free man.

I stayed in a nice hotel. My room was high. I had a view of the White House, the National Mall, and in the distance, like a spot of rust in all that white, the copper National Museum of African American History & Culture, still under construction. Twenty years before, near a gas station in a part of this town nobody ever visited, I had completed the downward spiral of my childhood by taking a life. Now I was going to the most important house in the nation, to meet the man who proved anything is possible in this country, even for a man who looked like me.

It should have been a happy day, but a couple days earlier, Darico's half brother had been shot and killed in my old neighborhood. It was another senseless death, the shadow that passes over us too often in the black community, or maybe I should say in *that* black community, the one I was born into and can never leave. I had a feeling, after he called me in pain and anger, that Darico was in trouble. He wasn't involved in the shooting, but he was standing too close to the kind of life we had to avoid.

The next morning, the Secret Service denied me entrance at the White House gate. I had an invitation. The ceremony was for me and other black role models. I wasn't a threat; I was an honored citizen. The Secret Service said my murder conviction made me a security risk.

"But I was invited *because* of my murder conviction," I argued. "I am being honored for turning my life around."

They wouldn't budge. Once a murderer, always judged. It was the lesson drilled into every returning citizen: some will give you a chance, but others will deny you rights, deny you jobs, and judge you forever on the worst thing you've ever done.

The only reason I got into my own ceremony was because one of my mentors made a few calls to the White House and threatened to have CNN run the story. I was admitted, finally, after a two-and-a-half-hour wait. If there's a more apt metaphor for modern society's contradictory approach to returning citizens, I don't know it.

Unless it's the fact that a ceremony to honor sixty-four African American men had to be rescheduled because a white man pulled a gun on Secret Service agents shortly before it was scheduled to start.

I could have booked ten speaking engagements that weekend. I was *in demand*, as they say, but I chose two events that mattered to me because they were part of my journey and Master Plan.

The first was at a church in Lincoln Heights. It was my first time speaking in my old neighborhood, and more than fifty people came.

Only two were young men. That was sadly typical. Most were mothers whose sons had been murdered or were in prison, and that was sadly typical, too.

I started behind the podium, but I could feel the hurt in the room, maybe because I was hurting over Darico and everybody else I had lost in that neighborhood. So I came out and sat on the edge of the stage, and those mothers and I, together, discussed our broken communities. Someone said the mother of a suspected killer had been shot in the head, point-blank, in her own home the previous night. My heart sank as I realized the murdered woman was connected to Darico's brother's death.

I went from the church to the Newseum, a museum near the National Mall dedicated to journalism. I was the keynote speaker at a BMe conference on black male achievement, the kind of event where waiters in tuxedos walk around with tiny food on trays. I told my story again, this time from a raised stage to five hundred of the most powerful people in Washington, DC. At the church, the mothers had given me tears and encouragement. We held hands as we talked about a better future. At the Newseum, they gave me a standing ovation. From that stage, standing above that crowd, the future felt big, like anything was possible, and these successful African Americans, mingling with their wealthy white friends, were the proof. It was two worlds, the National Mall and Division Avenue. Or really, two halves of a whole, and the only bridge between them, at least that night, was me.

It was 2:00 in the morning when I finally got back to my hotel. I was exhausted, but I couldn't sleep. My mind was reeling over the murder of the mother in DC, and I was hurting: for Darico, for the mothers at my event, for all the mothers and all the sons caught up in the endless violence pulling us down.

So instead of going to bed, I wrote a Facebook entry. I knew Darico would never contact me now, with the violence so close. But I also knew he read my posts. So I wrote to the world, with my son in my mind:

> I did not want to post this, but this is the only way I can reach a few of my brothers who are hurting right now (since I know y'all follow my page) . . . when you told me what happened it brought tears to my eyes . . . I felt your pain and you know how much I love you which is why I always secretly go out of my way to help you . . . yes he was too young to die . . . I didn't even know what to say to you other than I'm so sorry . . . but now there's a war . . . now the other side has suffered a loss, and we can't lose our humanity in moments like this . . . brothers please, please . . . just remember what we used to dream about when we'd sit around in my basement . . . remember what we planned to do . . . and just stop . . . no more bloodshed . . . just call it even and live.

Open Arms

IN PRISON, I read about a young woman named Sarah Hemminger. She was a genius, a PhD student in neuroscience at Johns Hopkins, on her way to becoming a top brain expert. But you can't go to Johns Hopkins without seeing poverty, because some of the worst neighborhoods in Baltimore are next to the campus. Unlike most of the students, Sarah couldn't look away. She gave up her neurology career to create Thread, a mentorship program for kids from the inner city. She was an inspiration to us, back in the cells. Steve and I talked about Sarah all the time.

A few years after I got out, I met her. We were seated next to each other at a dinner party. I told her how much I admired her, and I asked if she would mentor me. Of course she said yes. Anyone who knows Sarah knows how giving she is.

It was Sarah Hemminger who told me: *Take care of yourself, Chris.* "This work will hurt you," she said. "People you love and believe in will fail. Kids you care about will die. It will break your heart. It can ruin your family. It will take your health, if you let it, and your happiness, too. The only way to survive is to take care of yourself."

I had gone through down periods before. There were weeks when I felt hopeless and frustrated. Everybody who cares feels that way sometimes. But I didn't understand the crushing heartbreak—the real pain Sarah Hemminger was talking about—until Darico ran. I thought, *You're out here trying to help, thinking you're somebody, but look at you, you can't even help your own son.*

I fell into a depression, another thing I inherited from my mother. It wasn't just Darico. I lost employees every month, to prison or to the streets or to that hopeless feeling that it's not worth struggling, because you'll never make it, a feeling I've been referring to as "the cave." I lost employees to drug addiction, because opioids were ripping through our communities. I watched funeral processions down North Avenue, black men on motorbikes popping blocklong wheelies, because we got a badass bike culture in Baltimore, and then here comes the hearse, pulling a white casket, and it's half-size because it's a kid in there, not even grown.

I thought, *Too many. Too much.*

Since getting out of Patuxent, I had helped 256 people. Yes, I kept track. I followed up. I made sure they had what they needed to keep succeeding. 256 people . . . but there were tens of thousands who needed help just in the neighborhoods. There were 318 homicides in Baltimore in 2016 alone, the second year of a three-year period that saw more than 1,000 people killed. We lost more than 2,000 during that period to overdoses. That's 3,000 losses, in a city of 600,000. That's one in every two hundred people, so you can image how bad it was in our communities. The last time the situation was that bad was in 1993, the year Eric was murdered in DC.

I started taking my Mercedes out late at night, in the quiet, watching block after block of desolation slip slowly past. I felt like those conquistadors must have felt a week after burning their boats, when they realized *It's hot in this armor, this whole place is a sucking swamp, and everyone's dying of dysentery.*

One day, I was talking with a top city official. He was telling me how much he appreciated what I was doing. I said, "Honestly, I feel like this city is the *Titanic*, and we're the band. We're just playing our instruments to make ourselves feel better, but we know the ship is going down and there aren't enough lifeboats for everyone."

He jerked back, shocked. I never talked like that. Even when I was down, I always said positive things. Then he relaxed, almost like he realized we could truly be ourselves with each other, and he said, "You know, Chris, I often feel the same way."

Darico had left me crippled financially, as well as lost. I had to pay his lawyer and his fines, and I lost the money I put up for his bond. His cell phone was on my account, and he ran up an $800 bill, but I didn't cancel his service. If I did, how could I ever contact him?

Then a couple dudes hit me on the street. Darico had used my name to buy a motorcycle, but he hadn't been making his payments. They weren't with a bank, I'll put it that way. This was a Friday. They said I had to pay them more than $20,000 by Monday or they'd kill me.

I didn't have the money because I'd been letting my construction business slip. It took a tremendous amount of energy to secure contracts and oversee my crews. I had been a workaholic for four years. But after Darico ran, I didn't have the heart to push myself that hard. So I went to my friends. Ben Jealous gave me a loan. So did Fagan Harris. But ultimately, I had to see Jane Brown. She had always helped me, but this felt different. In the past, I needed her help to take my success to the next level. This time, I was on my knees.

"I'll pay you back," I said. "Whatever schedule you want."

She said, "Chris, don't worry. We'll work it out. You're like a son to me."

I had opportunities opening up to use my mind, not my hands. The Breakout people had loved my presentations in Baltimore and Miami, so they scheduled me for conferences in Los Angeles and Portland. BMe wanted me for Philly and Detroit, to inspire other black entrepreneurs in hard-hit neighborhoods. Bernie Sanders, who was running for the Democratic presidential nomination, shot a campaign commercial about me at a job site and against a bleak section of Reservoir Hill. My narration was simple: *I came from nothing, but I achieved great things because I educated myself.* As I posted on Facebook: "I do my best to stay politically neutral . . . but I really believe in the power of education . . . it has changed my life." The video was viewed more than two and a half million times.

In 2015, I maxed out at twenty-nine employees. By the late summer of 2016, that number had been cut in half. My goal had always been to push guys up into better jobs. I didn't want their endgame to be "receiving an hourly wage from Chris Wilson." I wanted them to learn and believe in their own greatness. Many took that opportunity, but the majority who left BIC never escaped the cave, and that hurt me, too. I was still working hard—fourteen employees is a lot—but I didn't go after new contracts as aggressively, and I didn't fill positions when people left. I wish that had been a business strategy, but it wasn't. I knew I could support myself with a dozen employees and some brain work, and for the time being, that seemed like enough. I'd been grinding at my Master Plan twelve hours a day, seven days a week, for twenty years. And I was tired.

But people in my life stepped up. When they realized I was hurting, friends like Ben Jealous, Fagan Harris, and Sarah Hemminger went out of their way to find my company work. Jane Brown pushed back the repayment of my loan. Jason Hardebeck hired a young returning citizen who I was struggling to keep fully employed.

The cofounder of Breakout, Michael Farber, invited me to stay with him in New York. Those guys had introduced me to so many people: a movie producer; my book agent; my amazing business adviser, Nathalie Molina Niño. I knew they were connected, but I didn't realize Michael was *that* connected until I saw the penthouse apartment he shared with three roommates in SoHo. There were models, modern furniture, a bumping stereo, and a huge rooftop deck with the whole city lit up around you. We sat out until sunrise, sipping wine, talking, and listening to music. It was the dream. It was the life I wrote into my first Master Plan.

With my Breakout group in Soho, New York
(YASMINE ADYITYA)

I had never taken weekends off before. That fall, I took the bus or train to New York almost every weekend to hang with my Breakout group.

"Move to New York," they said. "We'll hook you up. Baltimore is too dangerous." They didn't like me being on the corners in Barclay and the Eastside, caught between the drug dealers and the cops and not sure which was more hazardous to a man on parole.

I thought, *Maybe I should do that.* I had several offers to partner in my business. Larger firms wanted my contacts, and they wanted a minority owner to help them secure public contracts. Some offered me good money just to consult for them. But none were willing to employ my crews.

Was it worth it? Was it time to stop fooling myself and take a lifeboat?

For years, I had been collecting old furniture and broken things from the street. That fall, Jason Hardebeck gave me space at his high-tech workshop, the Foundery, where I could rehab those discarded things. I went at night, after work, when I could be alone with the tools and my thoughts, cutting and stitching and sanding wood until it was smooth like glass and stained to a shine. It was peaceful, like the Patuxent wood shop with Tooky on a Sunday afternoon, all those years ago. It was so quiet I could hear W. E. B. DuBois once again talking about the aristocracy of labor and the beauty of craftsmanship.

My friend Fagan's mother was terminally ill. She could have done anything with her remaining time. She chose to have someone drive her to the Foundery two or three evenings a week so she could sit with me and watch me work on furniture. She was getting weaker, it was heartbreaking, but she kept saying, "I love what you're doing, Chris. It's so important. You're such an inspiration."

Half of me wanted to say, *If you only knew how much pain and doubt I have. If you only knew how much I am letting everyone down.*

But the other half said, *I can't disappoint her. I have to be better.*

I went back to New York. I was spending time with artists and furniture makers, so I started a business transporting pieces between the cities for them. The first trip, I had my teenage work crew (the C team) load my truck. The second week, I brought them to New York with me. I showed them the SoHo penthouse. We went to a nice restaurant and a club. We walked Manhattan so they could see the architecture, the people, and the life on those streets. I saw the happiness and wonder on their faces. Barclay is a cave. But a city like Baltimore can be a cave, too.

"Don't forget this," I told them. "Bring it back with you. This is why you're working so hard. This is why you're striving, because life can be this good."

I thought, *Burn the lifeboats, Chris. Baltimore ain't sinking. Bring this energy and optimism back with you.*

I hate the holidays. Work slows down and people hole up. It's a hard time for someone with no family. I used to go to dinner every year at the Edwardses', but it never satisfied. They're special to me, especially Steve. We talk every day, and I often get texts like: *Dude, it's still hard to believe we both made it out! Seriously . . . I'm sitting in my backyard with a cup of tea right now, thinking . . . we free . . . we made it!*

That's Steve Edwards: a black guy drinking tea out of a little porcelain cup!

But that's Steve, too: the friend who was there with me. One of the few people on planet earth who can appreciate how incredible freedom feels after you were sentenced to die in prison. Sometimes, out of nowhere, an appreciation for the littlest things—a cup of tea, a walk down a city street—is so powerful, it almost knocks me down.

But that doesn't make us family. Especially after Steve came home, Thanksgiving and Christmas with the Edwardses was a reminder that, as much as I loved them, I was only a guest.

So I wasn't sure what to do with my holidays, until an artist friend,

Jeffrey Kent, offered me free painting lessons. I had known him for years because Jane Brown helped him, too. He had a rickety row house next to a gas station on the edge of Barclay. The front door was bolted shut; the windows were covered; but the little side door opened into an incredible, cluttered world of canvases, sketches, and paint. He was a black man, one generation older than me, and that house was a history lesson not only in art but in the African American experience. I spent many long slow nights in there, painting and talking. I bought a bunch of canvases and supplies, and whenever I wasn't working at my business, I worked on my art, painting scenes from my incarceration in primary colors. It wasn't easy. Christmas alone sucks. But I had a rhythm, I had a plan, and a purpose to every day.

Around the new year, Darico came home. The law had caught up with him that summer in DC, just before his son was born. He served six months in Patuxent for the domestic assault, and Tooky took care of him. The first thing Darico said to me when he got out was "They remember you in there, Pops. They love you in there." I could hear the admiration in his voice.

"That's the power of a Master Plan," I told him.

"Do you still have a job for me?" he asked.

"Of course. I'm building my business up. I've rededicated myself to the work. It's going to be a good year, son."

"I have a few things to take care of," he said. He was out in County with his girlfriend and their baby boy. "It won't take me long."

"You know where I am."

A few days later, on January 6, 2017, Darico was shot on a Baltimore street, less than two miles from my house. He lost part of his right lung, his intestine, and his colon. They had to remove his pancreas. He was unconscious for a week, and infections almost killed him several times. When he finally woke up, I was there at his side.

I told him, "You been given a second chance, son."

He said, "I know, Pops. I know. I don't want to die."

The cops were pressing him for information. They found a little marijuana in his pocket, so they threatened to arrest him if he didn't say who shot him. "What you think, Pops?"

"Don't tell them," I said. Telling meant becoming involved. Telling would make him a target. It would suck him back into the game. "This is your chance to walk away from the life, Darico. Don't take revenge. Don't testify. It's over. Walk away."

He fell back into a coma a few days later. Infections ravaged his internal organs, and once again, he almost died. He was in the hospital for two months. I visited him dozens of times, talking about the Master Plan and the life waiting for him with me, but by the time he was released he was back to talking about the streets.

I wanted him, but he chose to live out in County with his girlfriend and their son. That hurts my heart, but it doesn't break it. I'm stronger now. I'm not rushing. I'm not trying to solve everyone's problems, just my own. Like my sister said to me so many years ago: Darico's a grown man now. He's not my responsibility anymore.

The difference is: whenever he wants me, I'll be here, open arms, no questions asked, to welcome him home.

EPILOGUE

Moving Forward

My opinion is that in the world of knowledge
the idea of good appears last of all, and
is seen only with an effort.

—PLATO, "THE ALLEGORY OF THE CAVE"

April 8, 2017

APRIL'S A GOOD MONTH in Maryland. The sun is warming up. The leaves are coming back. It's too cold for the shore or the bay, but up in the prisons, the cells are starting to thaw. It's farmland in Howard County, the home of the Patuxent Institution. It was early, but some of the fields were already going green, and I was driving with the top down. I had been doing a lot of speaking and outreach, even as I ratcheted up my construction business. I had been everywhere, from meetings with the mayor of Detroit to the shantytowns of Puerto Rico. I have since been to France, Spain, Colombia, and Italy, where my sponsors put me up in a fifteenth-century castle, shared their traditional foods, and told me (in Italian of course), "We have many African migrants here. It's so important they see a face like yours, so they know they can be successful."

It's not just Baltimore. That's what I've come to realize. The things we need are needed all over the world. And if we can do it here—build a model halfway house for other Chris Wilsons, rehabilitate an entire block, bring a real grocery store with fresh food to the middle of the inner city, all current projects I'm working toward—that triumph won't be limited to these streets. It can grow and echo outward and inspire others to change lives, too.

I get notes from Patuxent inmates all the time. They say, "Hey, Chris, I've got the reading list you left. I'm the #1 Book Crusher!"

I write back, "Yeah, only because I'm not there anymore, ha, ha, but good for you!"

This is about so much more than reading, isn't it? There was no such thing as a Book Crusher before I created it. There was nothing called a Master Plan. No résumé workshops. No foreign language program.

This is for today's inmates, working their Master Plans. But it's also about tomorrow's bammas, the ones who say, "What up with all these strivers in here?" and the old head who replies, "Well, let me tell you, young, there used to be a guy in here, I can't remember his name, but he had no family, and he was carrying life. He started from nothing, worse than you, but he started all this. And you know what? He's out. They didn't want to let him go, but this place can't hold you, young, if your mind is right."

I thought about that when I saw Patuxent, squatting behind its double fence on that chilly April morning. Not the guards and the cells, but my people, the inmates, with their shorts made out of sewed-together state-issued sweatshirts and their rusty weight pit and their books. I thought about Tooky, still inside, despite everything he's done for people like me. His name is Arthur Miles. I know he hurt people, and I'm sorry about that. But he's a good man, and we need him out here.

#FreeTooky.

I thought about the assistant attorney general for the state of Maryland who pulled me aside one day after a speech. This woman's lifework was prosecuting young men like me. Prosecutors like her

stood before judges every day, all over the country, and called us los-
ers, animals, and hopeless criminals who should never be free. I
thought she was the enemy. But she'd been following my work, she
said, and she was moved by my success.

Then she put her arm around me and whispered something I'll
never forget. She said, "My younger brother is going through hard
times. He's making mistakes. Can you talk to him, Chris? I know you
help a lot of people, and I'm praying you can help him, too."

I thought, *If my story can reach this woman, and inmates, and returning citizens, and even people who have never thought about any of
these things before, then maybe it really can make a difference. Maybe
we can change the system.*

That's one reason I accepted an invitation to the annual Moving
Forward conference at the women's prison across the street from
Patuxent. I wanted to speak to those two hundred female inmates,
all nearing release, about seizing their second chance. I did my research; 85 percent of them were mothers. A majority were in for drug
offenses. That hit me hard, because I knew what it felt like to lose a
mother to drugs, to chase after her from the age of twelve but never
quite reach her, and never get to tell her how much she means. When
I stood in the common room at the prison, that's what I saw: all those
lost mothers, and all the children waiting for them on the other side.

"You got to get out," I told them. "You got to get straight, make a
plan, and stay out. Because we need you. You are the pillars of our
community. We're gonna hug you. We're gonna help you, I promise
you that, because we can't do it without you. We need our mothers
home."

Judge Serrette met me afterward in tears. That was the other reason I came: Judge Serrette was an organizer of the event, and I had
just come off my mandatory state supervision. My parole officer had

worked on that for three years, but there was paperwork, procedures . . .
Even when you earn it, the system pushes back. But Agent Mack was
relentless. She got it done. That meant, among others things, I was
allowed to speak to Judge Serrette for the first time since my court
date in 2006, when she gave me back my life.

"Oh, Chris," she said, and I knew that look. It was pride. "You
have no idea, Chris, how many people email and call me to rave
about you."

I stayed for another few hours, talking with the inmates. I listened
to their stories. I encouraged them. I gave a lot of those hugs I promised, too. At the end of the day, I walked out with Judge Serrette. We
made small talk until we got to our cars, where we said good-bye. I
opened my door to go, but then I stopped. I couldn't help myself; I
had to ask.

"Why did you do it?" I said. "I gotta know. Why'd you let me out?"

She thought about it for a second. It was a nice evening, quiet and
warm. She said, "I read all the letters you sent about your Master
Plan, Chris. I read everything in your file. A few days before the
hearing, I woke up in the middle of the night, thinking about those
letters. I said to myself, *I want to give this guy a chance.* But I needed
to see you first, to be sure. When you came into my courtroom, and
I heard you talk about how you changed your life, I believed you. It's
as simple as that, Chris. I believed in you." She smiled. "And I'm glad
I did."

Maybe I should leave you there.

Maybe I should close this book with that message: Choose faith,
not fear.

But I keep thinking, here at the end, about another night, a few
years ago, when two young black men cornered me outside a vacant
lot near my apartment on North Charles.

"What up, Chris?" they said, flashing guns. "We been looking for you."

I backed against the fence so they couldn't get behind me. This was the third time I'd had a gun pulled on me since getting out, not including cops, and it never gets easier.

"We heard you causing problems," they said.

I suspected this was about the Chinese restaurant—I had organized a boycott until they fired their kitchen staff for selling heroin—but I wasn't sure. When you're in the trenches, trying to destroy the cave, you make enemies. People have a lot invested in the way things are.

I said, "I don't know what you heard, homey, but it's a lie. I'm out here trying to help. Check me out online. You'll see."

They hesitated. I could tell they hadn't expected me to be so calm. They said a few more things, threatened to come back and finish me, then stuck their guns in their waistbands and walked away. I went to Tapas Teatro and had a drink or three to calm my nerves. I didn't even consider reporting it to the cops. I knew that would do more harm than good.

A few days later, I was driving in Harwood, a rough neighborhood next to Barclay, when I saw one of the young men go into a convenience store. I pulled over and called Steve.

"It's him, Steve. What should I do?"

"Let it go, Chris," he said. "Get the hell out of there."

I thought about it. Then I thought of the promise I had made to myself when I prayed over the neighborhood knucklehead as his life bled out.

"No," I said. "I can't do that."

I could tell from his shorts the guy wasn't packing, so I waited for him in the parking lot. When he saw me leaning on his car, he jumped back. I put my hands up to show I didn't have a gun. How high do you raise your hands to show you haven't touched a weapon since 1996?

I said, "I been where you are, homey. At seventeen, in a similar situation, I made a mistake. I pulled a gun and took a life. They sentenced me to die in prison, with no real shot at parole. It took me sixteen long, hard years to get my life back. I just wanted to tell you this ain't worth it. Don't make my mistake."

He nodded. "I know who you are," he said. "I googled you. I like what you're doing."

I told him I could get him a job, or whatever he needed.

He didn't take me up on the offer, but I see him and his friend every now and then, cruising Harwood and Barclay. They honk and nod, a sign of respect. So maybe he'll come around. I don't know.

But I'll keep putting it out there. I'll keep trying to make those connections. Because I want to change this system for every young man and woman in the streets. I want them to know they can break this cycle. They can make something beautiful of their lives. All they have to do is reach out, and we'll be there.

That's my endgame. That's why I'm out here today.

What's yours?

Q&A
Chris Wilson and Judge Cathy Hollenberg Serrette

In November of 2006, you reduced my sentence to twenty-four years. You gave me a second chance at life, and for that I will never be able to thank you enough. But I do want to know: Why did you set me free?

In the book, you noted the sentencing objectives established in Maryland case law that I discussed at your modification hearing. Additionally, among my considerations were the facts that you were an adolescent at the time of the offense and that you had matured and demonstrated empathy and remorse. Your accomplishments since the tragedy, under the most challenging circumstances, were extraordinary and indicative of an earnest intent to do well and to do good. I believed Mr. Showstack's representations and Mr. Mee's testimony, but far more importantly, I believed you and hoped you would continue to flourish.

Have you had the opportunity to help anyone else in a similar way?

I hear all types of criminal, civil, and family law cases, and in each, I am cognizant of my profound responsibility to apply the law fairly, equitably, humanely and with a deep commitment to justice for all. Therapeutic jurisdiction, a legal philosophy that asserts that courts can act as therapeutic agents, has been incorporated into the family law arena for some time. It has been incorporated in the criminal law arena in the form of "problem solving courts." I recently published an article in the Maryland Bar Journal regarding the traumatic impact of mass incarceration on the children of those incarcerated, suggesting, among other things, that therapeutic jurisdiction be further incorporated into criminal justice practices. It is my hope that my rulings in all arenas improve the lives of those involved.

Putting aside the specific details of my own story, do you have any criteria for reducing someone's sentence?

Maryland case law tells us that deterrence and rehabilitation are among the key objectives of sentencing. Therefore, when hearing a request for a modification, those objectives are among the key considerations in determining whether there is a reason to modify a previously imposed sentence. Each individual brings his or her own history to the modification hearing, and it is that history, including that which the individual has done since the original sentence, that will influence the outcome of the hearing. As well, we consider any victim impact statements. I would urge people to use their time inside to attain as much education as possible and to the extent possible, to address their particular struggles, whether mental health,

drug abuse, or something else. In addition to demonstrating intellectual achievement, it is important to demonstrate empathy and concern for others, for a judge must consider the safety of the community,
as well as the well-being of the applicant.

*Not everyone gets an opportunity like mine, to speak directly to
you. What advice would you give the many people out there who
hope and work for second chances?*

Chris, you are a model. The best advice I can give is for folks to respect themselves and respect others, help themselves and help others.
The previous question addresses my advice for those inside. Hopefully, any education and skills acquired inside will be useful in the
community. Take advantage of whatever tools and services are available, inside and out, to continue to grow. And as you have so success-
fully done, set goals and aspirations and reach out to organizations
and individuals who can help you achieve the goals you have set.

*We live in an era of mass incarceration. American jail and prison
populations have ballooned over the last twenty years, people (including non-violent offenders) are imprisoned for excessive dura-
tions, and all of those things disproportionately affect people of
color. In such a time, what in your opinion is the responsibility of
the law? And what is the responsibility of each individual judge?*

Brilliant lawyers and writers such as Judge A. Leon Higginbotham
Jr., Michelle Alexander, and Bryan Stevenson, to name a few, have
addressed the responsibility of the law. As per judges, we must apply

the law in a just and equitable manner that respects the dignity and humanity of every party that comes before us. Additionally, judges can participate in bar associations, their administrative offices, and a plethora of other organizations and initiatives to improve the administration of justice.

You have argued that international law should be considered in domestic advocacy. When it comes to issues of mass or excessive incarceration, what do you think the U.S. can learn from other countries?

Much has been written about our incarceration rates relative to those of countries throughout the world and the racial disparities in our criminal justice system. Thus, there is much to learn.

What I have argued is that international human rights standards are applicable domestically. In 2011, I published an article entitled *Invoking International Human Rights Law in Litigation: A Maryland Judge's Perspective*, in the Clearinghouse Review Journal of Poverty Law and Policy. As noted in the article, the United States Constitution provides that we are bound by all treaties to which we are a party. In addition to treaties, international customary law is a part of U.S. law, unless otherwise expressly provided. The Supreme Court cited the International Convention on the Elimination of All Forms of Racial Discrimination in examining the consideration of race in law school admission decisions, and the United States Court of Appeals for the Ninth Circuit noted a "clear and universally recognized norm prohibiting arbitrary arrest and detention" in a decision that was overturned by the Supreme Court, which nonetheless indicated that federal courts could properly identify some international norms as enforceable. Closer to home, in 1984, when the Maryland Court of Appeals considered whether capital punishment for juvenile offenders constituted cruel and unusual punishment, it examined the societal standards at home and abroad, including the International Covenant on Civil and Political Rights and the American Convention on Human Rights. And in 2010, the Supreme Court considered international norms in *Graham v. Florida*, in which the U.S. Supreme Court prohibited the imposition of a life sentence without parole on a juvenile offender who had not committed murder, which was followed by *Miller v. Alabama*, in which the Supreme Court found that mandatory life imprisonment without parole for those who were juveniles at the time of their crimes violated the Eighth Amendment's prohibition on cruel and unusual punishments.

In other words, international human rights laws are applicable domestically and may provide additional support in efforts to counter mass incarceration and racial disparities in the criminal justice system. Many international covenants, including but not limited to the International Convention on the Elimination of All Forms of Racial Discrimination, the International Covenant on Civil and Political Rights, the United Nations Standard Minimum Rules for the Treatment of Prisoners, the International Covenant on Economic, Social and Cultural Rights, and the Convention on the Rights of the Child, have set international norms which have resulted in practices and policies in many countries which have been less destructive than those that have been documented at home.

When you reduced my sentence, you told me that you expected me to follow my Master Plan. One of the most important things on my plan was to write a book—and now you're part of that book. I have done my best to honestly relate my experiences and to offer what advice I can to readers—whether they are adults or young readers, free or imprisoned. What do you hope this book can do for others?

I was deeply moved by *The Master Plan* for many reasons. One, of course, is your remarkable tenacity, intelligence, kindness, and insight. I learned much more about you than I had previously known even though I had read the letters you sent and listened intently to everything you and Mr. Showstack said at your reconsideration hearing. On a larger scale, I believe the book touchingly personifies issues of race, poverty, violence, trauma, mass incarceration, and the systemic degradation of those who are and have been incarcerated. And while much has been written in this regard, the actual impact can be lost in numbers and statistics. I also think the book is important because it provides hope and guidance, not only for those who are incarcerated and those returning to the community following a period of incarceration, but for struggling youth and young adults who have never been incarcerated. I hope the book sparks a light in its readers, educating, motivating, and inspiring them.

Recommended Reading

ONE OF the things I left behind in Patuxent was a reading list for other inmates, because reading leads to knowledge, and knowledge, as Frederick Douglass knew, is the pathway from slavery to freedom. I hope you go forward from this book and read everything you can get your hands on, and you make that quest for knowledge your own. But since there are millions of choices out there, here's a quick list of fundamental books that have helped me on my journey from imprisonment to purpose. I hope they help you on yours.

Aesop's Fables by Aesop

"The Allegory of the Cave" from *Plato's Republic*

The Heart of the Five Love Languages by Gary Chapman

Made to Stick by Chip Heath and Dan Heath

The Art of Seduction by Robert Greene

The Other Wes Moore by Wes Moore

Tattoos on the Heart by Greg Boyle

The Tipping Point by Malcolm Gladwell

Mastery by Robert Greene

Man's Search for Meaning by Viktor E. Frankl

How to Talk to Anyone by Leil Lowdes

The New York Times Guide to Essential Knowledge by The New York Times

The Singularity Is Near by Ray Kurzweil

The 33 Strategies of War by Robert Greene

Napoleon's Master by David Lawday

The New Jim Crow by Michelle Alexander

Giants by John Stauffer

How to Learn Any Language by Barry Farber

Emotional Intelligence by Daniel Goleman

Rich Dad, Poor Dad by Robert Kiyosaki

Philosophy by Manuel G. Velasquez

The 48 Laws of Power by Robert Greene

Classics of Strategy and Counsel by Thomas Cleary

Writing My Wrongs by Shaka Senghor

The Ascent of Money by Niall Ferguson

Flowers for Algernon by Daniel Keyes

The Undercover Economist by Tim Harford

Think and Grow Rich by Napoleon Hill

32 Things to Remember When Following Your Master Plan

Think about how you'd like to be remembered when you're gone.

Learn how to be memorable.

Read books that feed your soul.

Surround yourself with amazing people.

Always demand your worth in all aspects of your life.

Write down your plan.

Stay up on world events.

Get into good trouble.

Build a strong network and then feed it.

Live a balanced life.

Invest in your health.

Always dress and act like the boss.

Build your credit.

Brand yourself.

Be a good listener.

Imitate successful people.

Leave bread crumbs.

Learn how to write.

Understand relationship maintenance.

Know the data.

Become a lifelong student.

Slowly reread your emails before you send them.

Be an advocate for something.

Learn a second language.

Make stealthy partnerships.

Take notes and follow up.

Pay it forward.

Learn how to code-switch.

Respect others' time.

Always do your homework.

Be diplomatic.

Focus on the strategic stuff and delegate the small things.

A Note on Statistics

THIS IS NOT a research book. It is my story. But I did use several overviews of crime and punishment to try to put my situation in context, both for myself and the reader. For annual homicide rates in Washington, DC, and Baltimore, I relied on the largest papers in those cities, *The Baltimore Sun* and *The Washington Post*, which regularly feature articles citing those statistics. For the total prisoners in Maryland, the total prisoners in Patuxent, and those Maryland prisoners sentenced to life, I relied on publicly available numbers. Governor Glendening's "Life means life" speech was widely reported and has been widely debated since, and as recently as February 6, 2018, *The Washington Post* reported that no one in Maryland sentenced to life in prison as a juvenile has been paroled in more than two decades. I attempted to discover how many, like me, have been freed through sentence reductions and other nonparole methods. I consulted with several people devoted to this issue, including Nikola Nable-Juris at the Campaign for the Fair Sentencing of Youth, Sonia Kumar at the Maryland ACLU, and staffers in the Maryland Attorney General's office. The number is not tracked or published by the

Maryland DOC, nor, as far as I can tell, can it be calculated by other publicly disclosed records. At this writing, I have not found anyone who has any idea what the number is. I suspect: very small.

In 2016, sentencing juveniles under eighteen to life in prison without parole was declared illegal by the United States Supreme Court. However, it is still legal, as in Maryland, to sentence them to life without any *realistic chance* of being paroled.

Acknowledgments

THERE ARE PLENTY of people who helped me make this book happen. In my experience, being successful requires a team of supporters, or better yet, people who believe in you. I always strive to be the best I can be in life, but it is the people I surround myself with who deserve most of the credit.

Most important, I would like to thank God. I have struggled with my faith in God for most of my life. But it was in a prison cell that I asked God for a sign and in return, I would dedicate the rest of my life paying it forward by helping others. God, you have blessed me tenfold since then. To date, I have helped hundreds of people get jobs and improve their lives and I don't plan on stopping. Keep the blessings coming!

Leslie. You have been my rock for most of my life. There were many times when we were young and you stepped up and took care of me and our family during times of hardship. You never sugarcoated anything with me and you always told me what I needed to hear versus what I wanted. Thank you for encouraging me to never give up.

Stephen Edwards, my brother from another mother. I fell into a dark place at a point in my life but it was you and the rest of your family who helped restore my hope and showed me the light. Seems like it was just yesterday that we were sitting on milk crates in front of our cells, talking about what we'd do once we were free. We made it, brother! You have been my biggest supporter and I am forever grateful for your mentorship and love.

Judge Cathy Serrette, thank you for taking a chance on me. You gave me a second chance to live and it means everything to me. I won't let you down.

Erick Wright, there isn't a more loyal and solid person than you. We have a million stories to tell. You have had my back from day one. Real talk. I try my best to do for others the way you have for me, but it doesn't compare. It has also been a pleasure to watch you build your family and live your life to the fullest. Thank you for all you do for me, brother.

David Edwards, for more than a decade you came to visit me almost every weekend. When I came home, you helped me get on my feet. They don't make stand-up guys like you anymore. Thank you, brother.

Jane Brown, you have become like a mother to me over the years. It's people like you that make the world a better place. You have the biggest heart. I remember when we first sat down for coffee and I read my Master Plan to you. I said I wanted to start a company that helped people; I wanted to write a book and travel the world. You helped me start the company and told me to never stop being the person I am. It's because of your support and love that I have been able to help so many people in Baltimore. Thank you so much.

Michael Farber, I know you would say all of this would have happened regardless of me knowing you. But the truth is, you and the Breakout crew accelerated my Master Plan—from day one, when we sat on the curb for hours in Baltimore and talked about making a difference in the world. You let me crash at your place for months while I worked on getting this book deal. You gave me tons of advice and connected me to the most amazing people. I've also enjoyed watching you impact so many people's lives all over the country. It is an honor to call you my friend. Let's go, brother!!!

Nathalie Molina Niño, you have been like an angel in my life. You are the true mastermind behind this book. I admire your generosity and compassion for people in the world. You are family to me. I am forever grateful.

Jason Hardebeck, you were one of the first people I met when I got out of prison. You planted some powerful seeds in my mind and it gave me the courage to start my company and do work that made a difference. It feels really good to know you always have my back. Thanks, big brother.

Jeffrey Kent, I think we were meant to meet each other. We both have been at rock bottom but somehow we turned our lives around. Thank you for introducing me to the art world. We just getting started, brother.

Jason Timoll: Brother, you are amazing. Thank you so much for making this book happen. We were in the trenches together and you had my back. You are like family to me. Thank you.

Joy Gorman Wettels: Sister, you are so dope! The world needs more people like you. Your heart is always in the right place. Thank you so much for believing in me and helping me to tell my story.

Nina Shaw, I can't believe how blessed I am to have met you. Thank you so much for believing in me. You rock!

Peter McGuigan and Foundry Media. From the moment I met you, I liked you. I like how you take the time to get to know people.

Also, you are one of the hardest-working people I know. I am honored to be able to call you my friend.

Bret Witter: Thank you so much for going on this journey with me. This has been an adventure. You have an amazing life, too!

Leigh Blake and Earle Sebastian: I am so happy that I met you. The wisdom and creativity between you is incredible. I really appreciate all of the wisdom, advice, and love. As Leigh would say, "Mega!"

D. Watkins, thanks for advising me on this book, bro, but most important, for being my friend and always having my back.

Ben Jealous, you are the big brother I always wished I had. It don't matter where you are in the world, you always make sure I'm good. You are also one of the smartest and most caring brothers I've ever met. I am so blessed to know you. Thank you.

Fagan Harris: Dude, I love you. What more can I say? You are a blessing to the world. We have been through all kinds of stuff together and you always have my back. Thank you.

Wes Moore, you inspire me to be a better person and to demand my worth in life. Brother, you are my motivation. Thank you for helping me make this book happen. Let's get it, fam!

Harry Trainor, thank you so much for helping me. I am so lucky to know you.

Mark Tavani, I like how your mind works. It's like a chess player's mind. And most important, you get shit done. Thank you so much for believing in me. This book is dope! Thank you to everyone at Putnam—Ivan Held, Christine Ball, Sally Kim, Alexis Welby, Ashley McClay, Helen Richard, Danielle Dieterich, and all the rest of the great people I haven't met yet. You guys are the magic behind the scene that made this happen. Thank you!

Sarah Hemminger, I am so blessed to know you. You have been and continue to be my motivation. There is no heart bigger than yours. I love you to death, sister!

Treybian Shorters, I love you, brother! Thank you for reminding me of my true potential. You and the BMe family have been instrumental in my success.

I also have a few other people to thank for playing an instrumental role in my life (hopefully I don't forget anyone, but sorry in advance if I do). I am so blessed to have y'all in my life. Shout-outs to:

Karen Stokes, Taylor Branch, Tony Hawkins, Paula Rome, Deray Mckesson, Jim Sanit Jermain, Rakia Reynolds and Sky Blue Media staff, Allie Hoffman, Shaka Sengor, Keith Showstack, Tom Geddes, Jamie and Tom McDonald, Joe Jones and CFUF, Bob Embrey, John Brothers, Michael Pontecilli, Saffette, Eric H., Arthur Miles, Christina Yoo, Danielle Giles, University of Baltimore's School of Business, Betsy Nix, Kathy Anderson, Chester France, Mr. Pergerson, Rodney Foxworth, Dr. Fleming, Dr. Carter, Dr. Mason, Devin Allen, Julia Starks, Ian Newman, Tony "Slugg" Lewis Jr., Peggy Cafrizt, Ayana Lugo, Chris and Stephanie Streb, Alicia Keys, Nikia Kigler, Kara Brogden, Joey Malinski, Zach Garber, Konwandi Fidel, Eric Evans, Alia Malek, Angela Robinson, Michael Swirnow, Chris Adamo, Shal Ngo, Aditya Naik, Barco, Mike Shectir, Joe McNeely, Andrea Cantora, Andrew Coy, Andrew Hazlett, Andrew Rose, David Lingelbach, J. C. Weiss, Anne-Valerie Bernard, Donna Byrd, Ben Wrobel, Van Jones, Benjamin Evans, Senator Bernie Sanders, Marcus Allen, Larry and Jan Rivitz, Kate Cole, Rob the car dealer, Paul Rucker, Amy Sherald, David Sachs, Greg and Rick Segal, Kevin Shird, Starcia Scarborough, Jason and Sam Miskiri, Quincy Spruell and Telelissi, Ben Wobel, Harbor Bank, Zaccia Free, Christy Zuccarini,

Ricardo Basso, Sotto Sopra, Professor Bento, Raymond "Ray-Ray" Alderson, Genesis Be, all of my BMe family, Richard Leary, Kwamae Rose, Adman Jackson, Caryn York, the ACLU, Perfecto Sanchez, Jimmy Soni, The Root, Robert W. Deutsch Foundation, John Cammack, Darrah Burstein, Sarah B., Daniel Blackman, Wendy W., Scott Budnick and the ARC, Alicia Wilson, Dave Chapelle, Bowery Street Crew, Crickette and Brad Wolfson, Baltimore city, and New York City.